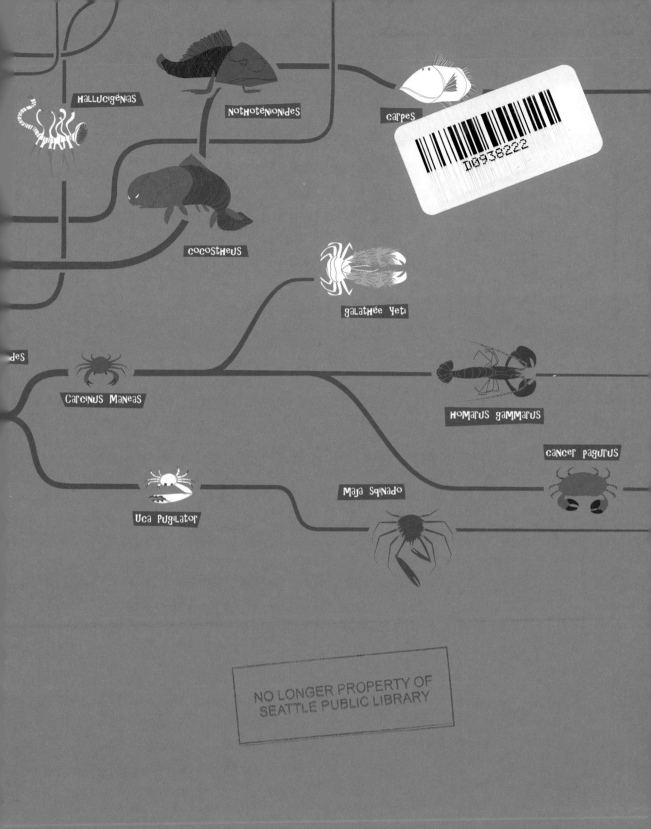

hallucigénias

nothoténionides

carpes

cocostheus

galathée yeti

des

carcinus maneas

homarus gammarus

cancer pagurus

uca pugilator

maja sqinado

THE MARCH OF THE CRABS

THE CRABBY CONDITION

ARTHUR DE PINS

Published by
ARCHAIA™

Ross Richie CEO & Founder
Mark Smylie Founder of Archaia
Matt Gagnon Editor-in-Chief
Filip Sablik President of Publishing & Marketing
Stephen Christy President of Development
Lance Kreiter VP of Licensing & Merchandising
Phil Barbaro VP of Finance
Bryce Carlson Managing Editor
Mel Caylo Marketing Manager
Scott Newman Production Design Manager
Irene Bradish Operations Manager
Christine Dinh Brand Communications Manager
Dafna Pleban Editor
Shannon Watters Editor
Eric Harburn Editor
Rebecca Taylor Editor
Ian Brill Editor
Chris Rosa Assistant Editor
Alex Galer Assistant Editor
Whitney Leopard Assistant Editor
Jasmine Amiri Assistant Editor
Cameron Chittock Assistant Editor
Kelsey Dieterich Production Designer
Jillian Crab Production Designer
Kara Leopard Production Designer
Devin Funches E-Commerce & Inventory Coordinator
Andy Liegl Event Coordinator
Aaron Ferrara Operations Assistant
José Meza Sales Assistant
Michelle Ankley Sales Assistant
Elizabeth Loughridge Accounting Assistant
Stephanie Hocutt PR Assistant

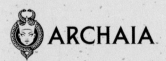

ARCHAIA

Written and Illustrated by
ARTHUR DE PINS

Translation by
EDWARD GAUVIN

Letters by
DERON BENNETT

FRENCH EDITION

Editor
CLOTILDE VU
Design by
DIDIER GONORD and **ADELINE RICHET**

ENGLISH EDITION

Design by
JILLIAN CRAB

Editors
IAN BRILL and **REBECCA TAYLOR**

This trilogy is dedicated to Captain Erwan Donnelly.

Thank you to Jérémy, Olivia, and above all Clotilde.
— Arthur De Pins

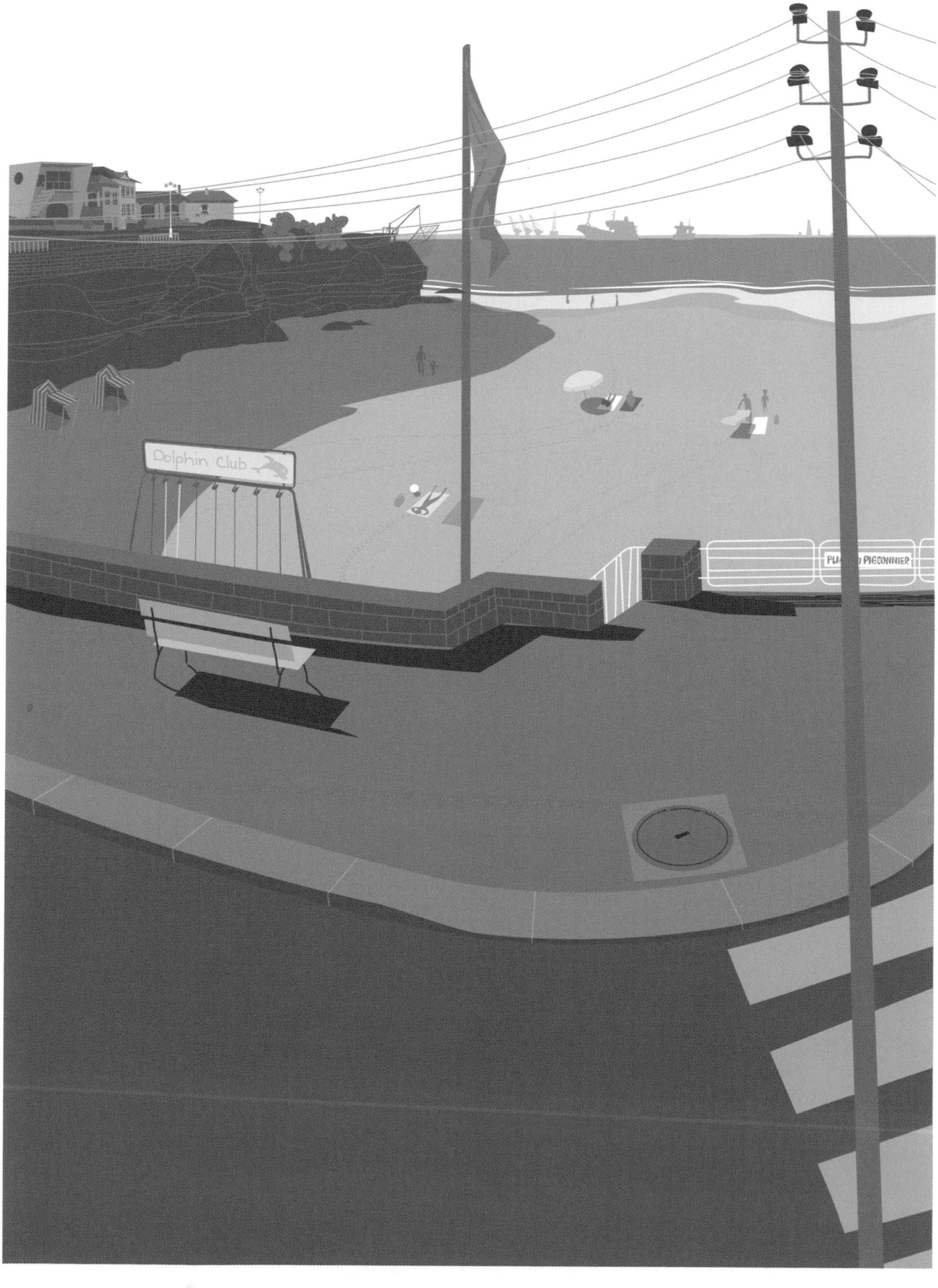
Dolphin Club
PIGEONNIER

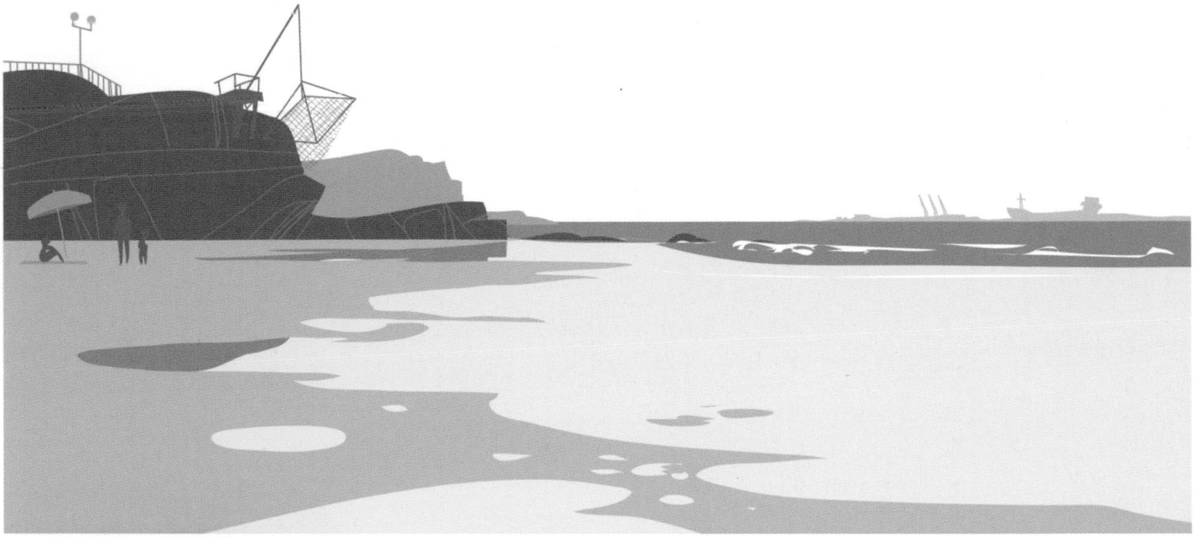

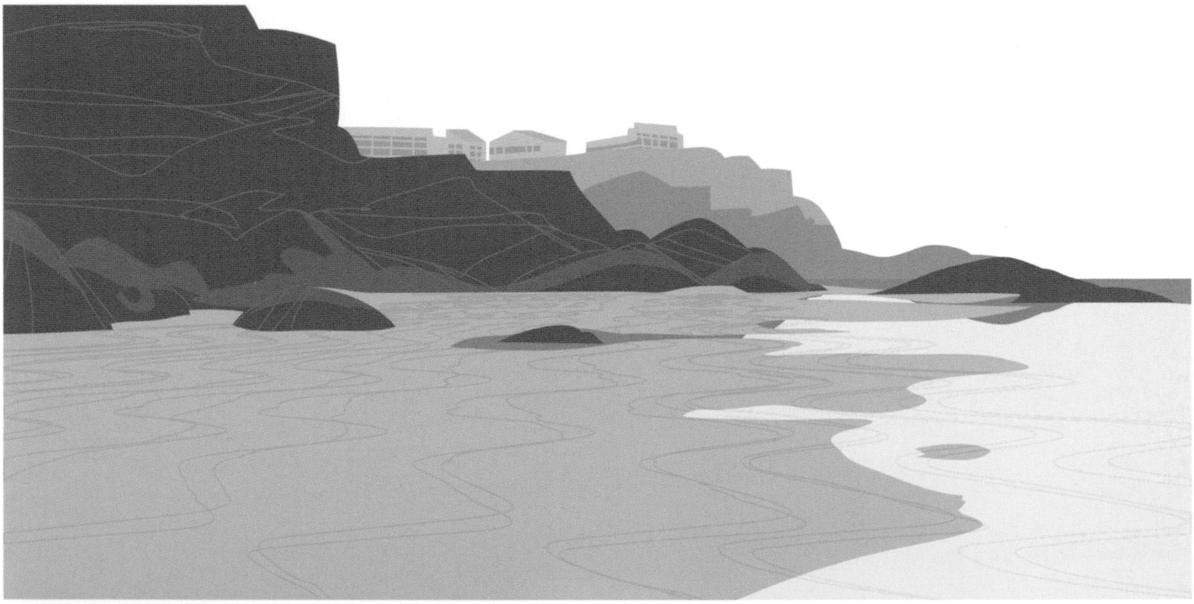

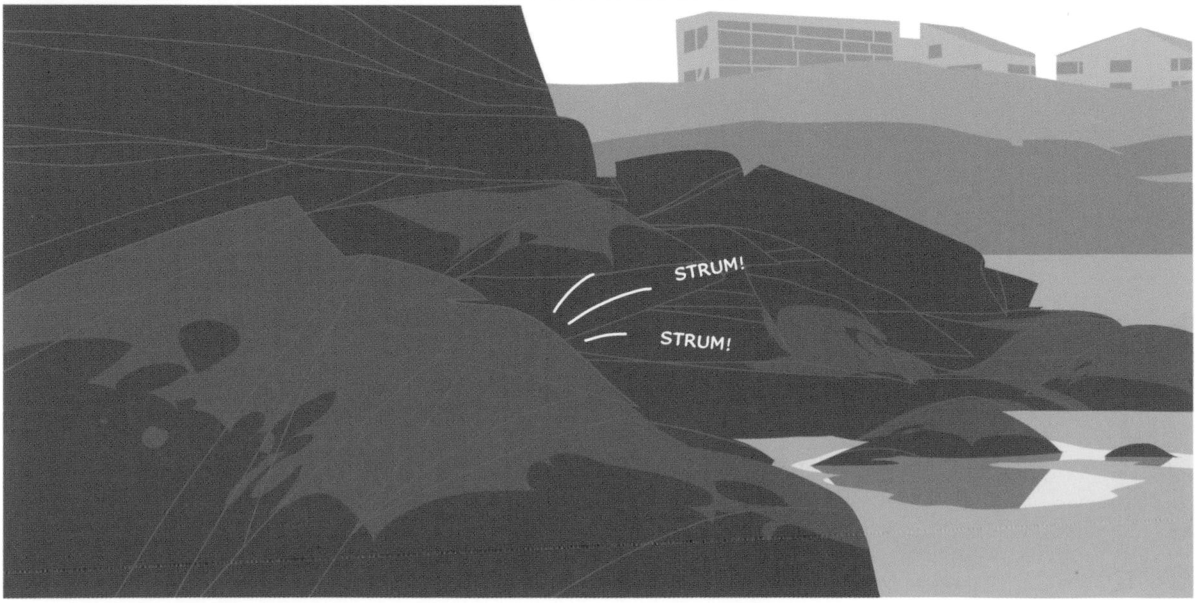
STRUM!
STRUM!

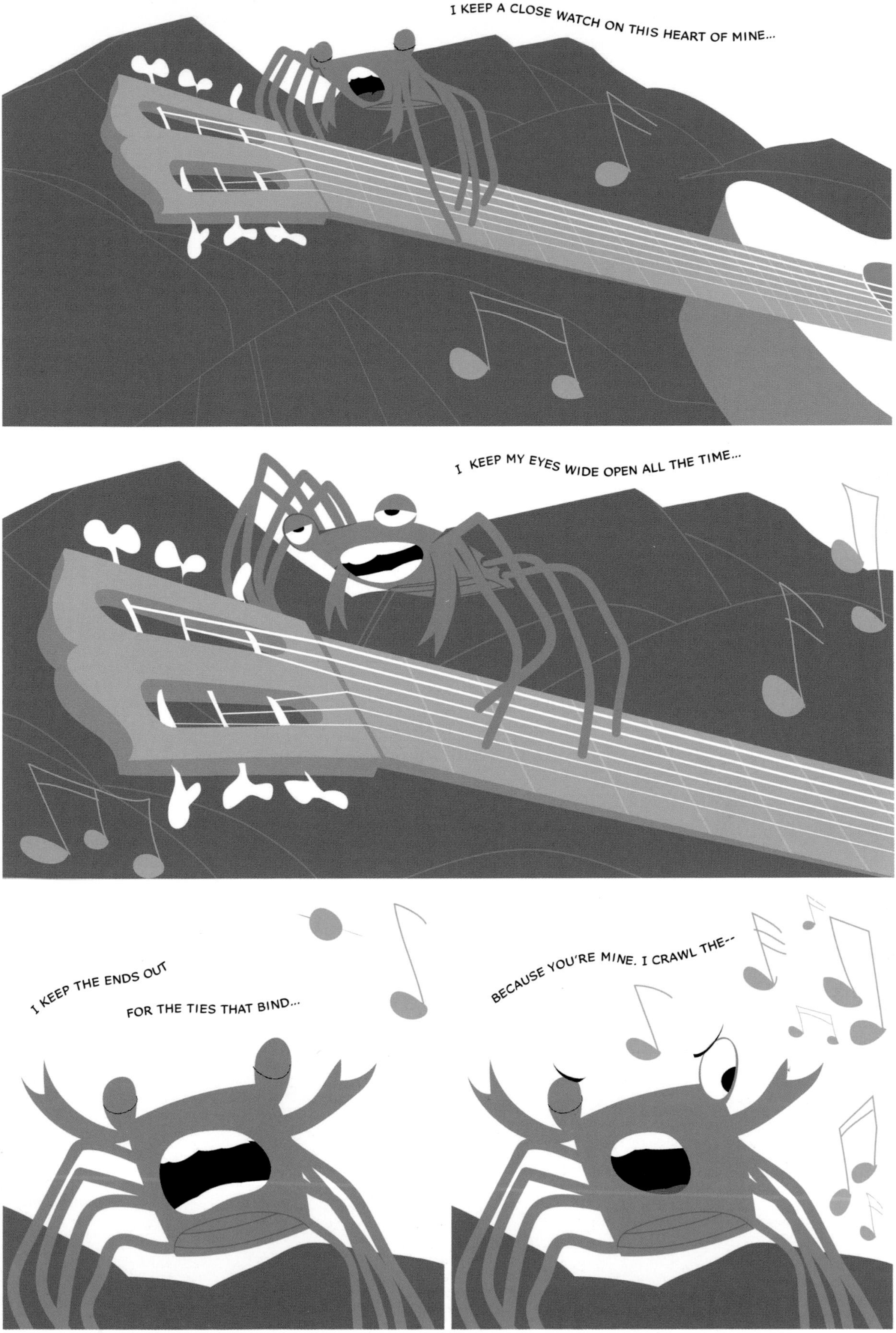
I KEEP A CLOSE WATCH ON THIS HEART OF MINE...
I KEEP MY EYES WIDE OPEN ALL THE TIME...
I KEEP THE ENDS OUT
FOR THE TIES THAT BIND...
BECAUSE YOU'RE MINE. I CRAWL THE--

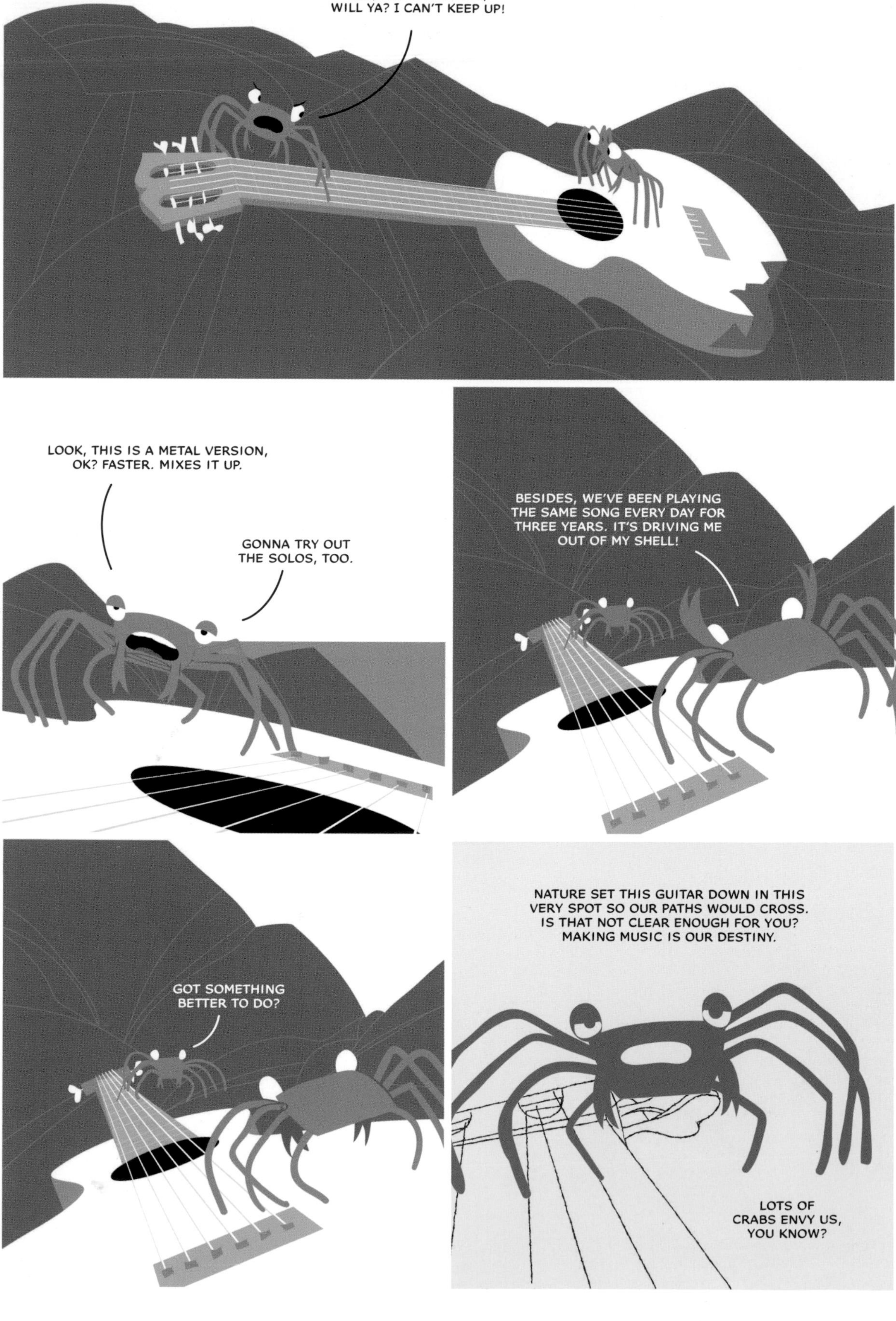
HEY, SLOW IT DOWN, WILL YA? I CAN'T KEEP UP!
LOOK, THIS IS A METAL VERSION, OK? FASTER. MIXES IT UP.
GONNA TRY OUT THE SOLOS, TOO.
BESIDES, WE'VE BEEN PLAYING THE SAME SONG EVERY DAY FOR THREE YEARS. IT'S DRIVING ME OUT OF MY SHELL!
GOT SOMETHING BETTER TO DO?
NATURE SET THIS GUITAR DOWN IN THIS VERY SPOT SO OUR PATHS WOULD CROSS. IS THAT NOT CLEAR ENOUGH FOR YOU? MAKING MUSIC IS OUR DESTINY.
LOTS OF CRABS ENVY US, YOU KNOW?

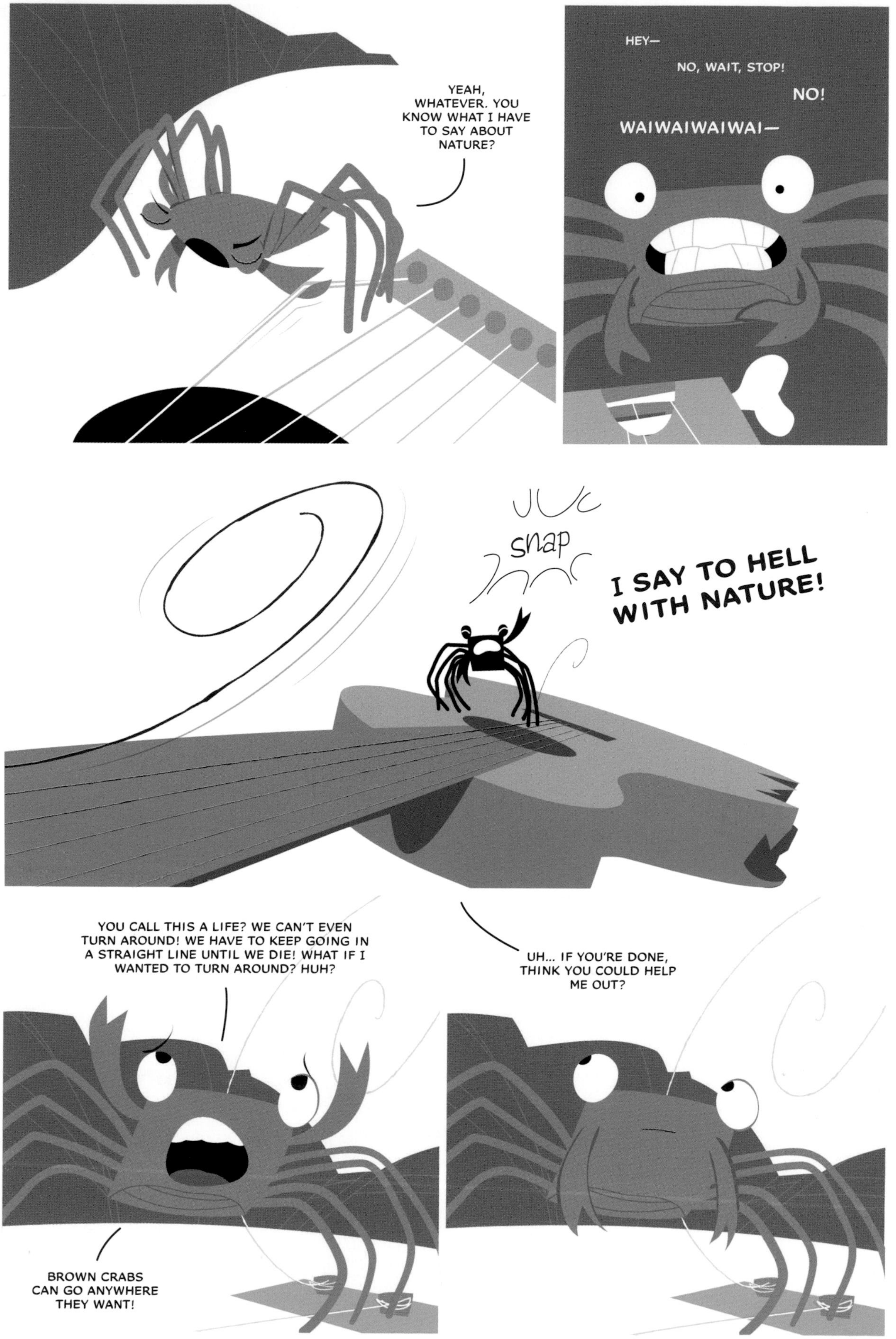
YEAH, WHATEVER. YOU KNOW WHAT I HAVE TO SAY ABOUT NATURE?
HEY—
NO, WAIT, STOP!
NO!
WAIWAIWAIWAI—
snap
I SAY TO HELL WITH NATURE!
YOU CALL THIS A LIFE? WE CAN'T EVEN TURN AROUND! WE HAVE TO KEEP GOING IN A STRAIGHT LINE UNTIL WE DIE! WHAT IF I WANTED TO TURN AROUND? HUH?
BROWN CRABS CAN GO ANYWHERE THEY WANT!
UH... IF YOU'RE DONE, THINK YOU COULD HELP ME OUT?

OH, MAN! SORRY, DUDE! I GET ALL OUT OF CONTROL WHEN I'M UPSET.
I'D COME GET YOU OUT OF THERE...
... BUT YOU'RE NOT IN MY PATH.
TERRIFIC!
WELL, AT LEAST FROM HERE I'VE GOT A GREAT VIEW OF—
OH, NO!
WHAT?
HUMANS!
HUMAN KIDS!
THEY'RE COMING!
THEY'RE GONNA PULL MY CLAWS OFF!

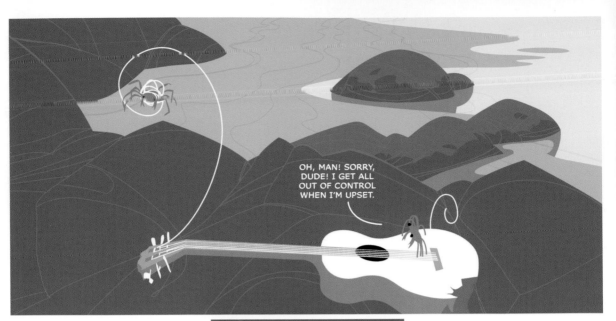

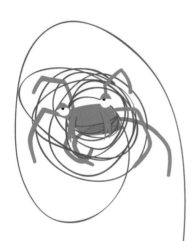

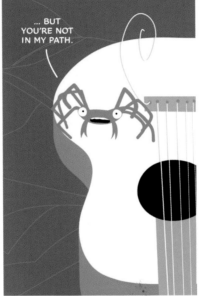

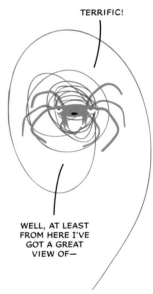

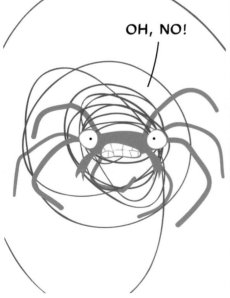

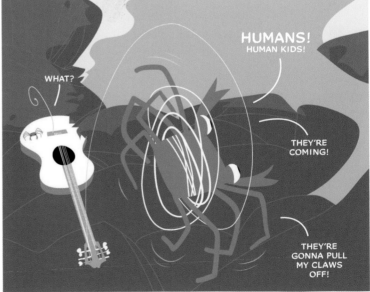

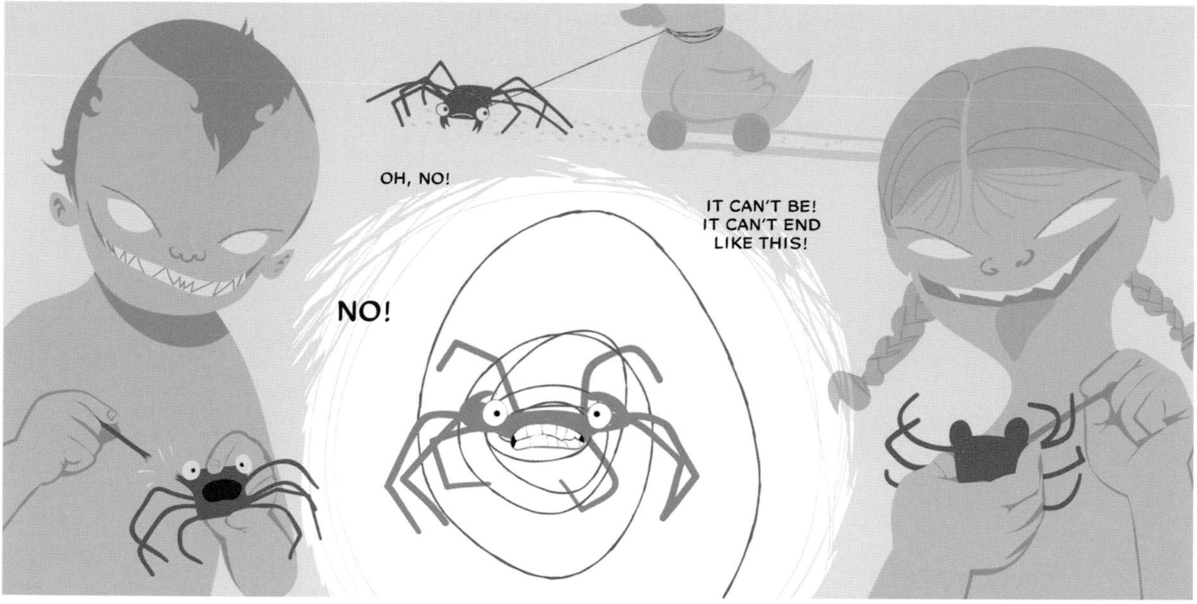
OH, NO!
NO!
IT CAN'T BE!
IT CAN'T END
LIKE THIS!

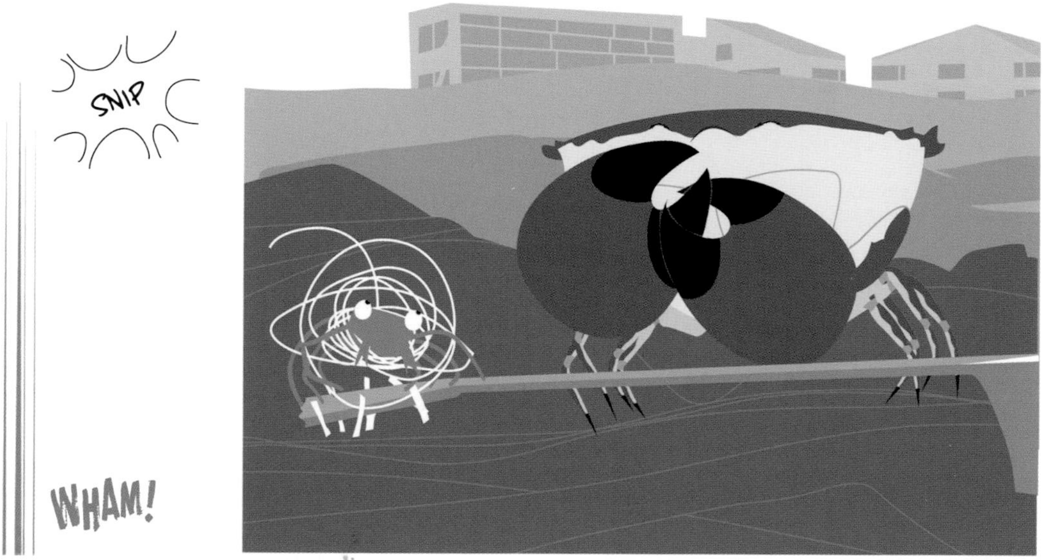
SNIP
WHAM!

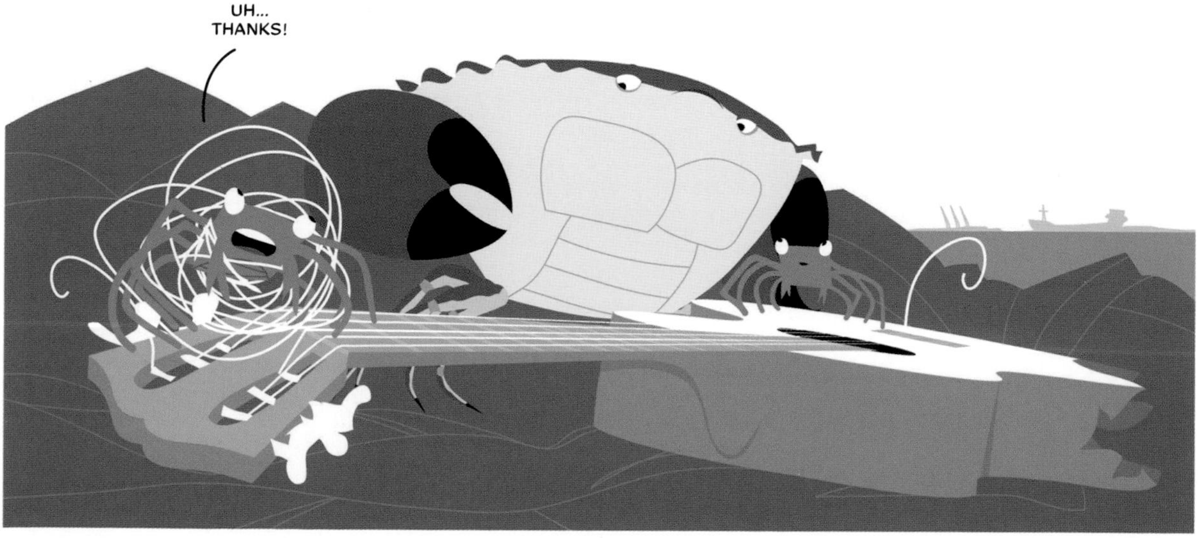
UH...
THANKS!

SPROING!
snip!
I HATE MUSIC!
I HATE YOUR SONGS. THEY BUM ME OUT.
GO ON, BEAT IT! SCRAM! SATAN'S COMING AT 2 O'CLOCK!

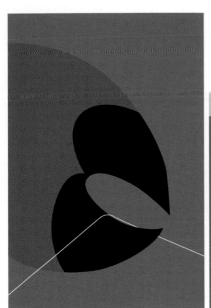

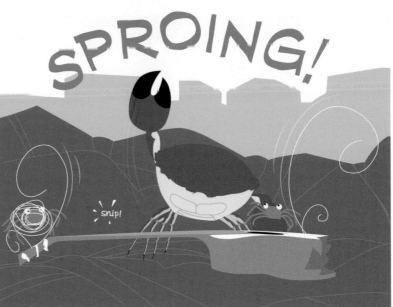

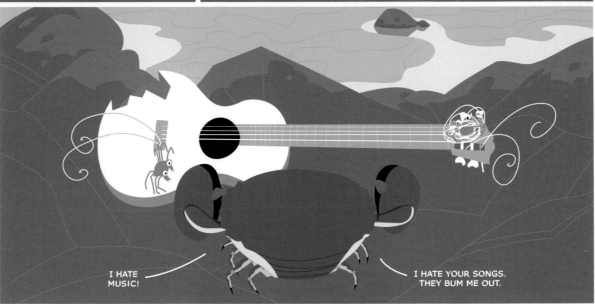

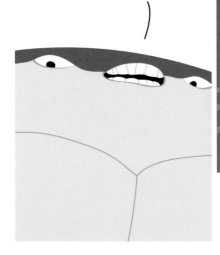

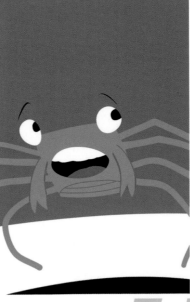

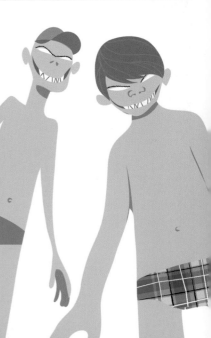

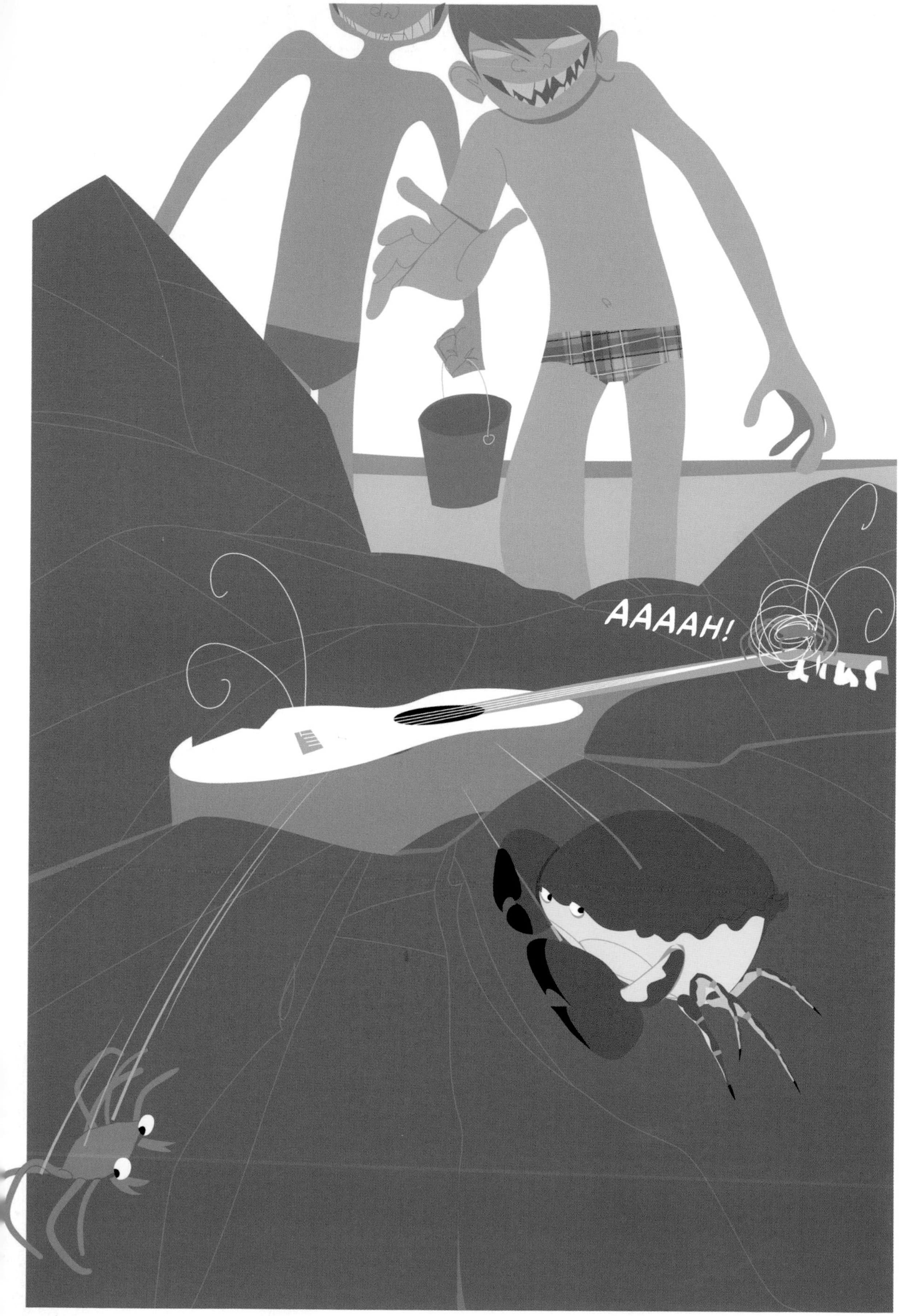
AAAAH!

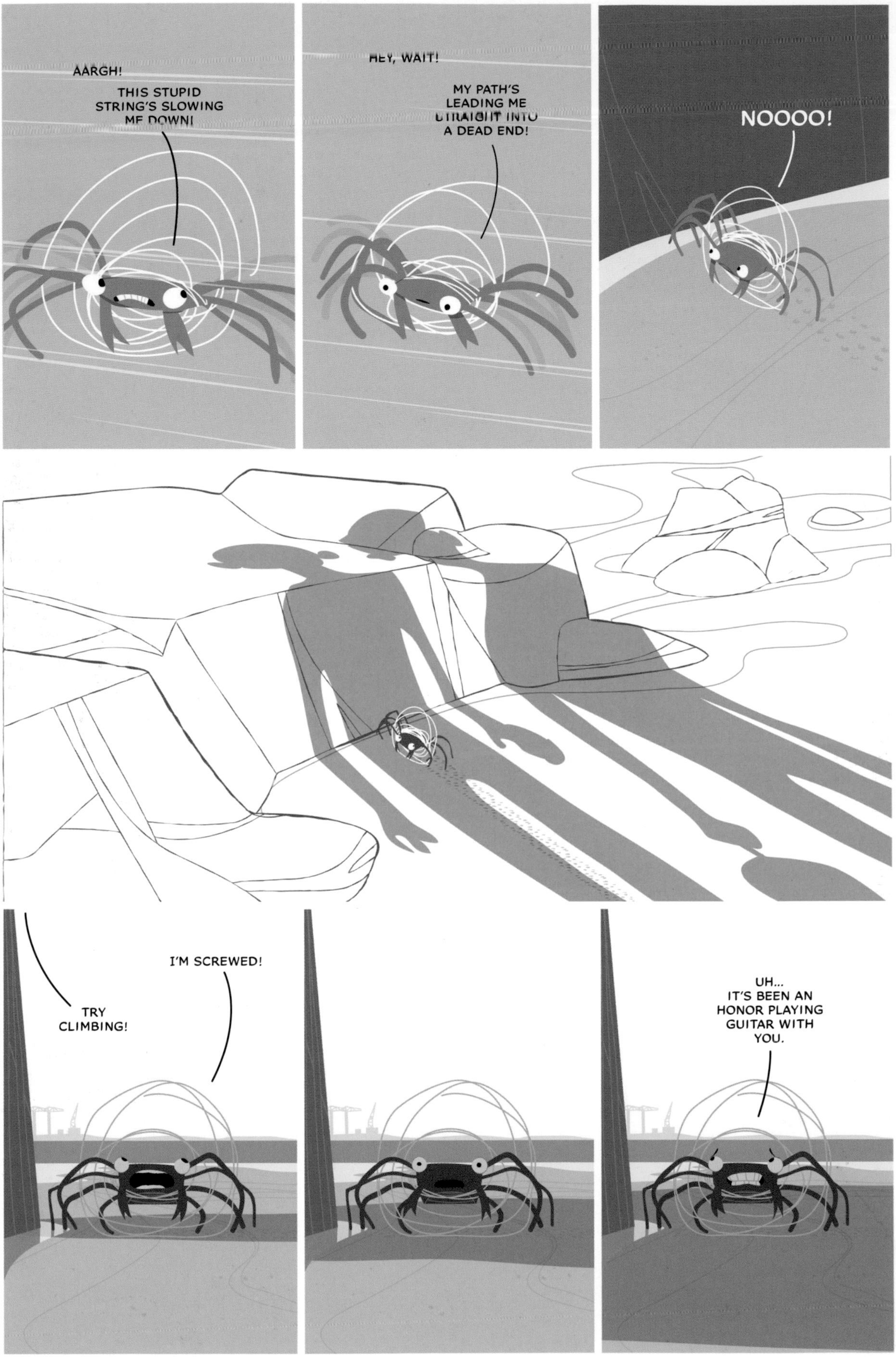

AARGH!
THIS STUPID STRING'S SLOWING ME DOWN!
HEY, WAIT!
MY PATH'S LEADING ME STRAIGHT INTO A DEAD END!
NOOOO!
TRY CLIMBING!
I'M SCREWED!
UH... IT'S BEEN AN HONOR PLAYING GUITAR WITH YOU.

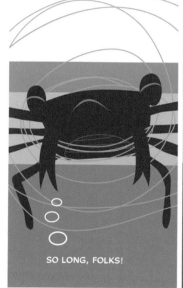

SO LONG, FOLKS!

SORRY ABOUT YOUR PAL.

WHAT WAS HIS NAME?

UH... DUNNO. WE DON'T HAVE NAMES.

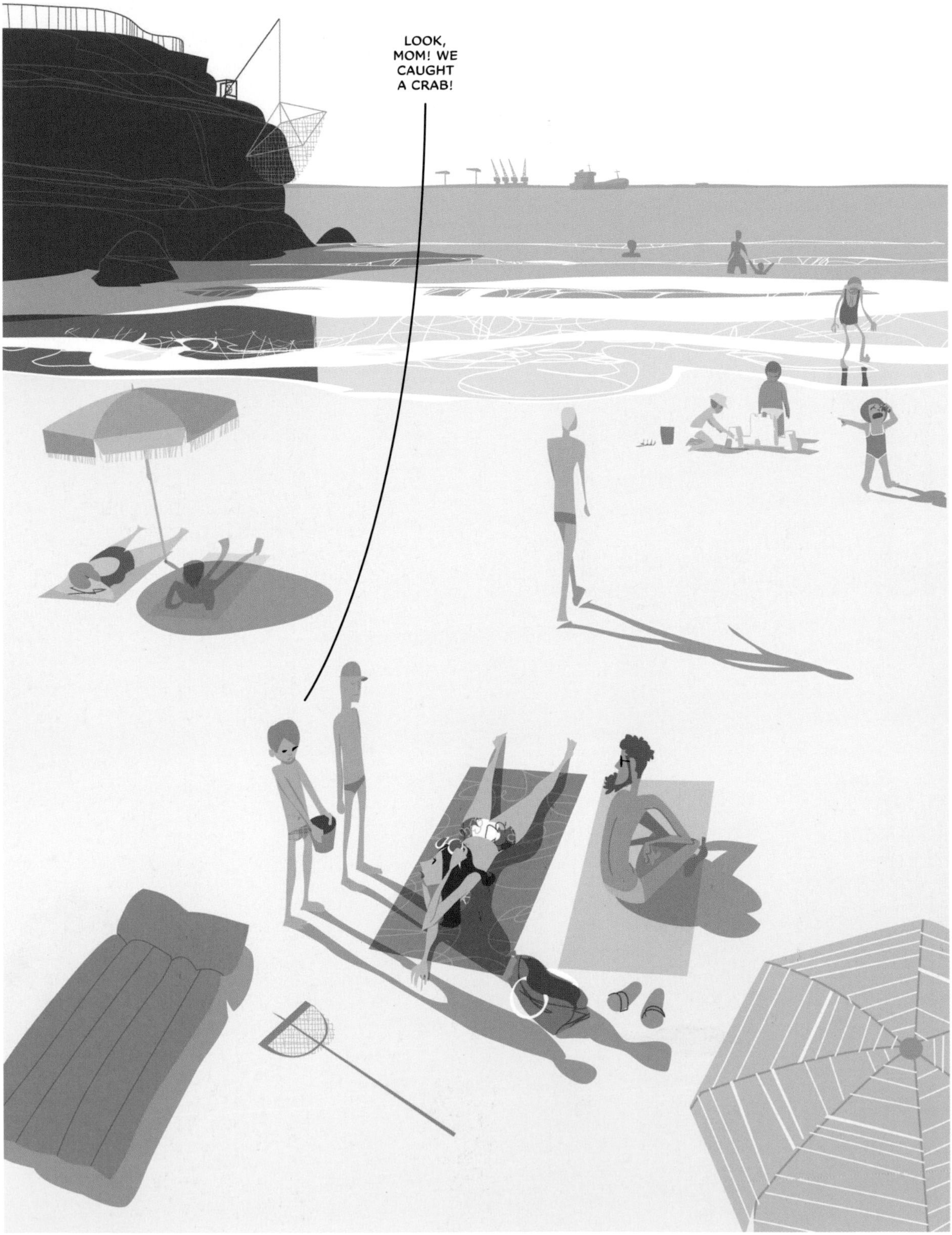
LOOK, MOM! WE CAUGHT A CRAB!

AH, DISCOVERING THE JOYS OF NATURE!

SWEETIE, THERE ARE AQUARIUMS FOR THAT KIND OF THING.

CAN WE ADOPT IT?

HUH, MOM?

NO WAY! THAT THING STINKS AND... IT'LL BE UNHAPPY.

LET ME SEE WHAT KIND IT IS.

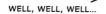

WELL, WELL, WELL...

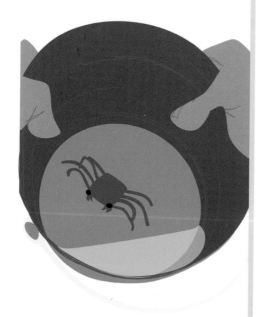

CANCER SIMPLICIMUS VULGARIS... THE MARBLED CRAB. THE ONLY SPECIES THAT CAN ONLY MOVE IN ONE DIRECTION.

AND SMELL LIKE ROTTEN MILK.

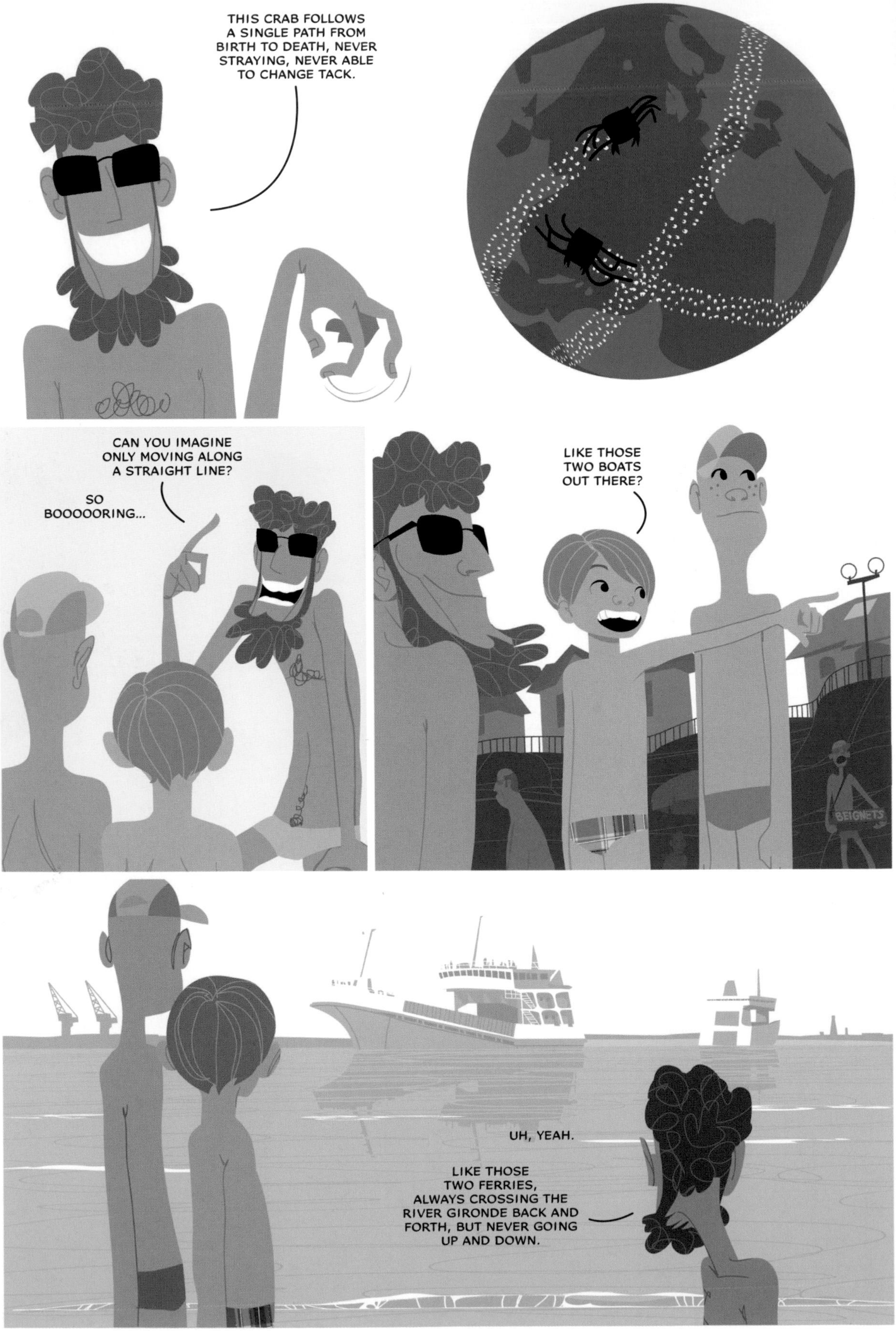
THIS CRAB FOLLOWS A SINGLE PATH FROM BIRTH TO DEATH, NEVER STRAYING, NEVER ABLE TO CHANGE TACK.
CAN YOU IMAGINE ONLY MOVING ALONG A STRAIGHT LINE?
SO BOOOOORING...
LIKE THOSE TWO BOATS OUT THERE?
BEIGNETS
UH, YEAH.
LIKE THOSE TWO FERRIES, ALWAYS CROSSING THE RIVER GIRONDE BACK AND FORTH, BUT NEVER GOING UP AND DOWN.

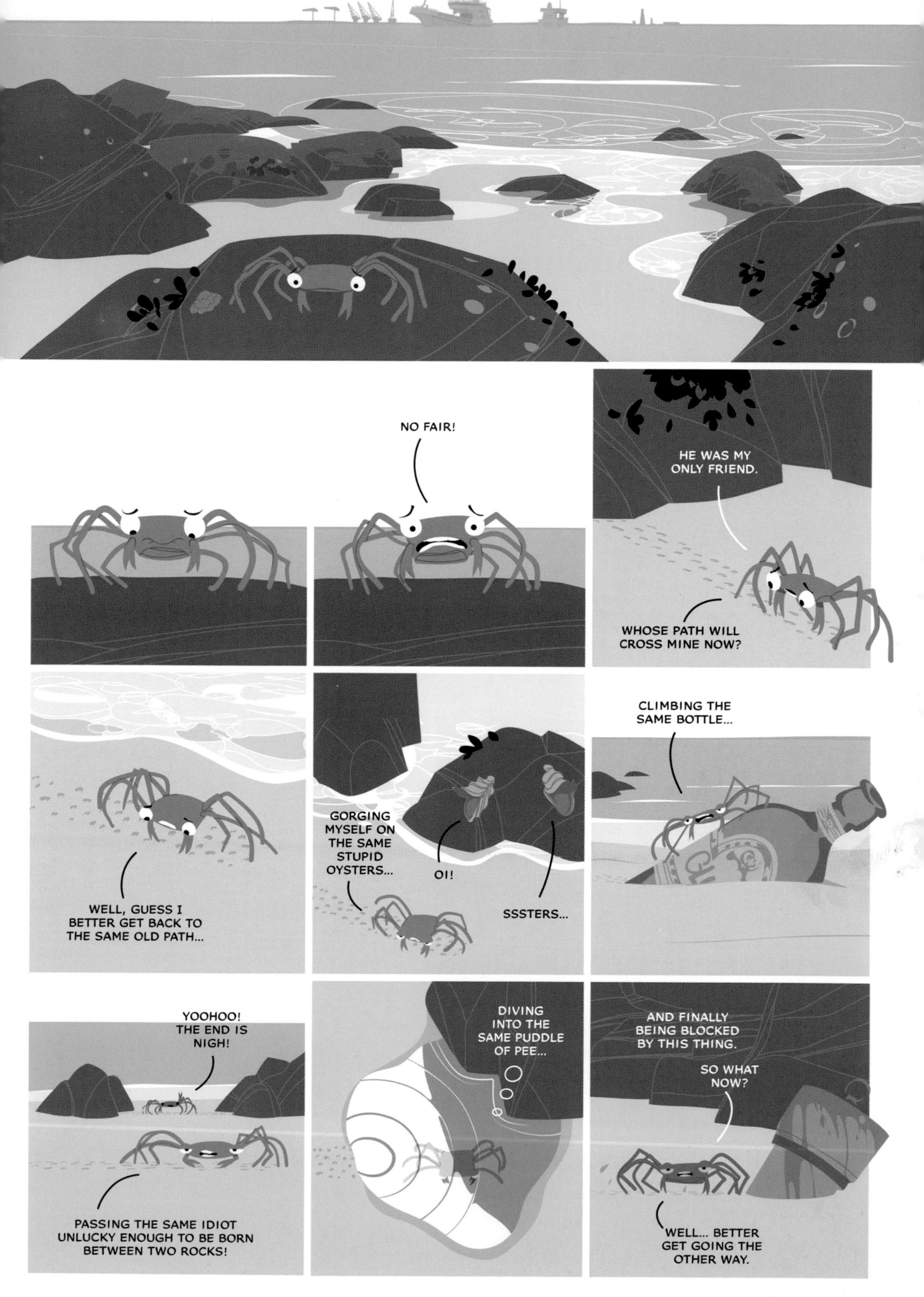
NO FAIR!
HE WAS MY ONLY FRIEND.
WHOSE PATH WILL CROSS MINE NOW?
WELL, GUESS I BETTER GET BACK TO THE SAME OLD PATH...
GORGING MYSELF ON THE SAME STUPID OYSTERS...
OI!
SSSTERS...
CLIMBING THE SAME BOTTLE...
YOOHOO! THE END IS NIGH!
PASSING THE SAME IDIOT UNLUCKY ENOUGH TO BE BORN BETWEEN TWO ROCKS!
DIVING INTO THE SAME PUDDLE OF PEE...
AND FINALLY BEING BLOCKED BY THIS THING.
SO WHAT NOW?
WELL... BETTER GET GOING THE OTHER WAY.

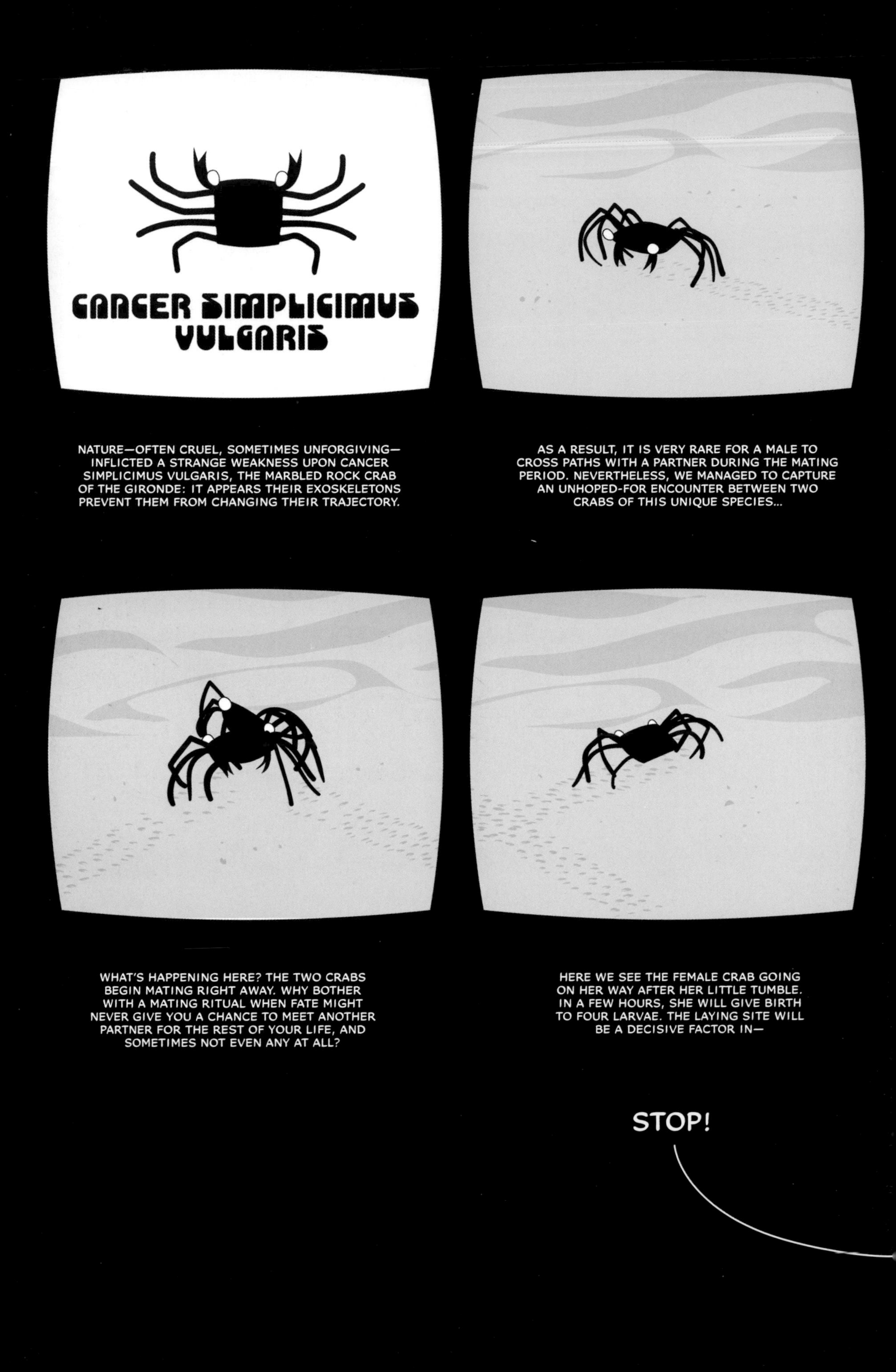
CANCER SIMPLICIMUS VULGARIS
NATURE—OFTEN CRUEL, SOMETIMES UNFORGIVING—INFLICTED A STRANGE WEAKNESS UPON CANCER SIMPLICIMUS VULGARIS, THE MARBLED ROCK CRAB OF THE GIRONDE: IT APPEARS THEIR EXOSKELETONS PREVENT THEM FROM CHANGING THEIR TRAJECTORY.
AS A RESULT, IT IS VERY RARE FOR A MALE TO CROSS PATHS WITH A PARTNER DURING THE MATING PERIOD. NEVERTHELESS, WE MANAGED TO CAPTURE AN UNHOPED-FOR ENCOUNTER BETWEEN TWO CRABS OF THIS UNIQUE SPECIES...
WHAT'S HAPPENING HERE? THE TWO CRABS BEGIN MATING RIGHT AWAY. WHY BOTHER WITH A MATING RITUAL WHEN FATE MIGHT NEVER GIVE YOU A CHANCE TO MEET ANOTHER PARTNER FOR THE REST OF YOUR LIFE, AND SOMETIMES NOT EVEN ANY AT ALL?
HERE WE SEE THE FEMALE CRAB GOING ON HER WAY AFTER HER LITTLE TUMBLE. IN A FEW HOURS, SHE WILL GIVE BIRTH TO FOUR LARVAE. THE LAYING SITE WILL BE A DECISIVE FACTOR IN—
STOP!

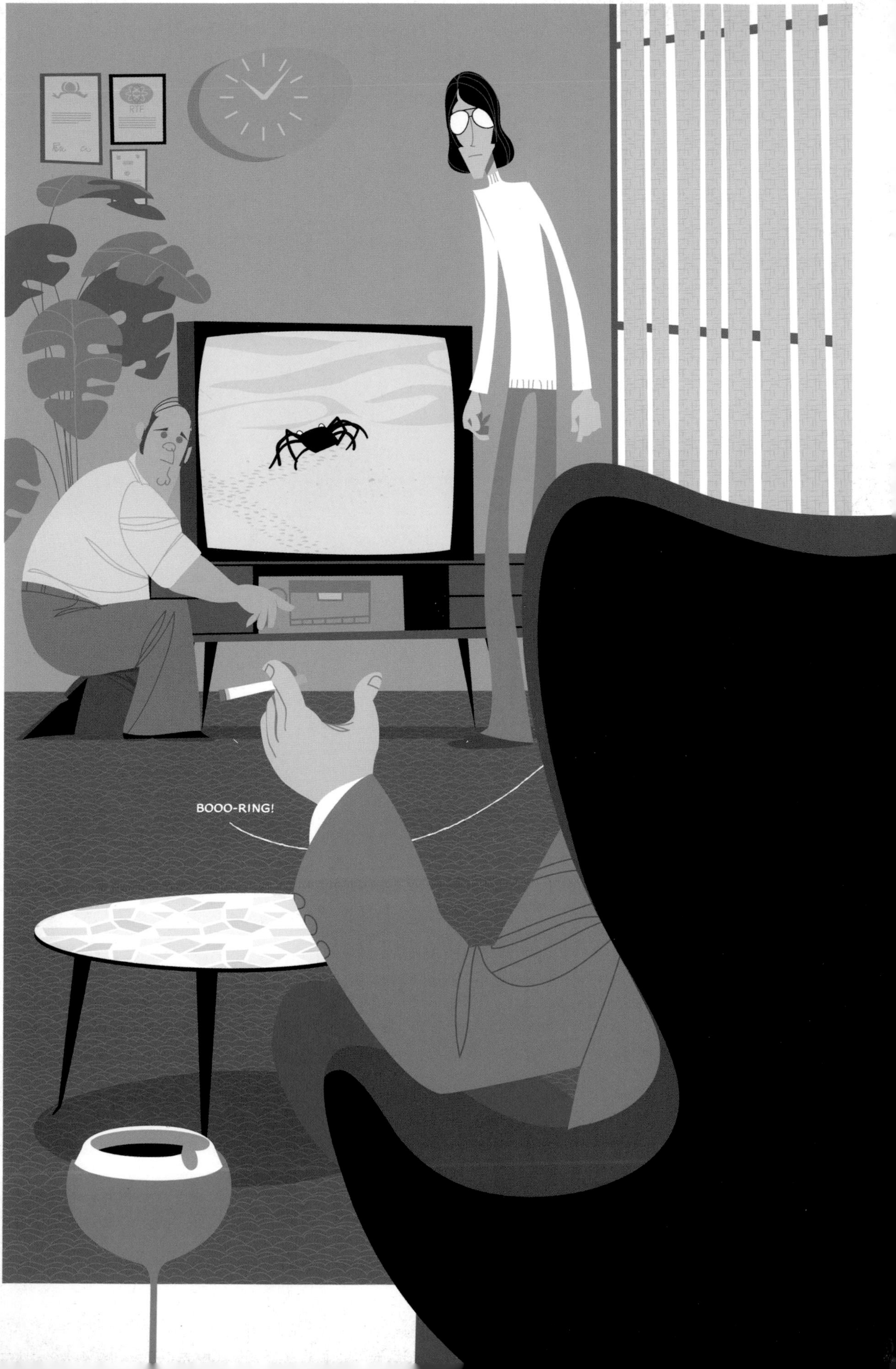
BOOO-RING!

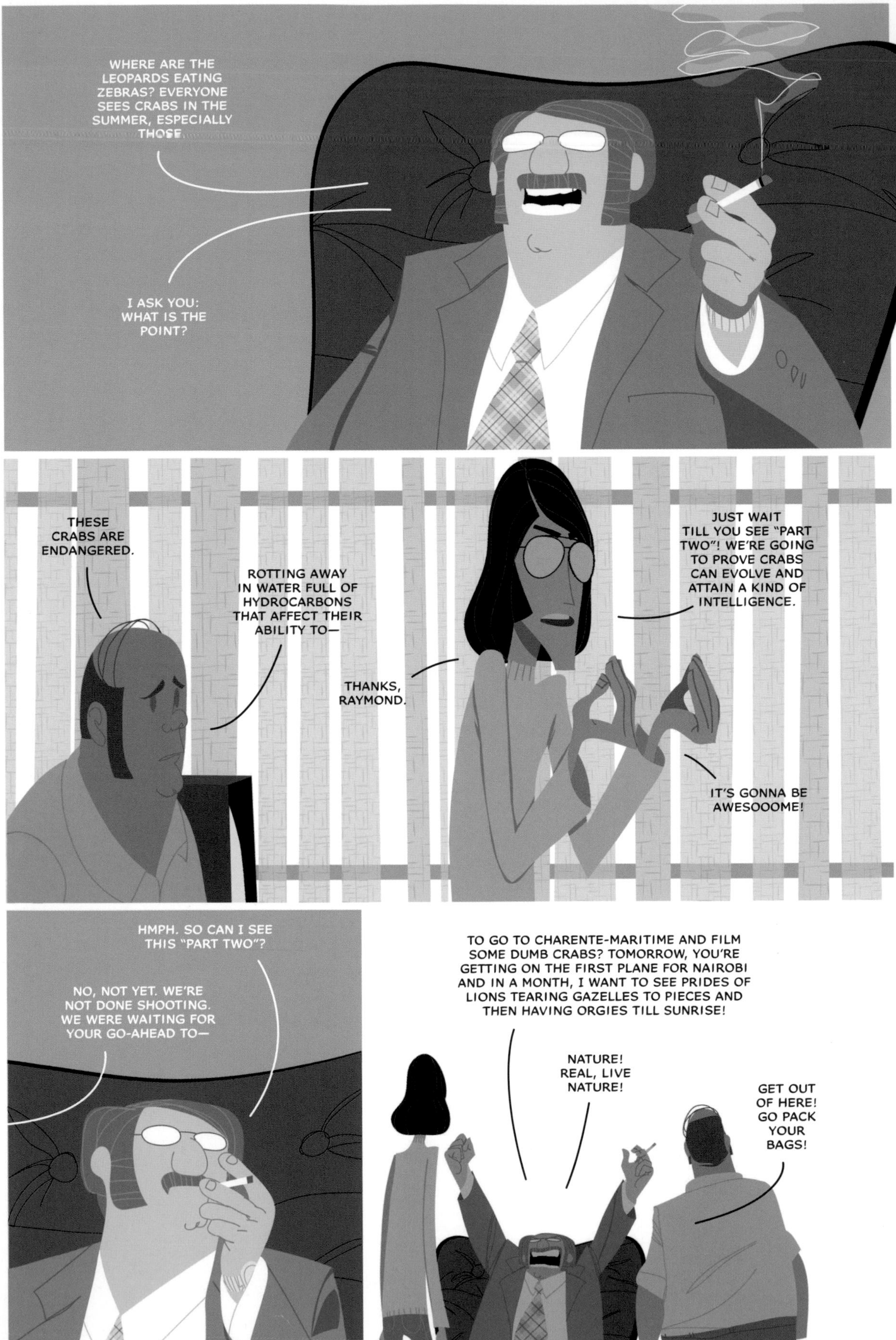
WHERE ARE THE LEOPARDS EATING ZEBRAS? EVERYONE SEES CRABS IN THE SUMMER, ESPECIALLY THOSE.
I ASK YOU: WHAT IS THE POINT?
THESE CRABS ARE ENDANGERED.
ROTTING AWAY IN WATER FULL OF HYDROCARBONS THAT AFFECT THEIR ABILITY TO—
THANKS, RAYMOND.
JUST WAIT TILL YOU SEE "PART TWO"! WE'RE GOING TO PROVE CRABS CAN EVOLVE AND ATTAIN A KIND OF INTELLIGENCE.
IT'S GONNA BE AWESOOOME!
HMPH. SO CAN I SEE THIS "PART TWO"?
NO, NOT YET. WE'RE NOT DONE SHOOTING. WE WERE WAITING FOR YOUR GO-AHEAD TO—
TO GO TO CHARENTE-MARITIME AND FILM SOME DUMB CRABS? TOMORROW, YOU'RE GETTING ON THE FIRST PLANE FOR NAIROBI AND IN A MONTH, I WANT TO SEE PRIDES OF LIONS TEARING GAZELLES TO PIECES AND THEN HAVING ORGIES TILL SUNRISE!
NATURE! REAL, LIVE NATURE!
GET OUT OF HERE! GO PACK YOUR BAGS!

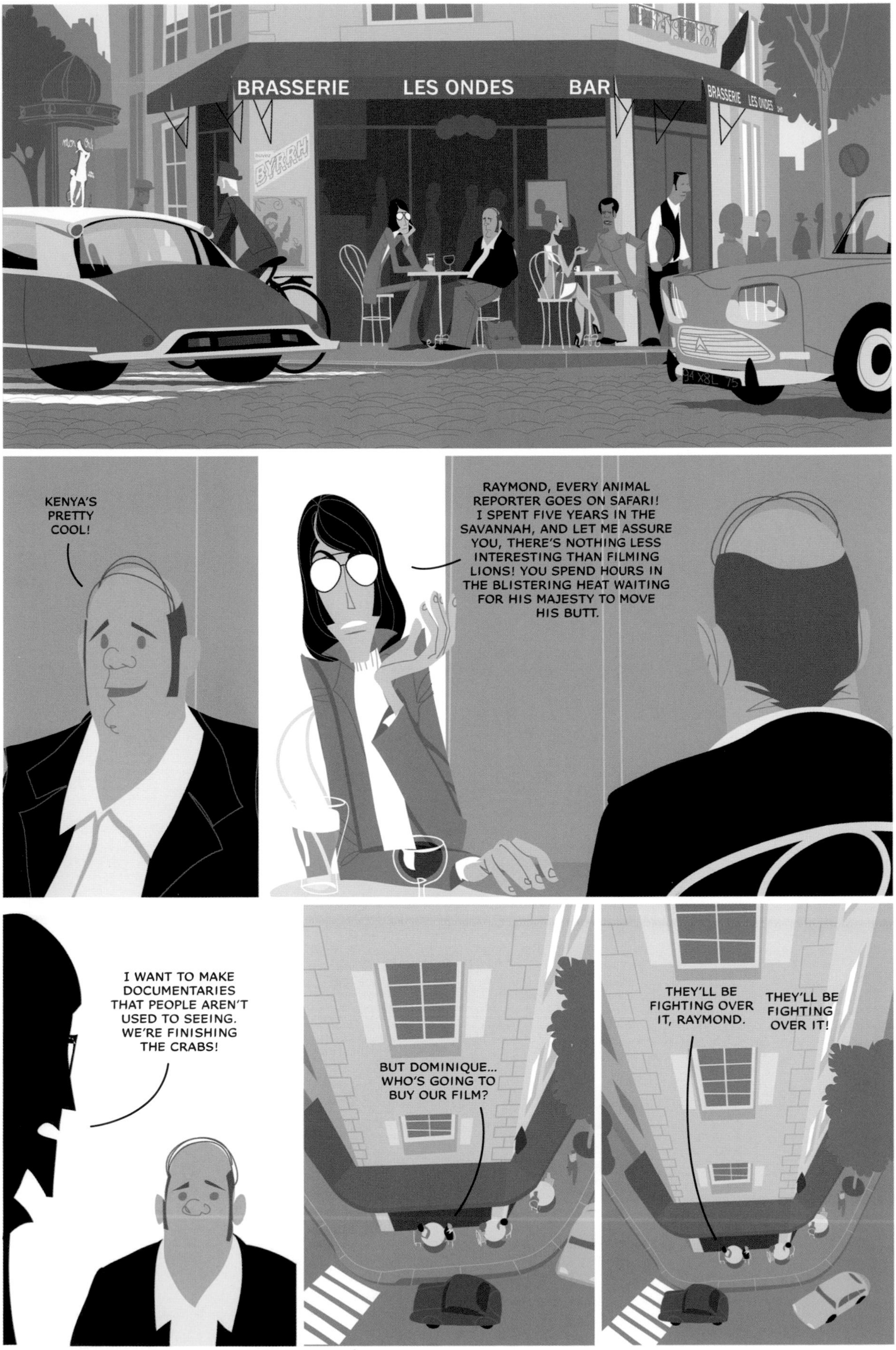
BRASSERIE LES ONDES BAR
BYRRH
KENYA'S PRETTY COOL!
RAYMOND, EVERY ANIMAL REPORTER GOES ON SAFARI! I SPENT FIVE YEARS IN THE SAVANNAH, AND LET ME ASSURE YOU, THERE'S NOTHING LESS INTERESTING THAN FILMING LIONS! YOU SPEND HOURS IN THE BLISTERING HEAT WAITING FOR HIS MAJESTY TO MOVE HIS BUTT.
I WANT TO MAKE DOCUMENTARIES THAT PEOPLE AREN'T USED TO SEEING. WE'RE FINISHING THE CRABS!
BUT DOMINIQUE... WHO'S GOING TO BUY OUR FILM?
THEY'LL BE FIGHTING OVER IT, RAYMOND.
THEY'LL BE FIGHTING OVER IT!

YOOHOO! DID YOU KNOW THE END IS NIGH? PREPARE YOURSELF FOR WHAT LIES BEYOND, FOR SOON THERE SHALL BE NO MORE WATER IN THE GREAT POOL OF LIFE...

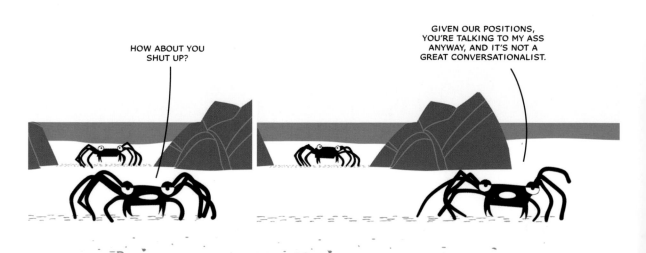

HOW ABOUT YOU SHUT UP?

GIVEN OUR POSITIONS, YOU'RE TALKING TO MY ASS ANYWAY, AND IT'S NOT A GREAT CONVERSATIONALIST.

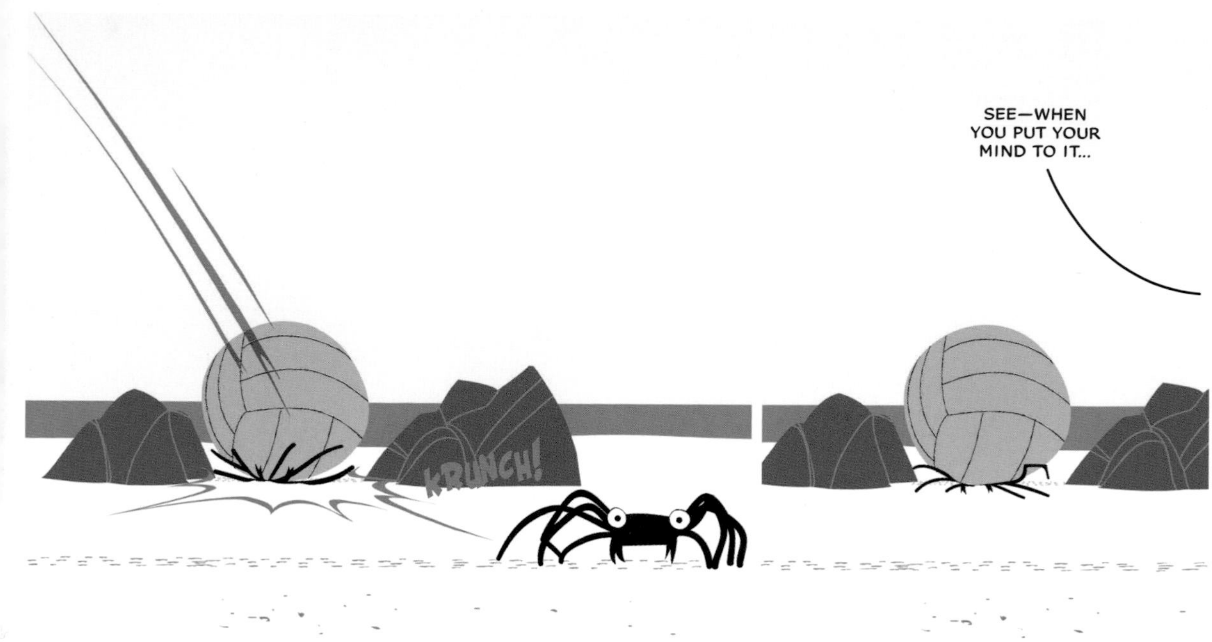
KRUNCH!
SEE—WHEN YOU PUT YOUR MIND TO IT...

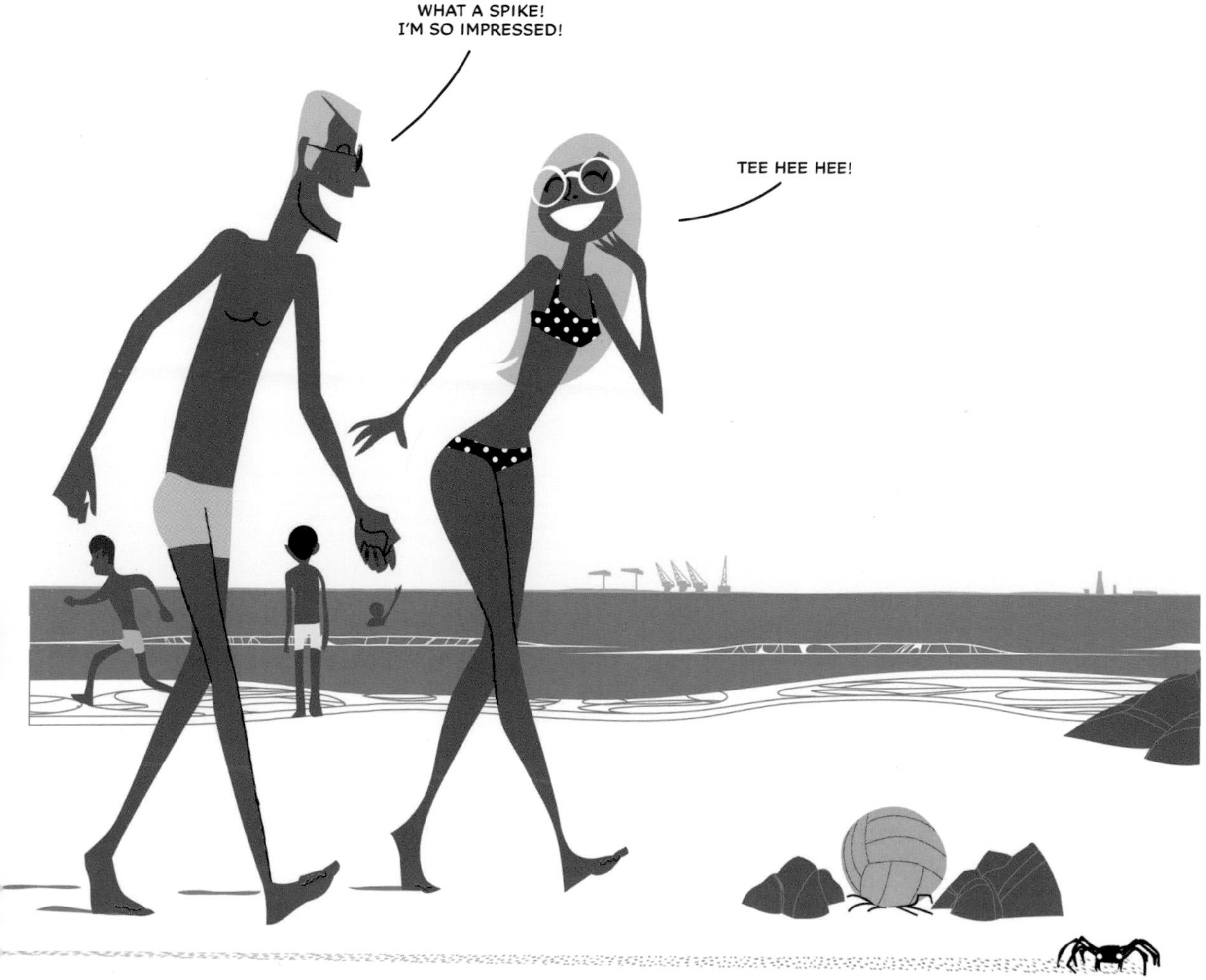
WHAT A SPIKE! I'M SO IMPRESSED!
TEE HEE HEE!

OH, LOOK! YOU SQUASHED A CRAB! GROSS! HA HA!
HUMANS!
GLUG
GLUG
JUST WHERE ARE YOU TAKING ME?
LET'S JUST TELL THEM IT TOOK US A WHILE TO FIND THE BALL...
OH, YOU NAUGHTY— NOT HERE! PEOPLE WILL SEE US!
PANT!
PANT!
AW, C'MON, VERONICA!
JEAN-LUC, I JUST—
NO!
C'MON!
NO.
HOW ABOUT HERE? IS THIS FAR ENOUGH?!
WELL OK, BUT JUST THIS ONCE......
... YES!
YES.
YES.
MMMM... OHHH
YESSSS...
?

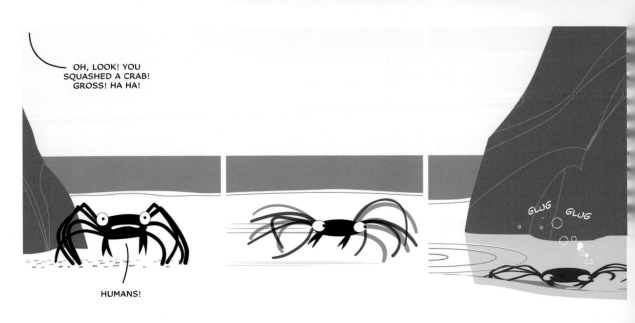

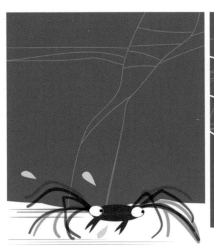

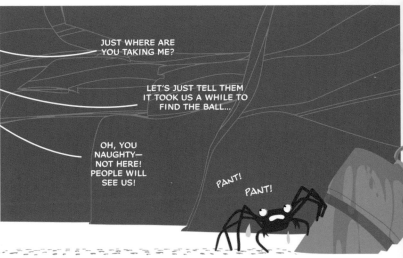

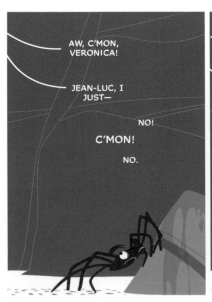

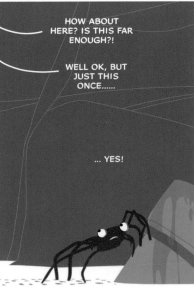

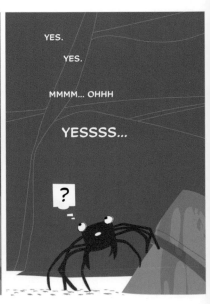

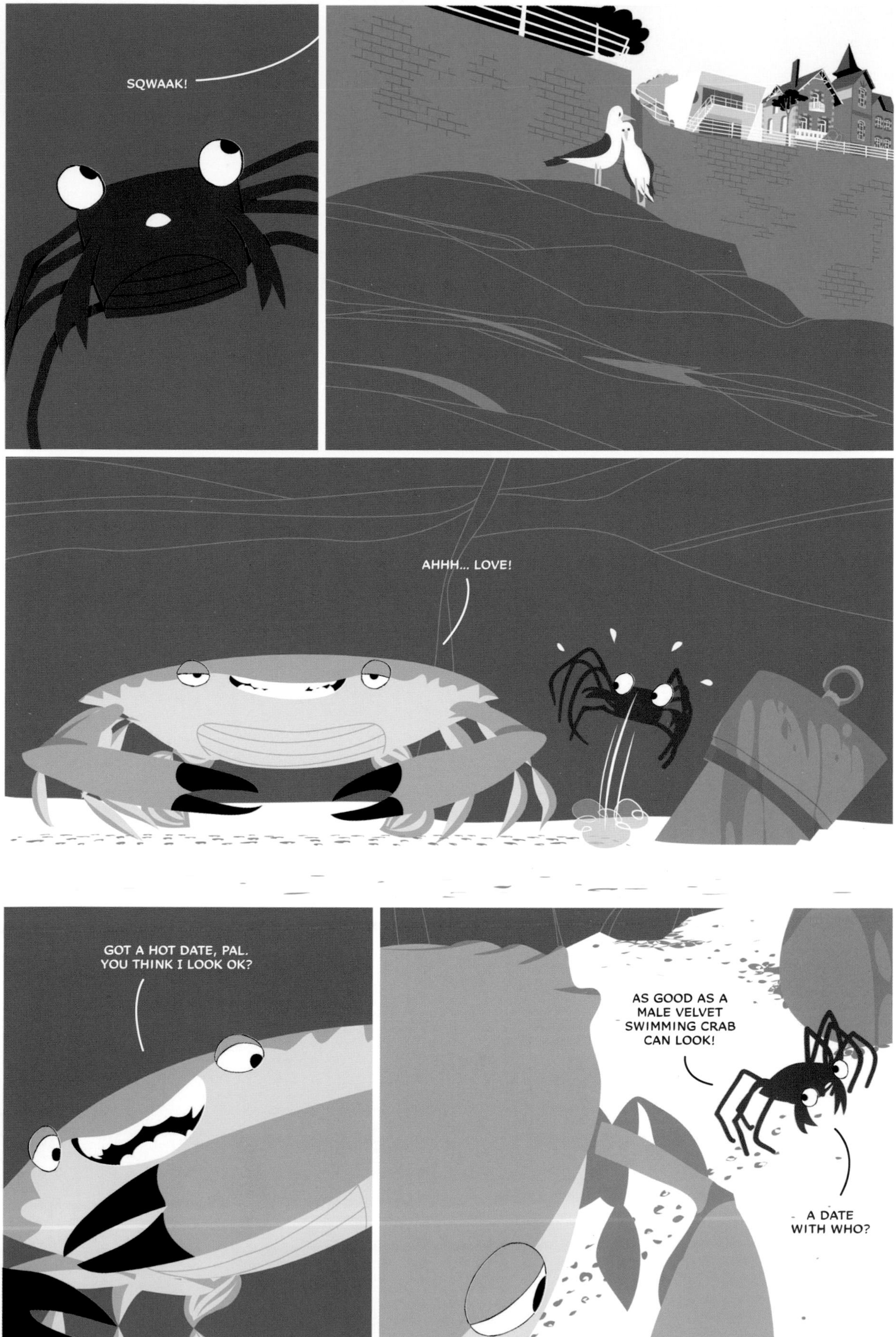
SQWAAK!
AHHH... LOVE!
GOT A HOT DATE, PAL. YOU THINK I LOOK OK?
AS GOOD AS A MALE VELVET SWIMMING CRAB CAN LOOK!
A DATE WITH WHO?

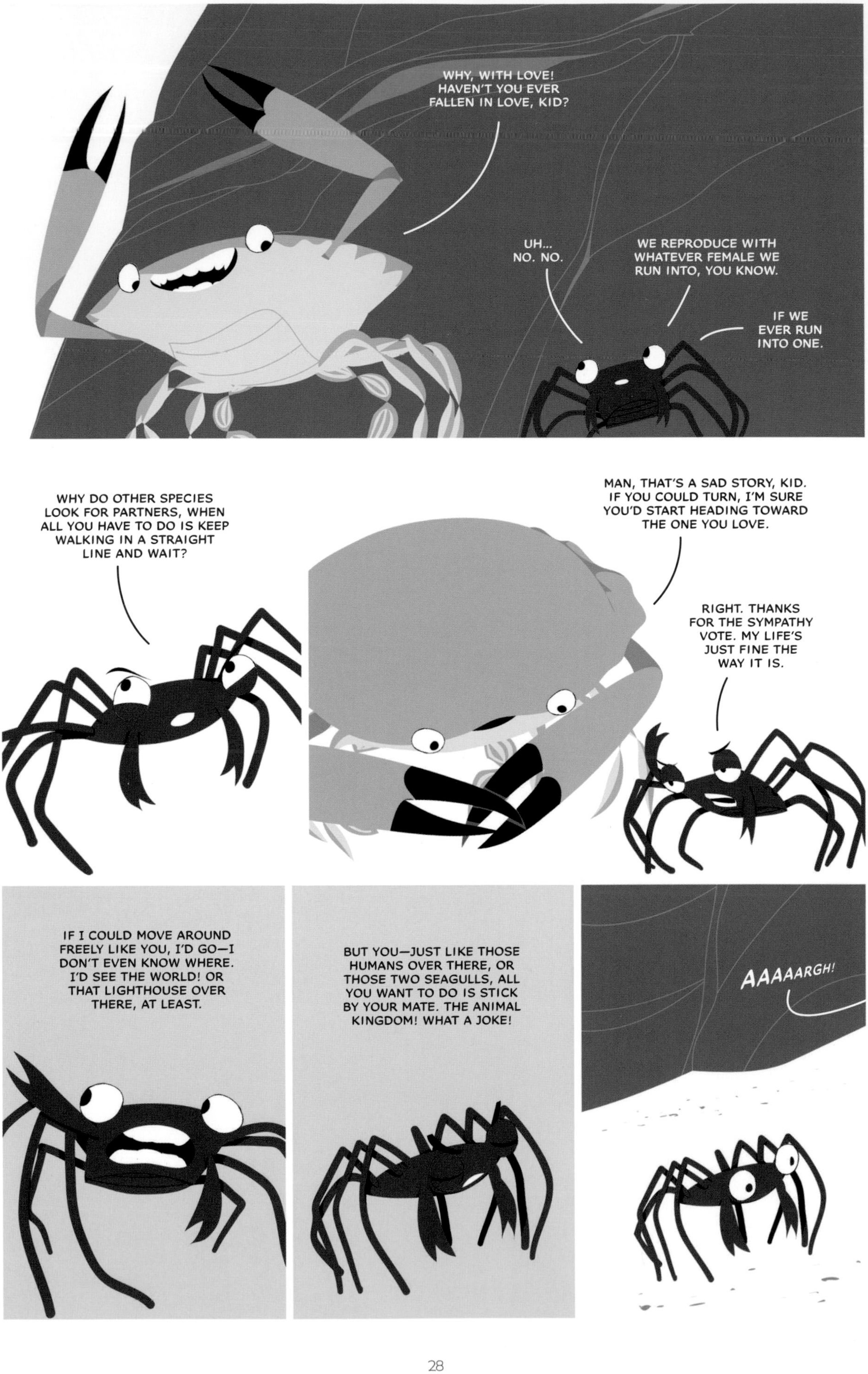
WHY, WITH LOVE! HAVEN'T YOU EVER FALLEN IN LOVE, KID?
UH... NO. NO.
WE REPRODUCE WITH WHATEVER FEMALE WE RUN INTO, YOU KNOW.
IF WE EVER RUN INTO ONE.
WHY DO OTHER SPECIES LOOK FOR PARTNERS, WHEN ALL YOU HAVE TO DO IS KEEP WALKING IN A STRAIGHT LINE AND WAIT?
MAN, THAT'S A SAD STORY, KID. IF YOU COULD TURN, I'M SURE YOU'D START HEADING TOWARD THE ONE YOU LOVE.
RIGHT. THANKS FOR THE SYMPATHY VOTE. MY LIFE'S JUST FINE THE WAY IT IS.
IF I COULD MOVE AROUND FREELY LIKE YOU, I'D GO—I DON'T EVEN KNOW WHERE. I'D SEE THE WORLD! OR THAT LIGHTHOUSE OVER THERE, AT LEAST.
BUT YOU—JUST LIKE THOSE HUMANS OVER THERE, OR THOSE TWO SEAGULLS, ALL YOU WANT TO DO IS STICK BY YOUR MATE. THE ANIMAL KINGDOM! WHAT A JOKE!
AAAAARGH!

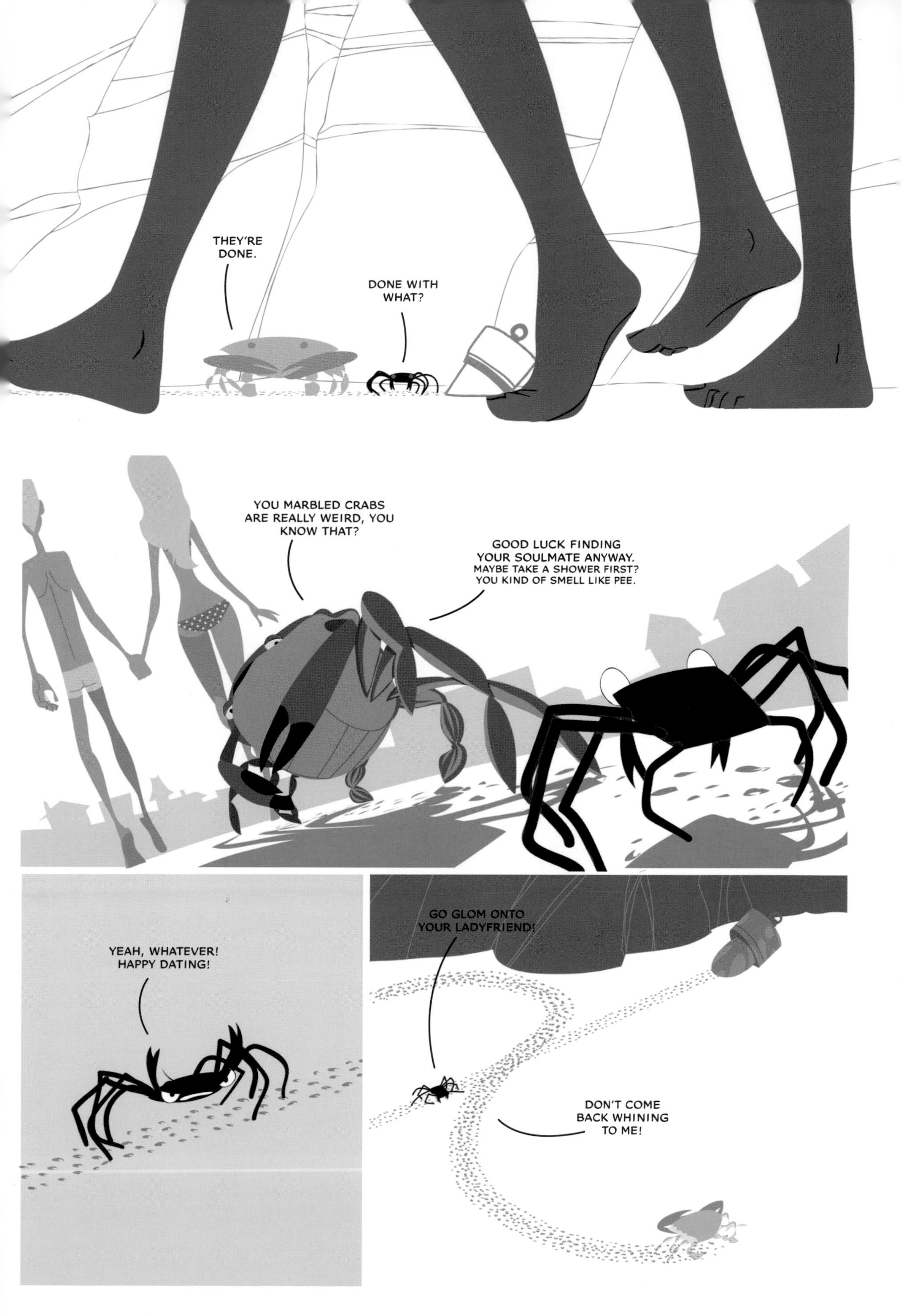
THEY'RE DONE.
DONE WITH WHAT?
YOU MARBLED CRABS ARE REALLY WEIRD, YOU KNOW THAT?
GOOD LUCK FINDING YOUR SOULMATE ANYWAY. MAYBE TAKE A SHOWER FIRST? YOU KIND OF SMELL LIKE PEE.
YEAH, WHATEVER! HAPPY DATING!
GO GLOM ONTO YOUR LADYFRIEND!
DON'T COME BACK WHINING TO ME!

YEAH YEAH YEAH... IF YOU COULD TURN YADDA YADDA THE ONE YOU LOVE YADDA
I DON'T GIVE A DAMN ABOUT WEDDING BELLS!
... EDDING BELLS
... BELLS
SHUT UP!
ME, I HAD A FRIEND ONCE...
DUDE, YOU STILL ALIVE?
OW! LEAVE ME ALONE!

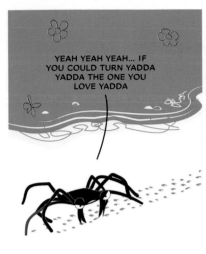

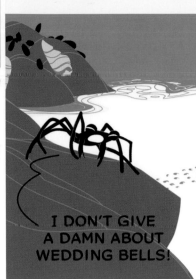

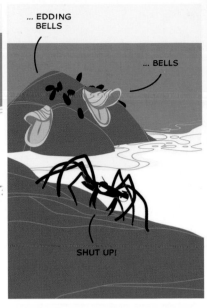

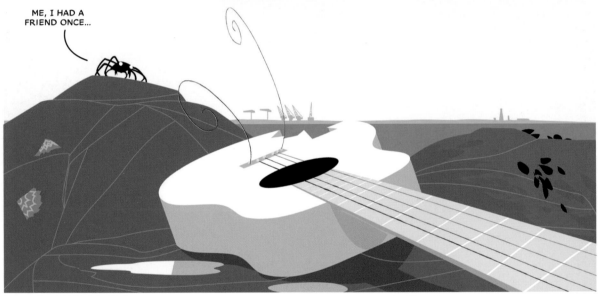

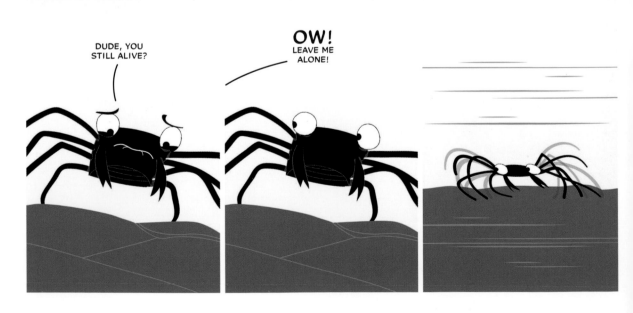

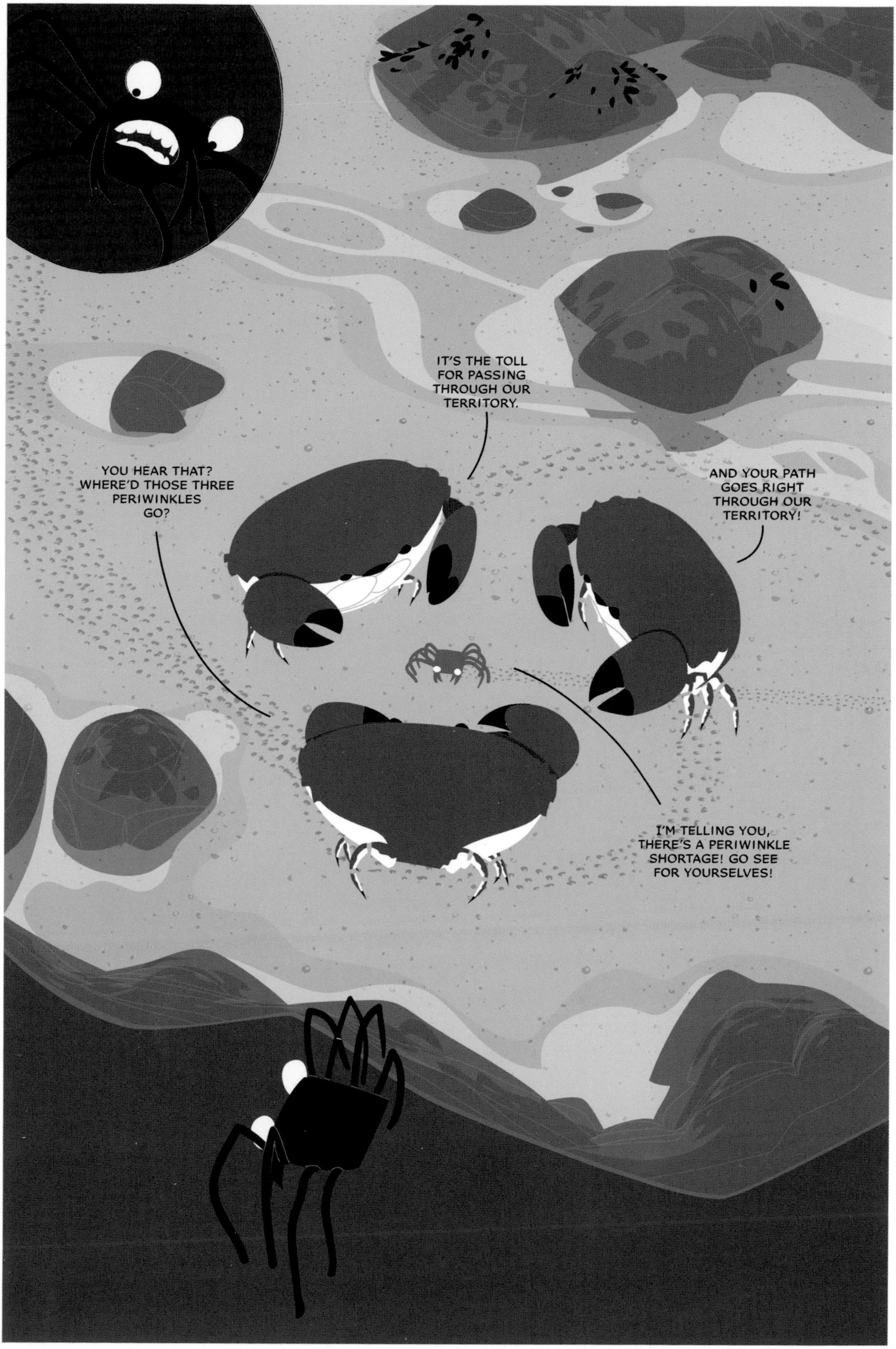
IT'S THE TOLL FOR PASSING THROUGH OUR TERRITORY.
AND YOUR PATH GOES RIGHT THROUGH OUR TERRITORY!
YOU HEAR THAT? WHERE'D THOSE THREE PERIWINKLES GO?
I'M TELLING YOU, THERE'S A PERIWINKLE SHORTAGE! GO SEE FOR YOURSELVES!

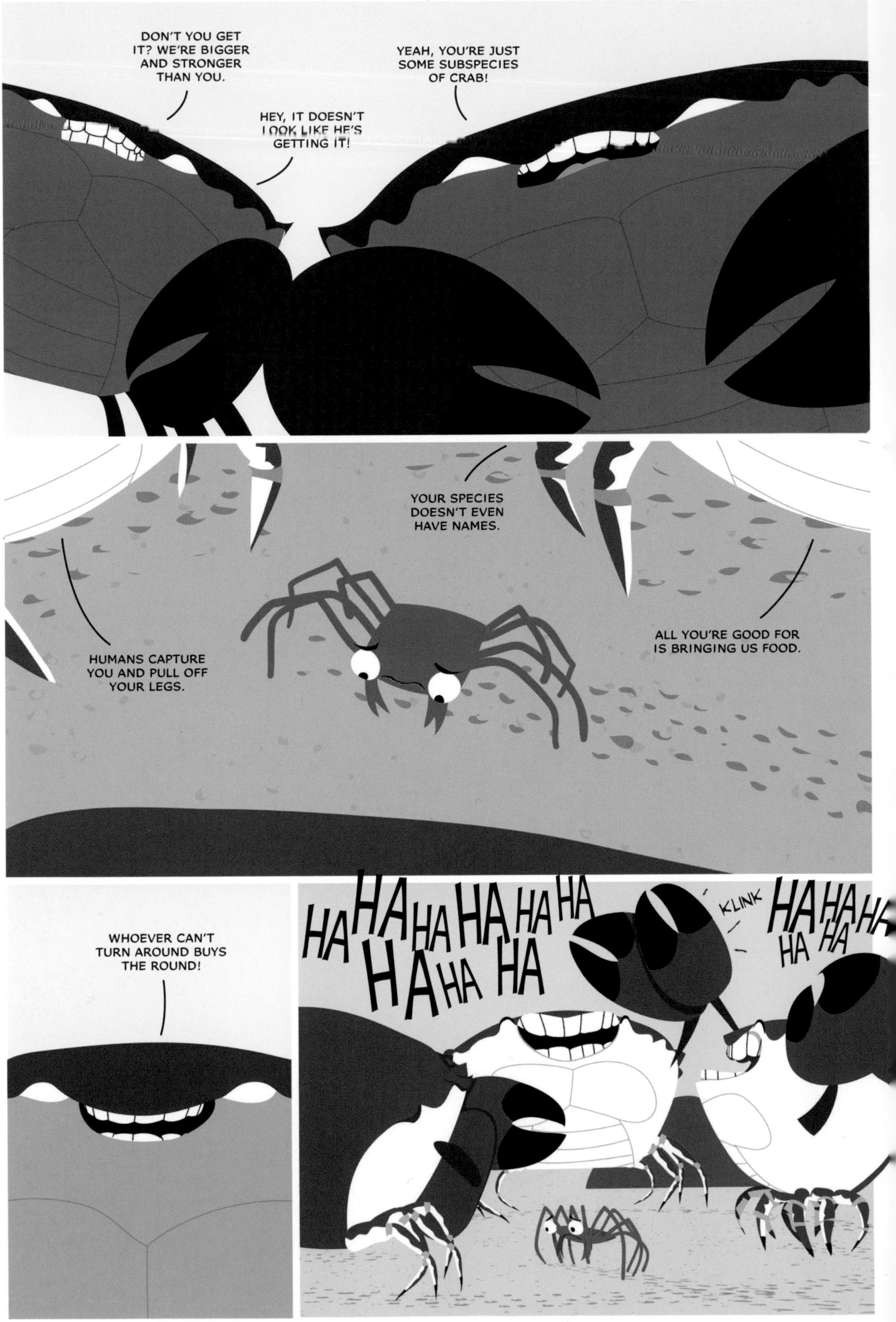
DON'T YOU GET IT? WE'RE BIGGER AND STRONGER THAN YOU.
HEY, IT DOESN'T LOOK LIKE HE'S GETTING IT!
YEAH, YOU'RE JUST SOME SUBSPECIES OF CRAB!
YOUR SPECIES DOESN'T EVEN HAVE NAMES.
HUMANS CAPTURE YOU AND PULL OFF YOUR LEGS.
ALL YOU'RE GOOD FOR IS BRINGING US FOOD.
WHOEVER CAN'T TURN AROUND BUYS THE ROUND!
HA HA HA HA HA HA HA HA HA HA HA
KLINK
HA HA HA HA HA

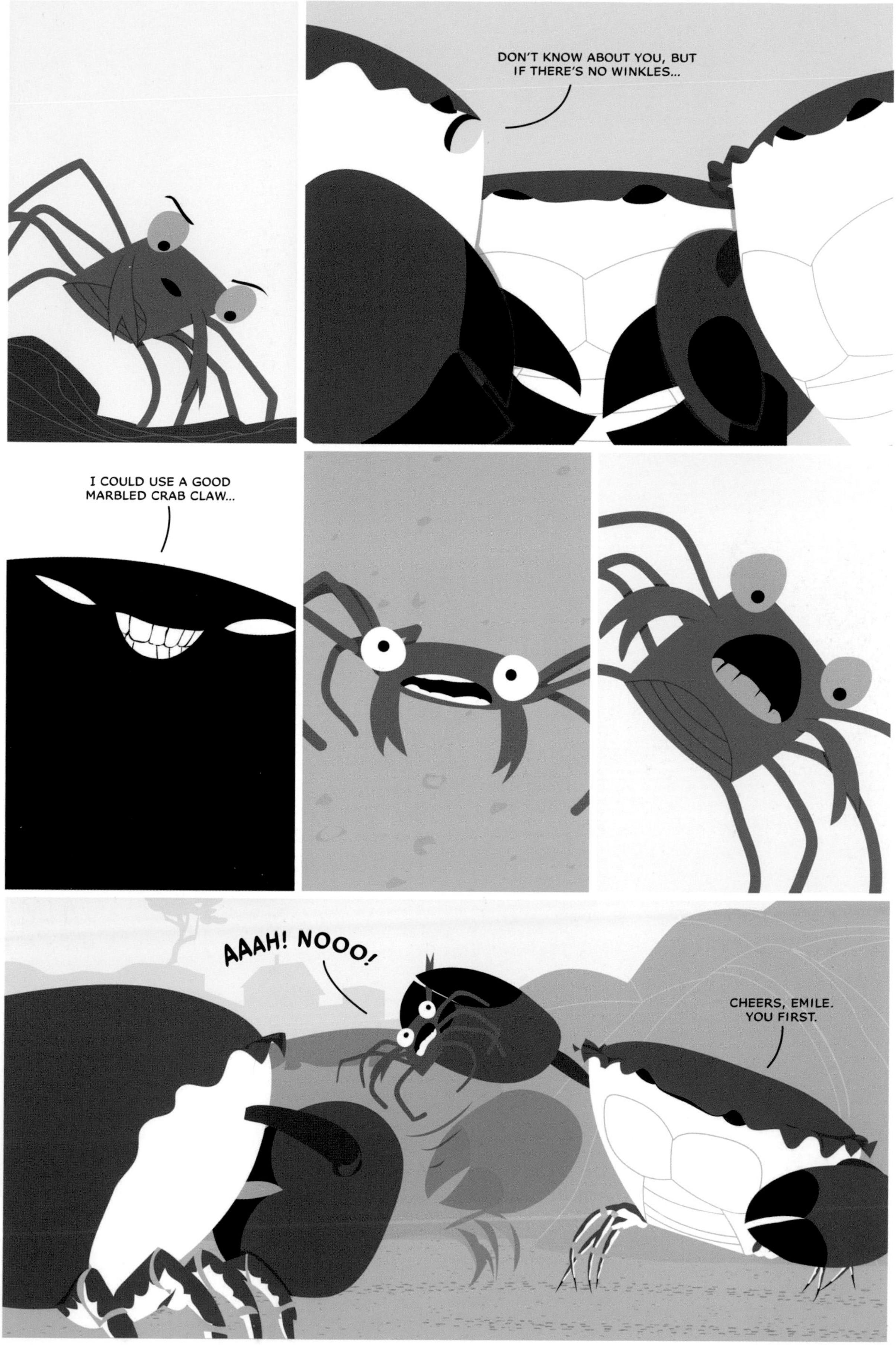
DON'T KNOW ABOUT YOU, BUT IF THERE'S NO WINKLES...
I COULD USE A GOOD MARBLED CRAB CLAW...
AAAH! NOOO!
CHEERS, EMILE. YOU FIRST.

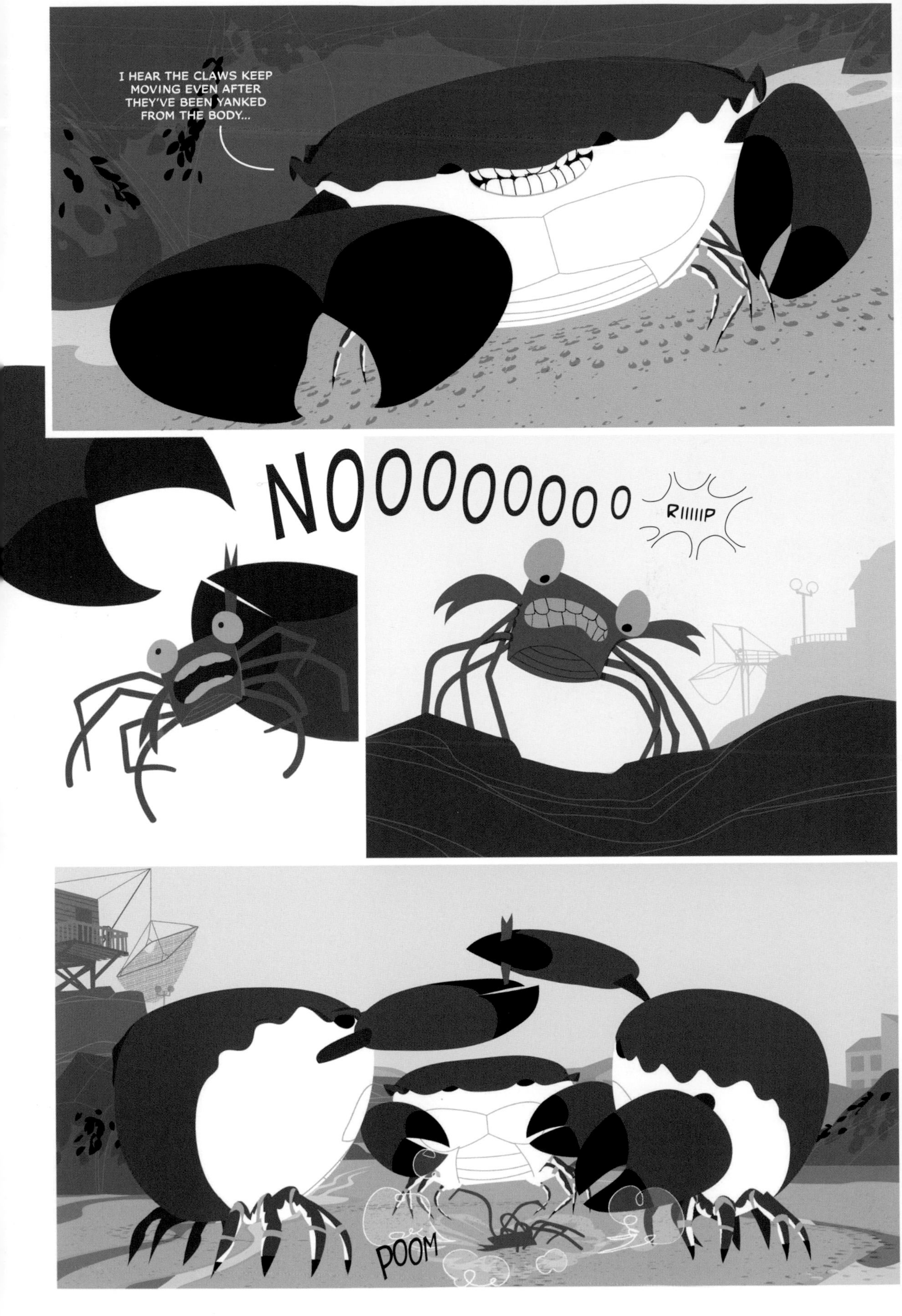
I HEAR THE CLAWS KEEP MOVING EVEN AFTER THEY'VE BEEN YANKED FROM THE BODY...
NOOOOOOOO
RIIIIIP
POOM

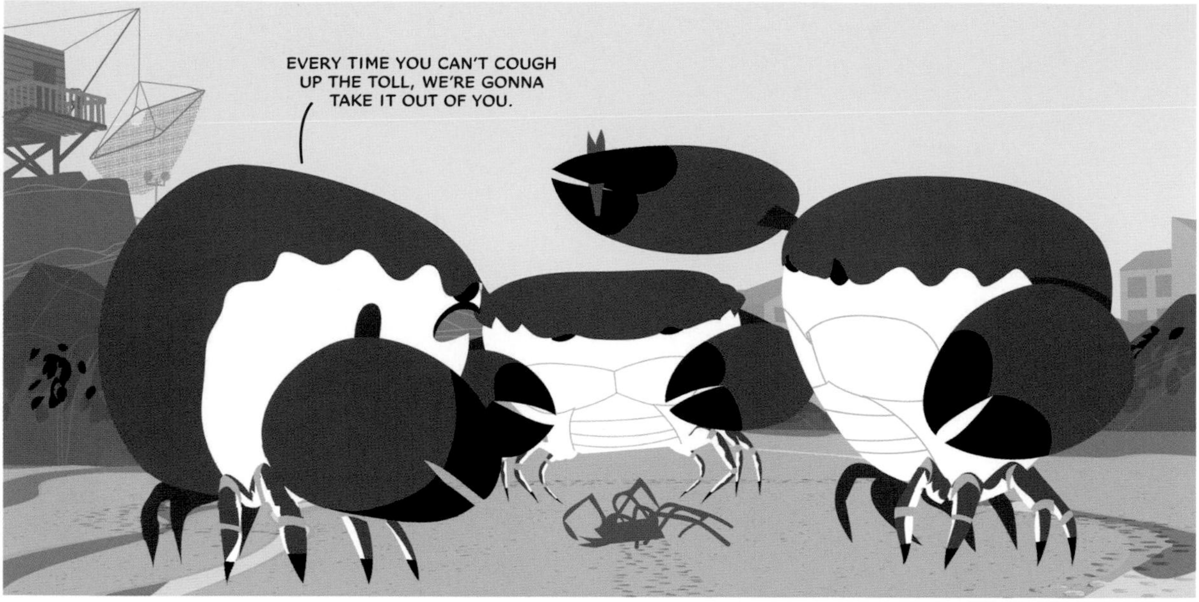
EVERY TIME YOU CAN'T COUGH UP THE TOLL, WE'RE GONNA TAKE IT OUT OF YOU.

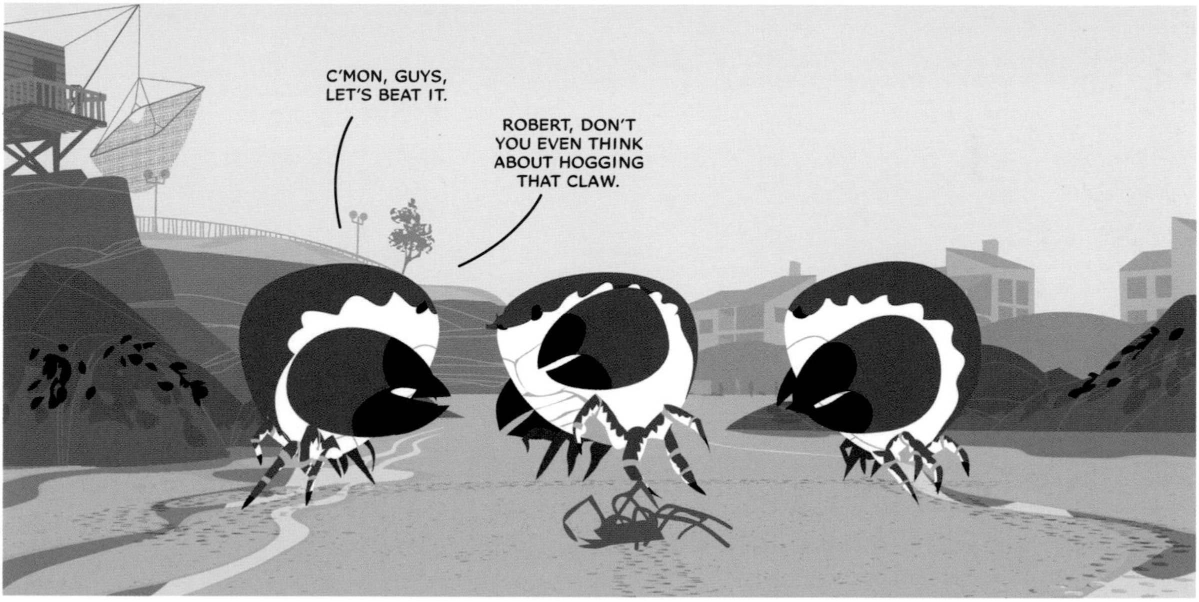
C'MON, GUYS, LET'S BEAT IT.
ROBERT, DON'T YOU EVEN THINK ABOUT HOGGING THAT CLAW.

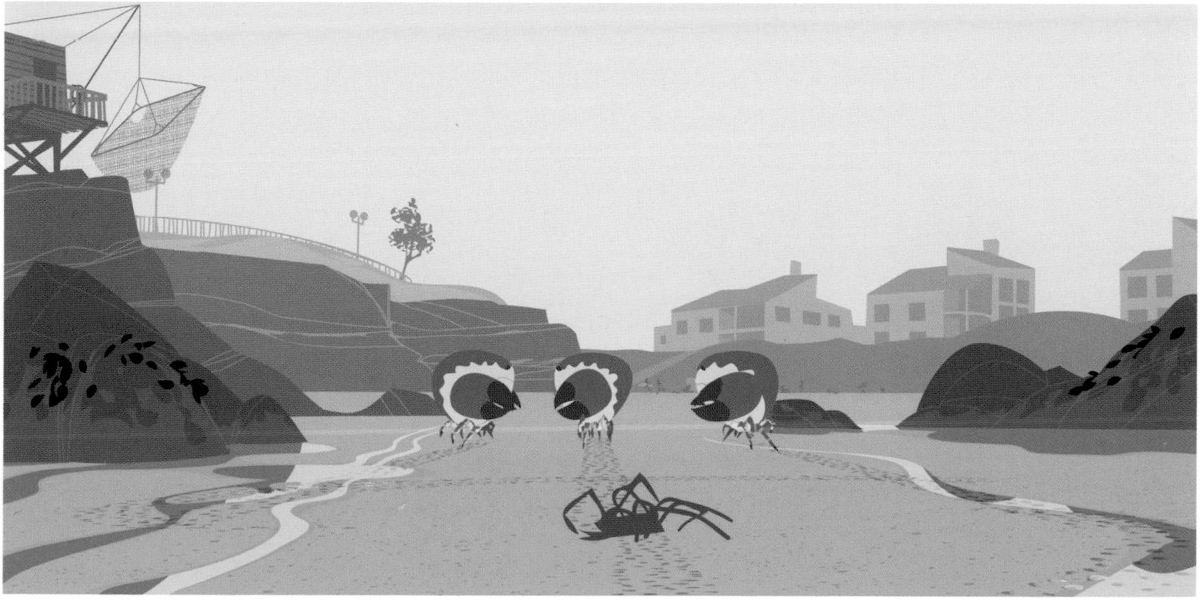

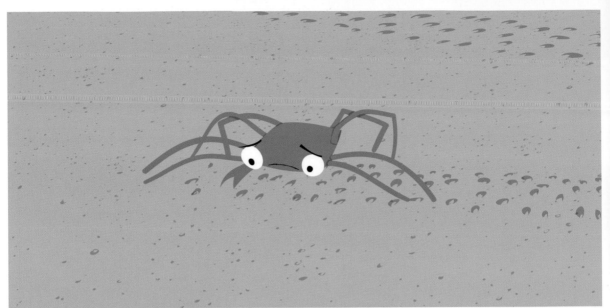

WHY?

WHY DID NATURE MAKE US LIKE THIS?

WHY US?

IS THIS OUR PURPOSE IN LIFE?

TO TAKE CRAP FROM EVERYONE ELSE?

OH, MARBLED CRABS ARE SO FUNNY! LOOK: THEY CAN'T TURN! HILARIOUS!

PATHETIC! A WHOLE LIFE SPENT MOVING IN A STRAIGHT LINE. AND WORST OF ALL, LADIES AND GENTS, IS THEY MEET SO RARELY...
THEY DON'T EVEN BOTHER HAVING NAMES.
HEY!
WHAT'S HAPPENING? HEY, CUT IT OUT DOWN THERE!

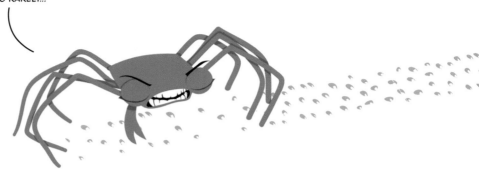

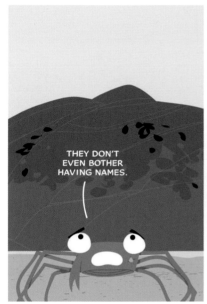

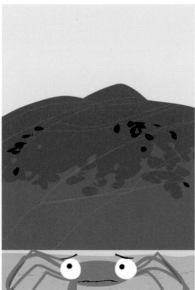

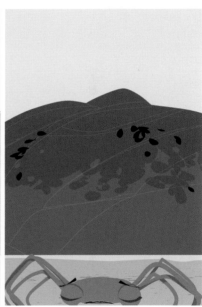

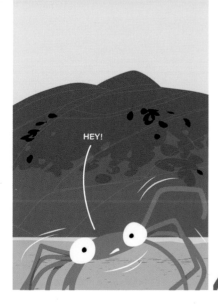

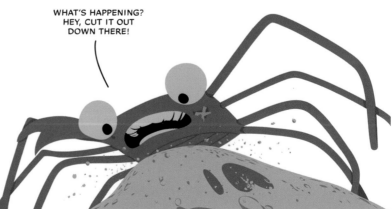

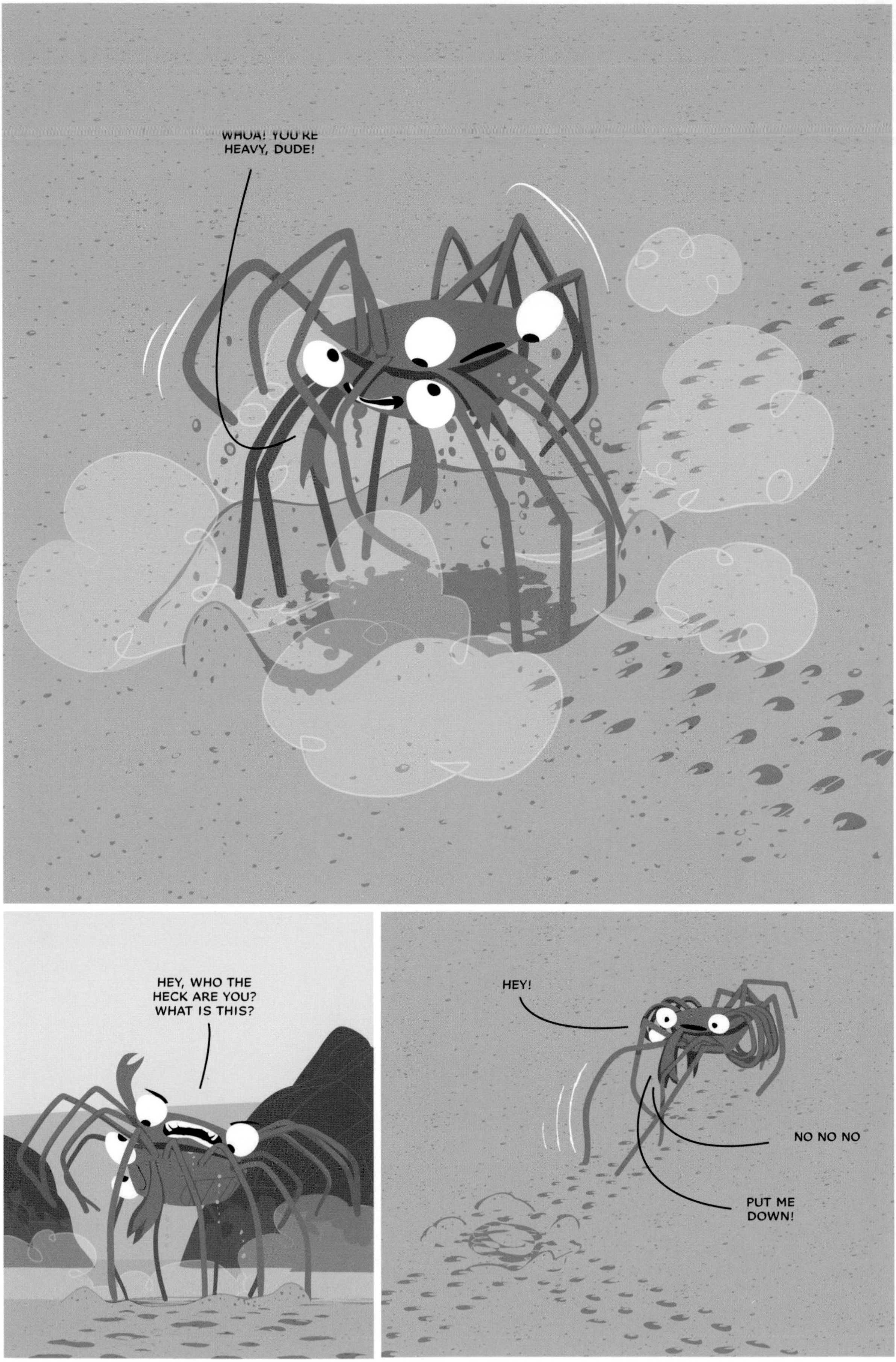
WHOA! YOU'RE HEAVY, DUDE!
HEY, WHO THE HECK ARE YOU? WHAT IS THIS?
HEY!
NO NO NO
PUT ME DOWN!

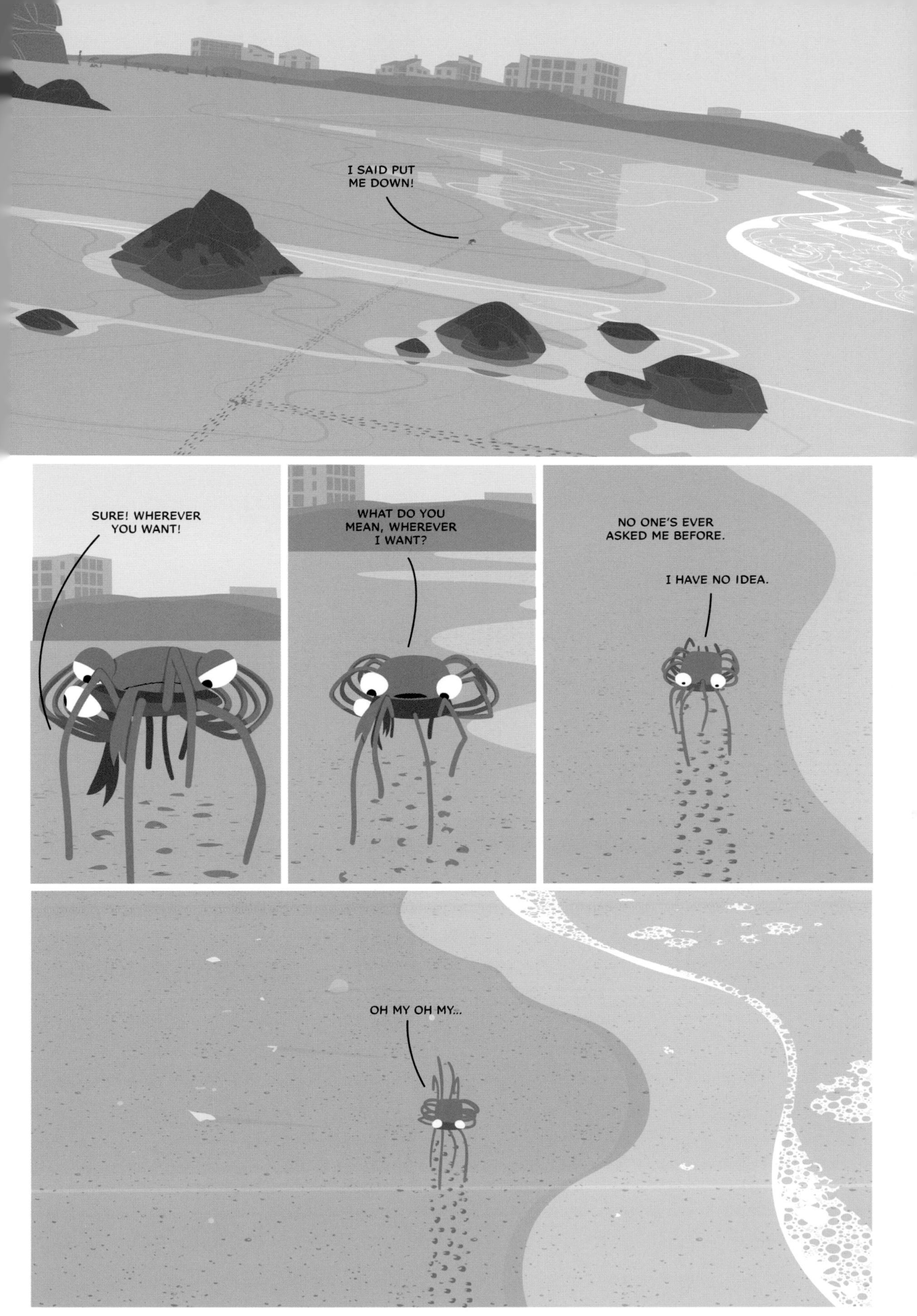
I SAID PUT ME DOWN!
SURE! WHEREVER YOU WANT!
WHAT DO YOU MEAN, WHEREVER I WANT?
NO ONE'S EVER ASKED ME BEFORE.
I HAVE NO IDEA.
OH MY OH MY...

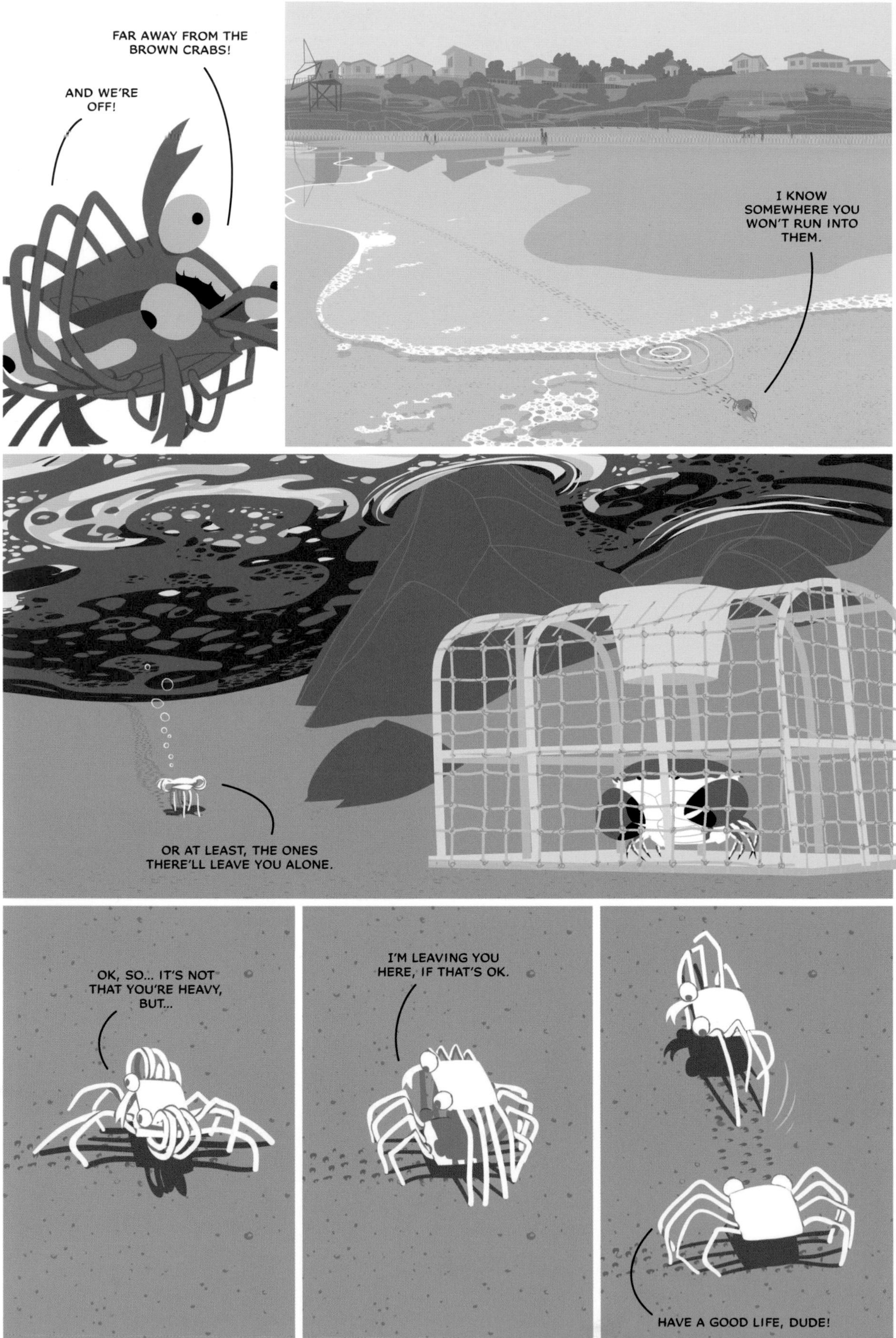
AND WE'RE OFF!
FAR AWAY FROM THE BROWN CRABS!
I KNOW SOMEWHERE YOU WON'T RUN INTO THEM.
OR AT LEAST, THE ONES THERE'LL LEAVE YOU ALONE.
OK, SO... IT'S NOT THAT YOU'RE HEAVY, BUT...
I'M LEAVING YOU HERE, IF THAT'S OK.
HAVE A GOOD LIFE, DUDE!

THANKS!

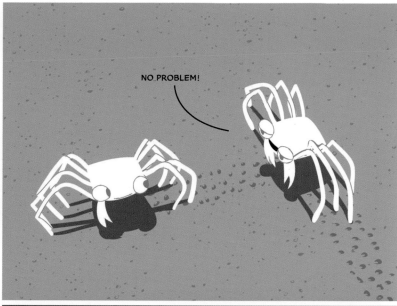

NO PROBLEM!

THIS IS A FIRST FOR ME, SO I WASN'T REALLY SURE WHAT TO MAKE OF IT, Y'KNOW?

WHAT'S A FIRST?

WELL, USUALLY WHEN I CROSS PATHS WITH ANOTHER MARBLED CRAB...

NOTHING HAPPENS. WE JUST CROSS PATHS.

WE NEVER SAY "SEE YOU LATER" BECAUSE WE DON'T KNOW IF WE WILL.

THAT'S WHY WE DON'T HAVE NAMES, Y'KNOW.

SO WHY DON'T WE GIVE EACH OTHER NAMES?

SINCE WE'RE GOING TO SEE EACH OTHER AGAIN.
GOOD IDEA!
GREAT, LET'S DO IT!
I KNOW! SINCE YOU ONLY HAVE ONE CLAW, LET'S CALL YOU "CLAW"!
UH... THAT'S SWEET, BUT I'D RATHER FORGET THAT EVER HAPPENED.
OOPS. SORRY.
I'M STILL GRIEVING, Y'KNOW?
OH, I KNOW! SINCE YOUR PATH GOES FROM EAST TO WEST LIKE THE SUN, WE'LL CALL YOU "SUNNY"!
ZZZ..
NIIIIICE! AND SINCE YOU GO THE SAME WAY AS THE BIG SHIPS ALONG THE ESTUARY...
... WE'LL CALL YOU "BOATER"!

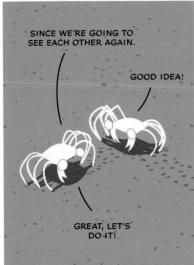

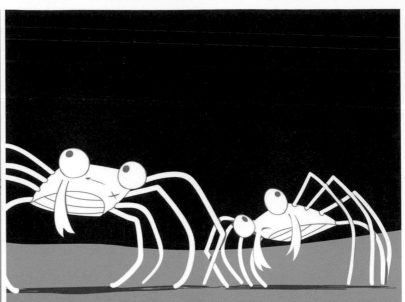

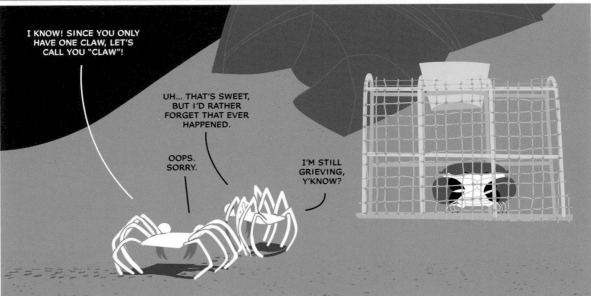

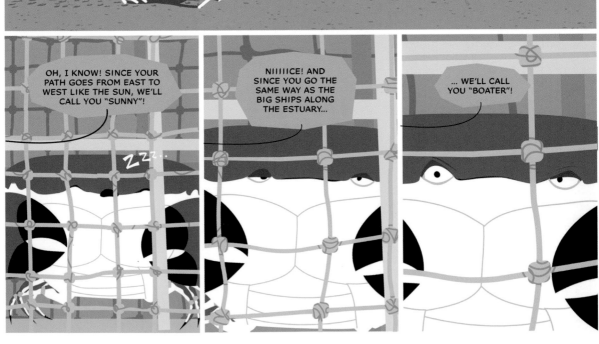

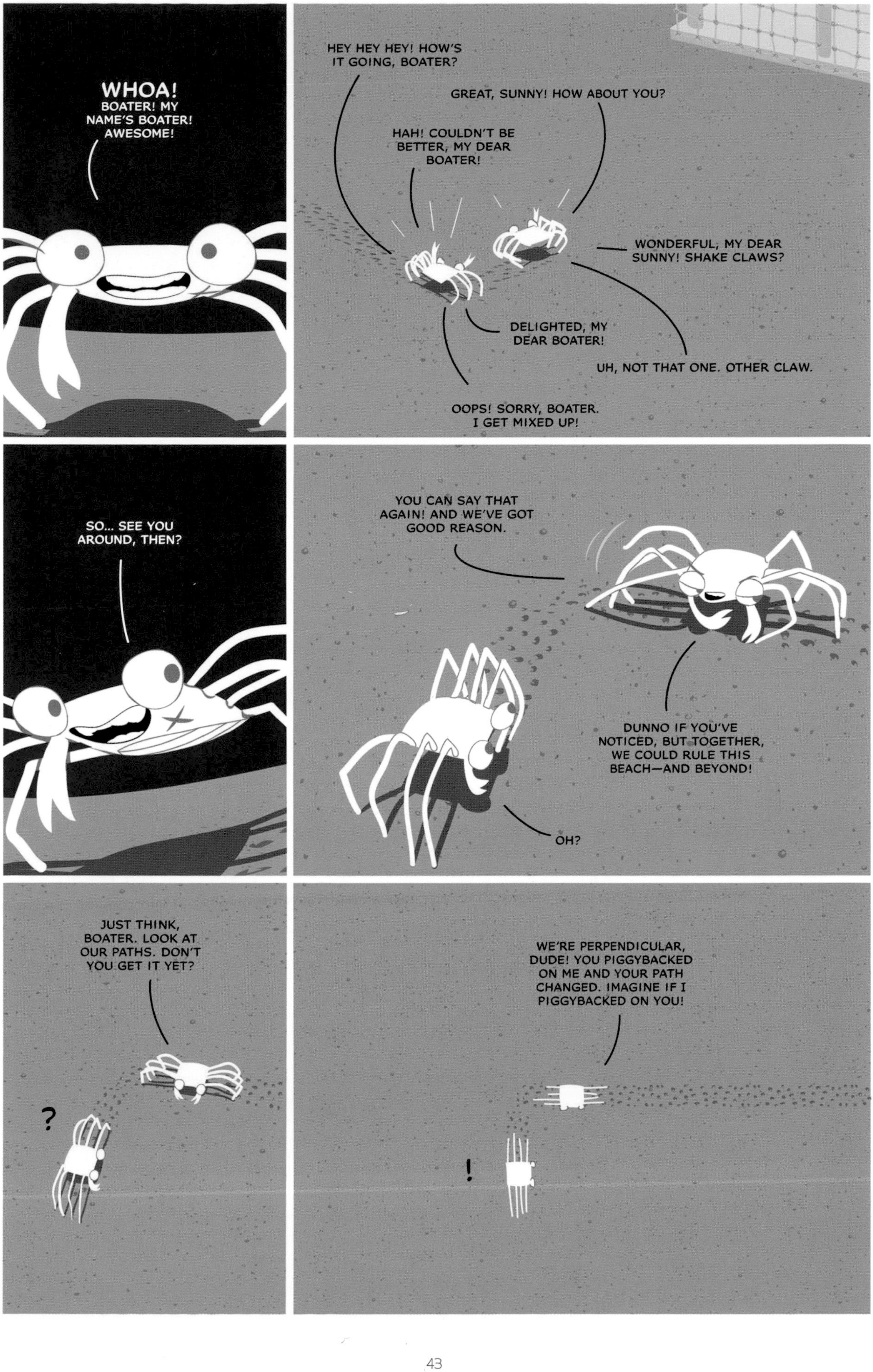
WHOA!
BOATER! MY NAME'S BOATER! AWESOME!
HEY HEY HEY! HOW'S IT GOING, BOATER?
GREAT, SUNNY! HOW ABOUT YOU?
HAH! COULDN'T BE BETTER, MY DEAR BOATER!
WONDERFUL, MY DEAR SUNNY! SHAKE CLAWS?
DELIGHTED, MY DEAR BOATER!
UH, NOT THAT ONE. OTHER CLAW.
OOPS! SORRY, BOATER. I GET MIXED UP!
SO... SEE YOU AROUND, THEN?
YOU CAN SAY THAT AGAIN! AND WE'VE GOT GOOD REASON.
DUNNO IF YOU'VE NOTICED, BUT TOGETHER, WE COULD RULE THIS BEACH—AND BEYOND!
OH?
JUST THINK, BOATER. LOOK AT OUR PATHS. DON'T YOU GET IT YET?
?
WE'RE PERPENDICULAR, DUDE! YOU PIGGYBACKED ON ME AND YOUR PATH CHANGED. IMAGINE IF I PIGGYBACKED ON YOU!
!

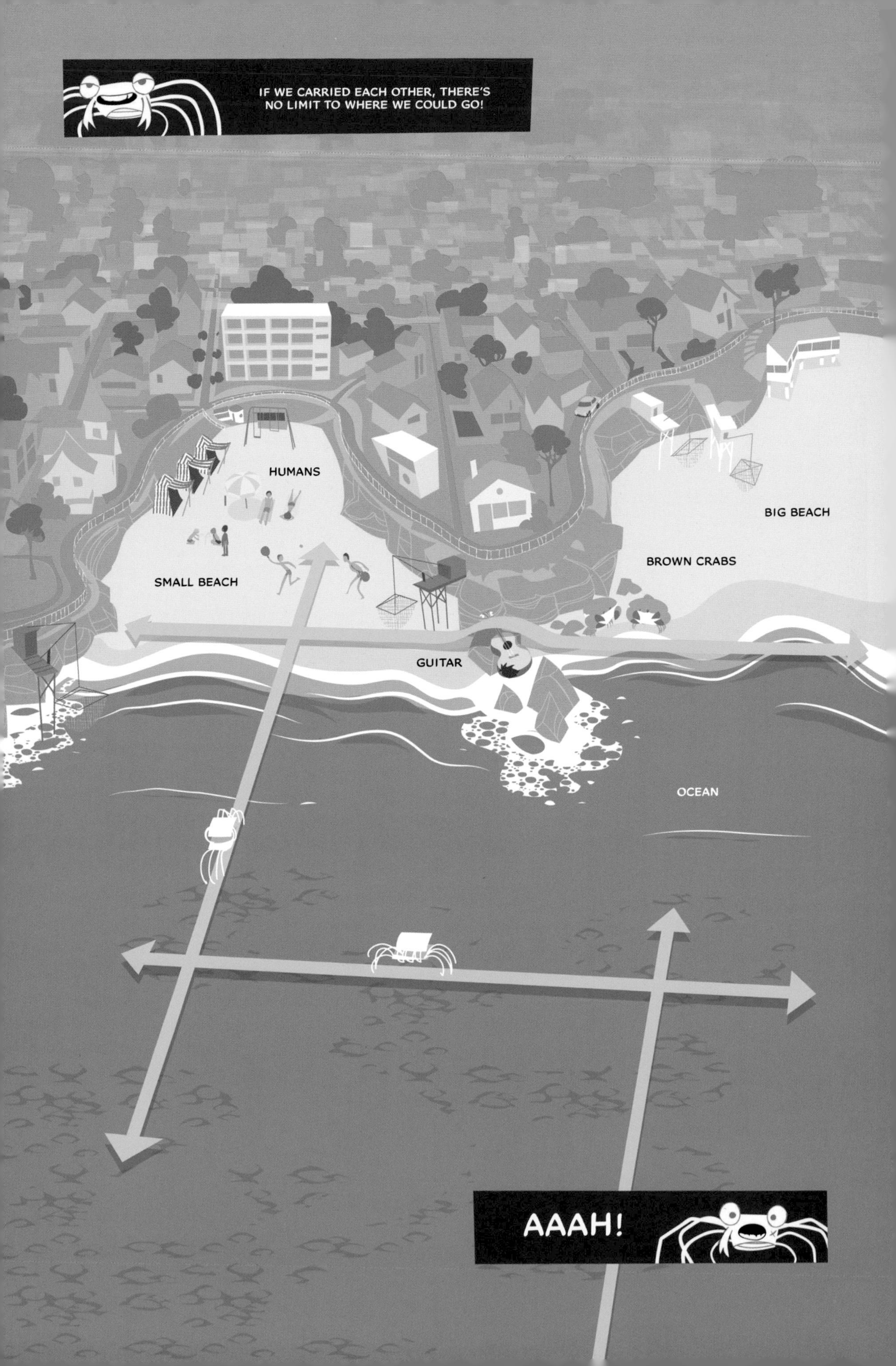
IF WE CARRIED EACH OTHER, THERE'S NO LIMIT TO WHERE WE COULD GO!
HUMANS
SMALL BEACH
BIG BEACH
BROWN CRABS
GUITAR
OCEAN
AAAH!

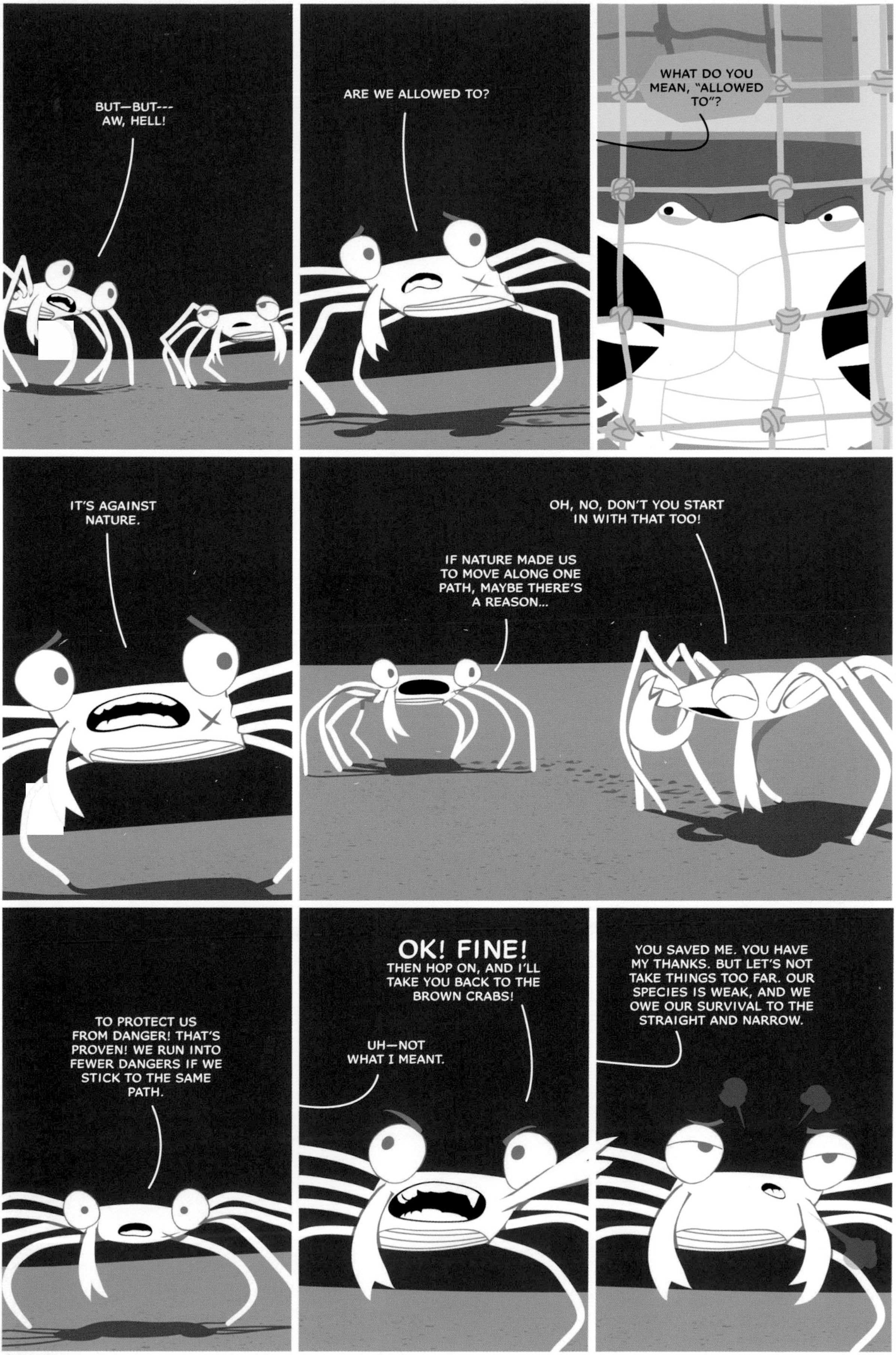
BUT—BUT---
AW, HELL!
ARE WE ALLOWED TO?
WHAT DO YOU MEAN, "ALLOWED TO"?
IT'S AGAINST NATURE.
IF NATURE MADE US TO MOVE ALONG ONE PATH, MAYBE THERE'S A REASON...
OH, NO, DON'T YOU START IN WITH THAT TOO!
TO PROTECT US FROM DANGER! THAT'S PROVEN! WE RUN INTO FEWER DANGERS IF WE STICK TO THE SAME PATH.
UH—NOT WHAT I MEANT.
OK! FINE! THEN HOP ON, AND I'LL TAKE YOU BACK TO THE BROWN CRABS!
YOU SAVED ME. YOU HAVE MY THANKS. BUT LET'S NOT TAKE THINGS TOO FAR. OUR SPECIES IS WEAK, AND WE OWE OUR SURVIVAL TO THE STRAIGHT AND NARROW.

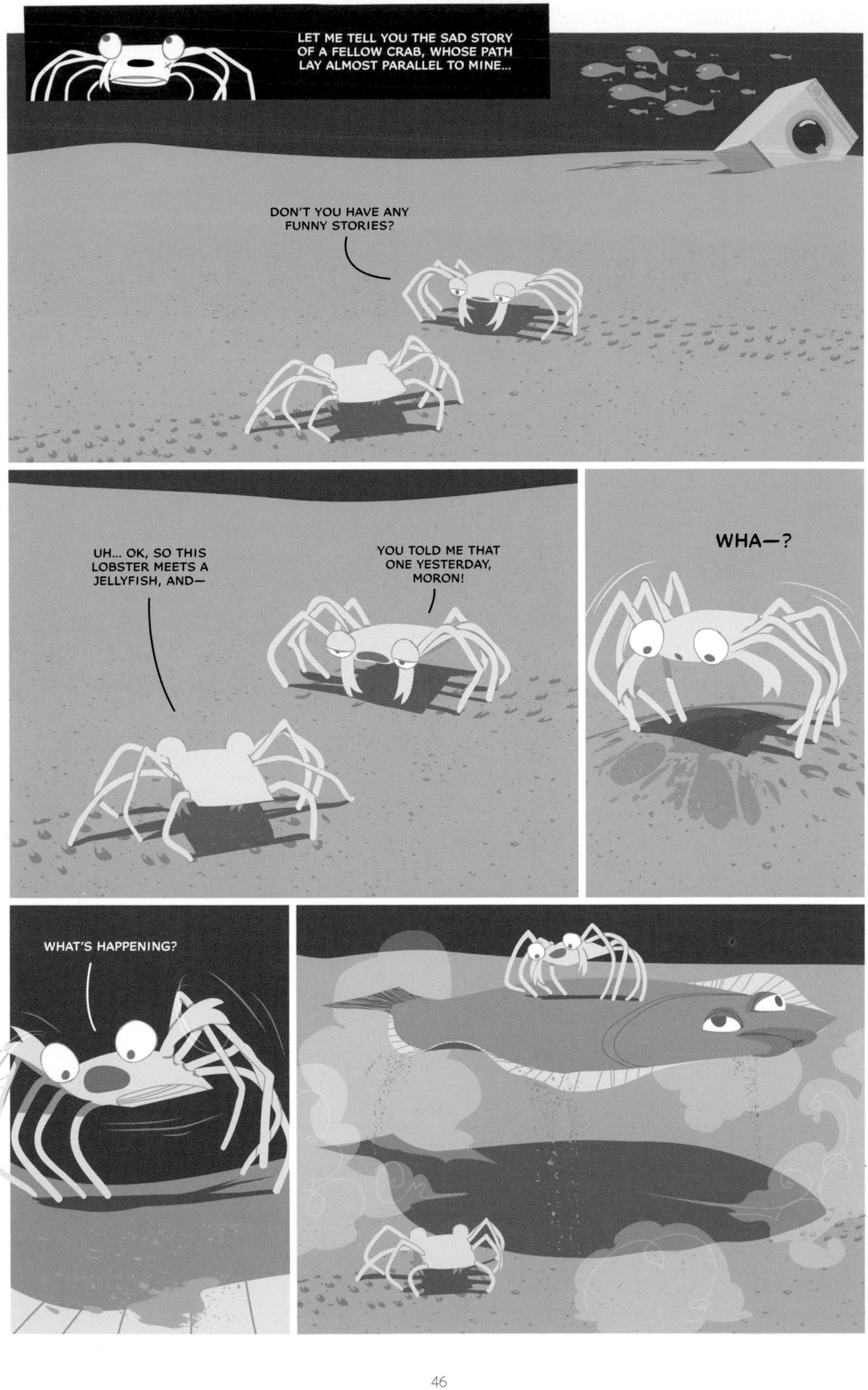
LET ME TELL YOU THE SAD STORY OF A FELLOW CRAB, WHOSE PATH LAY ALMOST PARALLEL TO MINE...
DON'T YOU HAVE ANY FUNNY STORIES?
UH... OK, SO THIS LOBSTER MEETS A JELLYFISH, AND—
YOU TOLD ME THAT ONE YESTERDAY, MORON!
WHA—?
WHAT'S HAPPENING?

LOOKS LIKE THIS IS MY LUCKY DAY!
WOOHOO! DID YOU SEE THAT, BRO? I JUST CHANGED PATHS!
YOU LUCKED OUT!
WHEEEE! SO LONG, OLD LIFE!
BRAAAZIIIL... LA LA LA LA
VVVVvvvrrraoum!
KRUNCH!
SEE? IT'S DANGEROUS! WE'RE NOT MEANT FOR SUCH THINGS! IN THE END, WE'RE BETTER OFF STICKING TO WHAT WE'VE GOT.

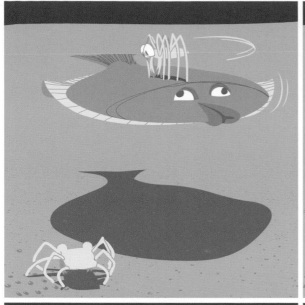

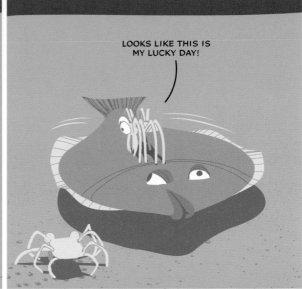

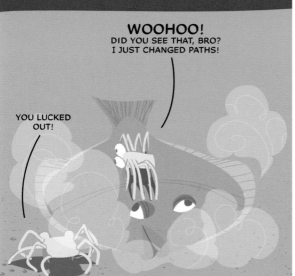

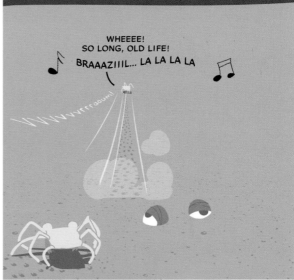

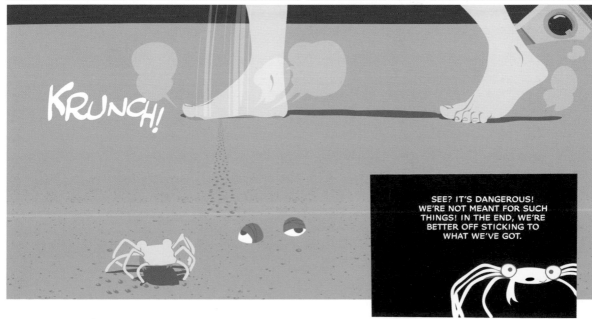

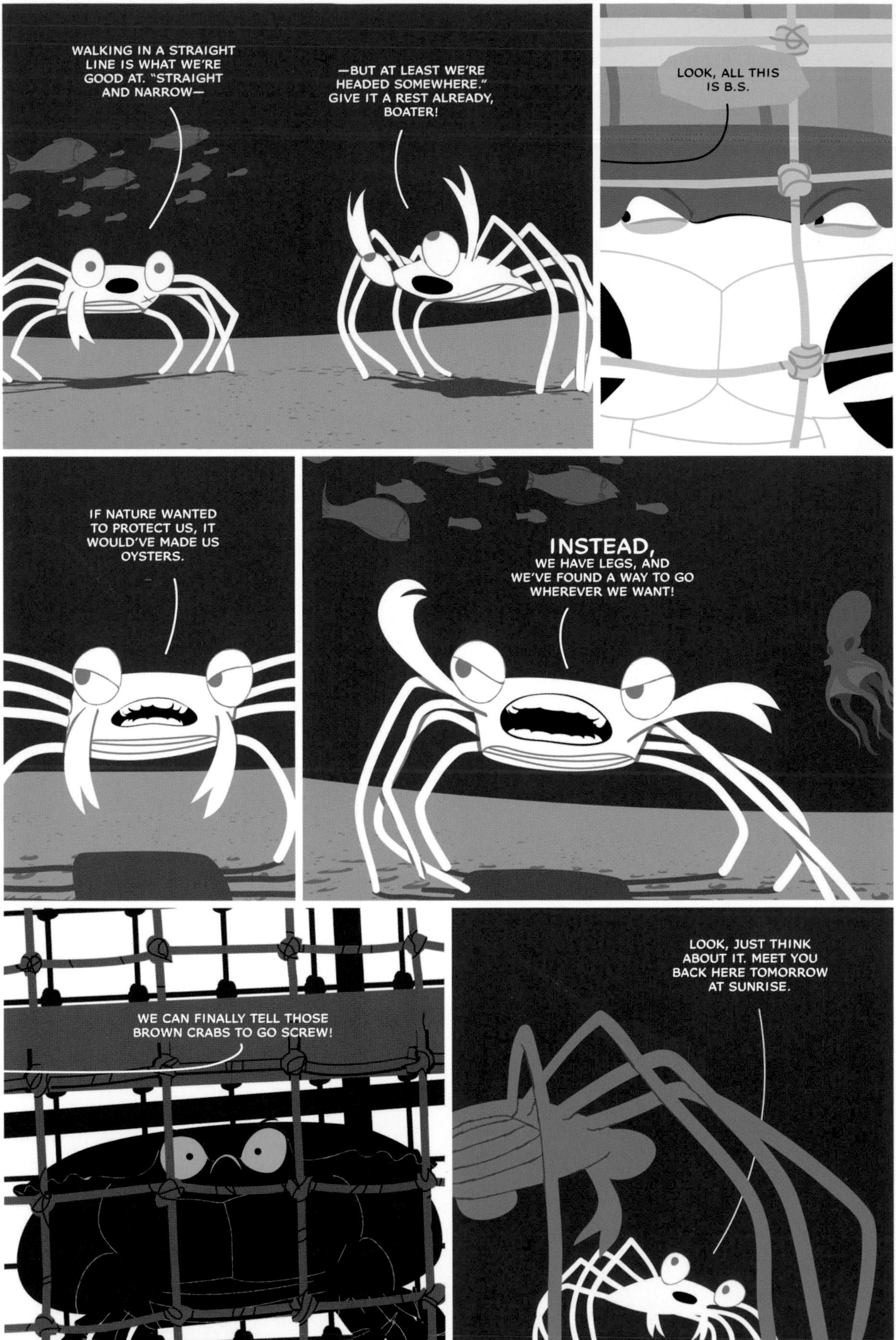
WALKING IN A STRAIGHT LINE IS WHAT WE'RE GOOD AT. "STRAIGHT AND NARROW—
—BUT AT LEAST WE'RE HEADED SOMEWHERE." GIVE IT A REST ALREADY, BOATER!
LOOK, ALL THIS IS B.S.
IF NATURE WANTED TO PROTECT US, IT WOULD'VE MADE US OYSTERS.
INSTEAD, WE HAVE LEGS, AND WE'VE FOUND A WAY TO GO WHEREVER WE WANT!
WE CAN FINALLY TELL THOSE BROWN CRABS TO GO SCREW!
LOOK, JUST THINK ABOUT IT. MEET YOU BACK HERE TOMORROW AT SUNRISE.

OK. SEE YOU TOMORROW, SUNNY!
HEY! PSSST!
TELL ALL THE BROWN CRABS TO MEET ME HERE! GOT SOMETHING TO TELL THEM.
AND WHILE YOU'RE AT IT, BRING THE LOBSTERS TOO!

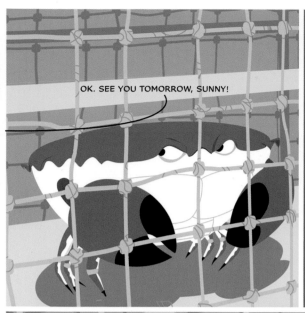

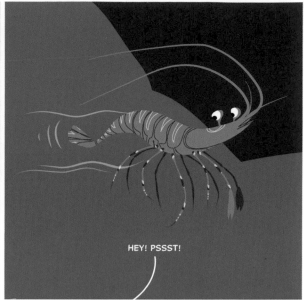

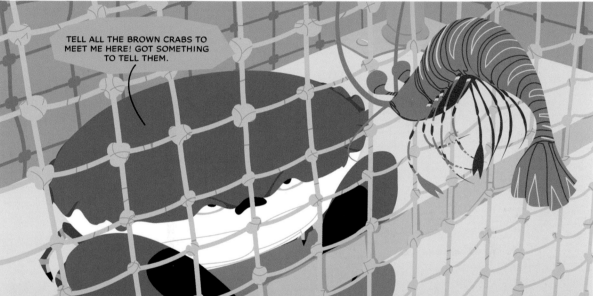

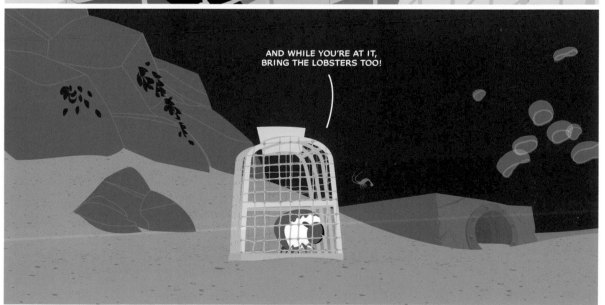

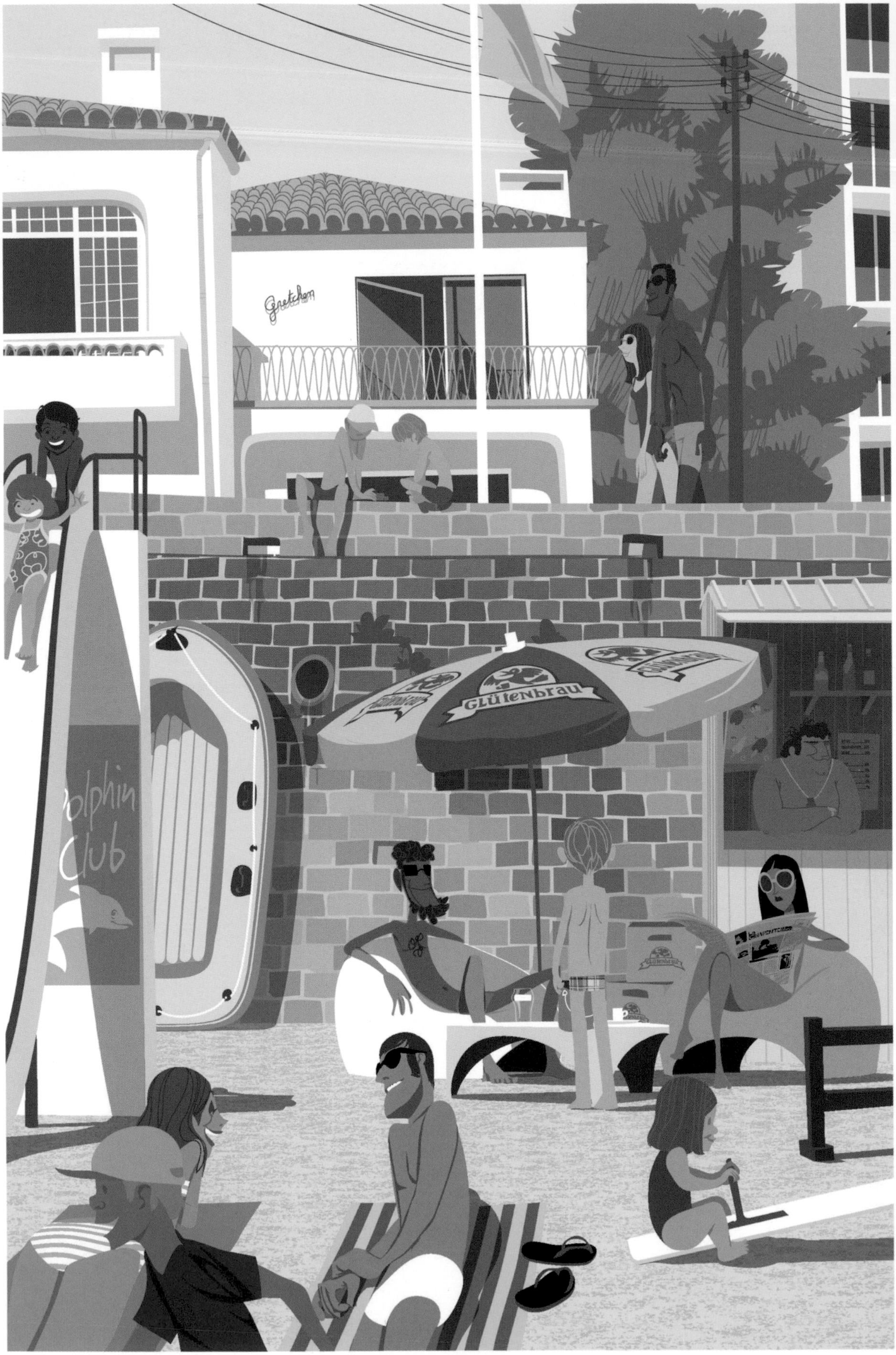
Gretchen
GLÜtenbrau
olphin
Club

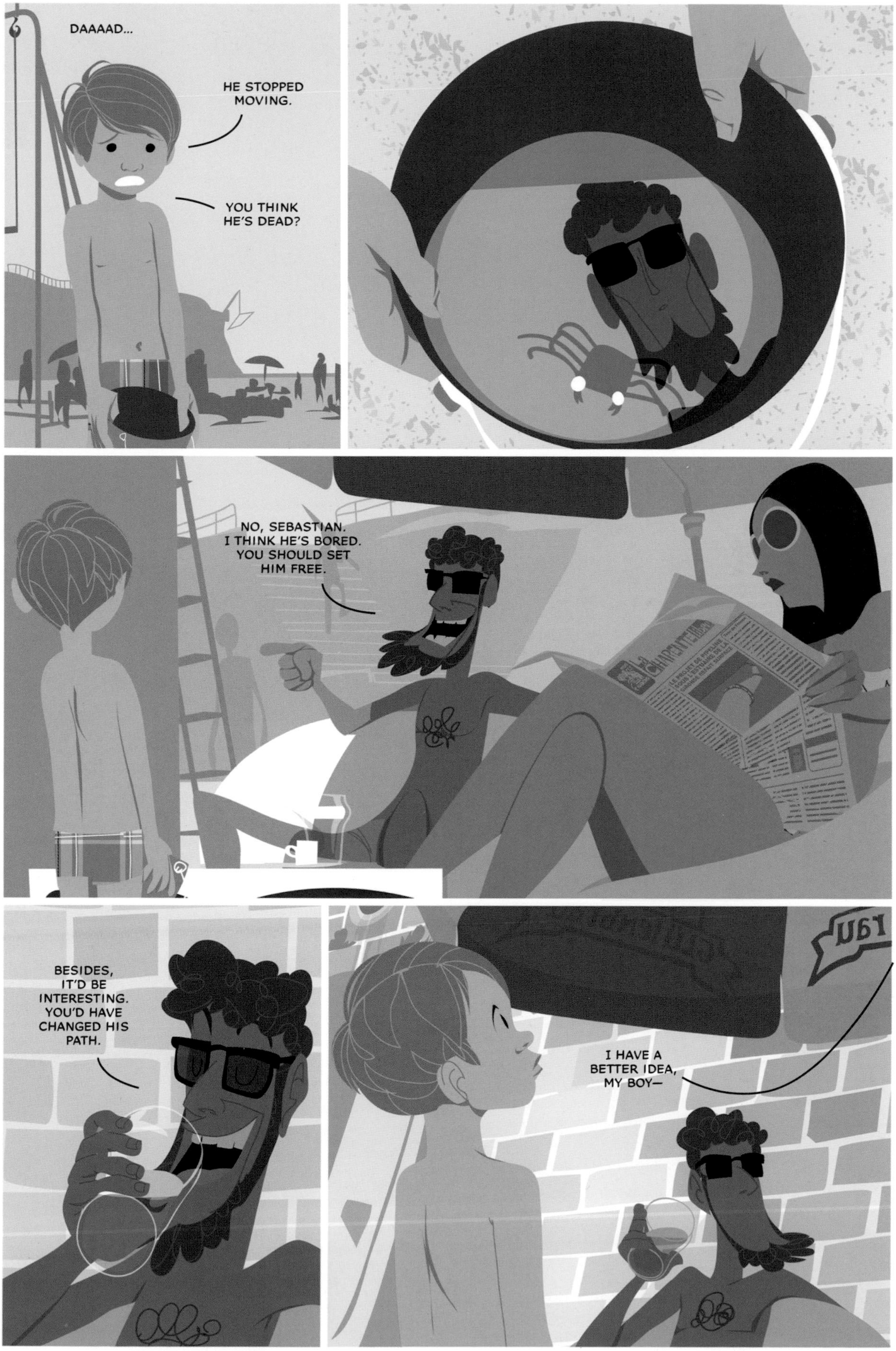
DAAAAD...
HE STOPPED MOVING.
YOU THINK HE'S DEAD?
NO, SEBASTIAN. I THINK HE'S BORED. YOU SHOULD SET HIM FREE.
BESIDES, IT'D BE INTERESTING. YOU'D HAVE CHANGED HIS PATH.
I HAVE A BETTER IDEA, MY BOY—

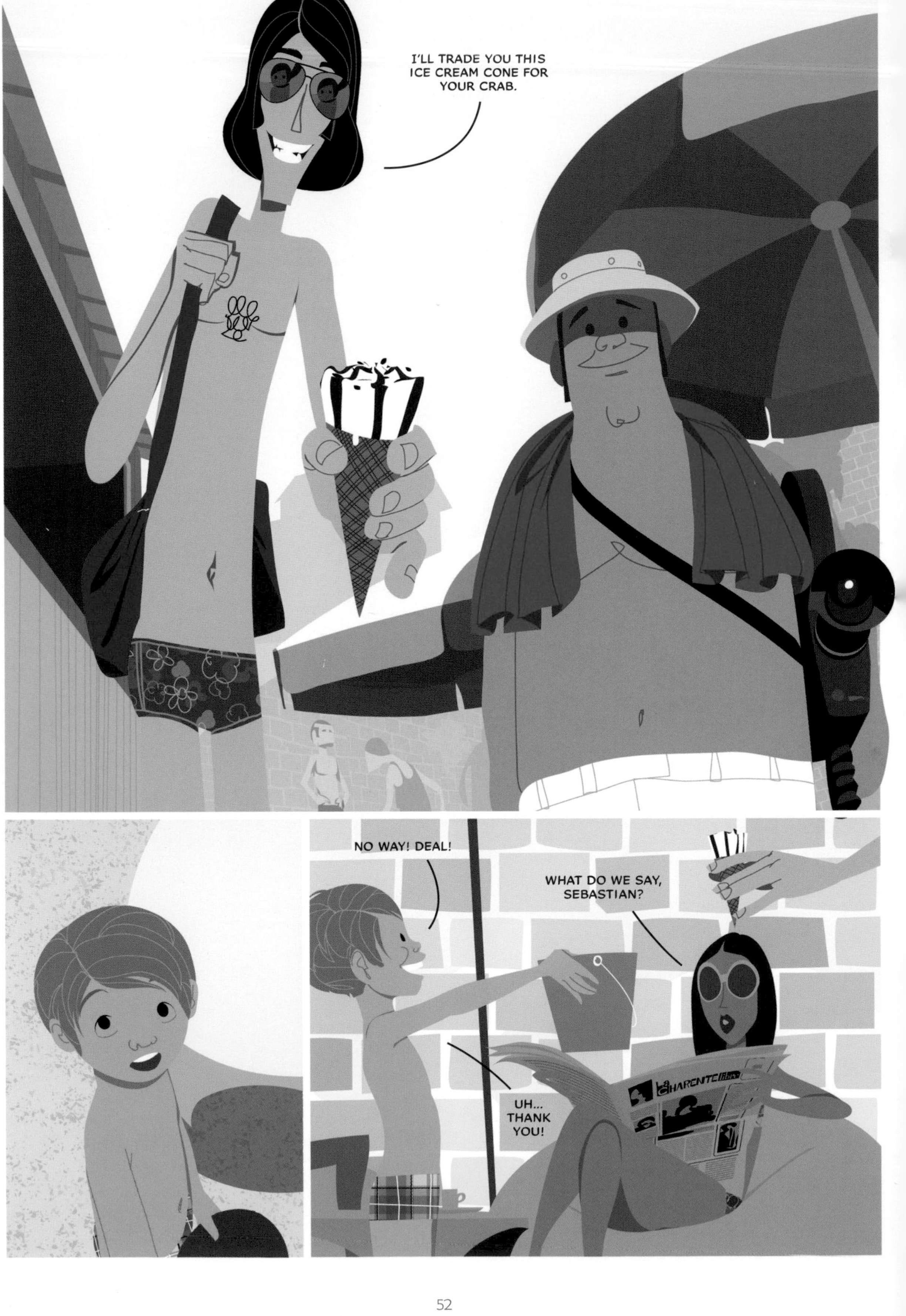
I'LL TRADE YOU THIS ICE CREAM CONE FOR YOUR CRAB.
NO WAY! DEAL!
WHAT DO WE SAY, SEBASTIAN?
UH... THANK YOU!

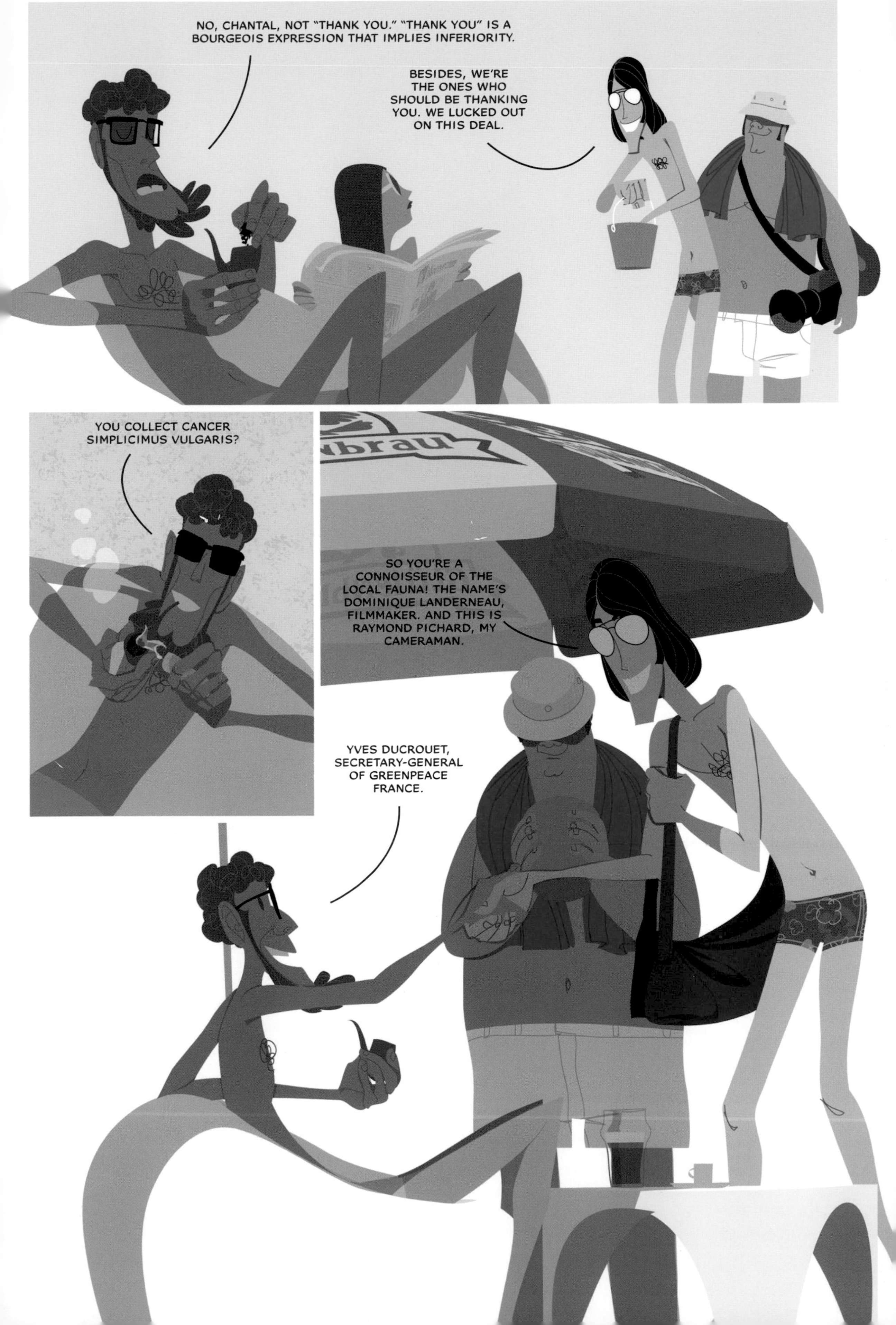
NO, CHANTAL, NOT "THANK YOU." "THANK YOU" IS A BOURGEOIS EXPRESSION THAT IMPLIES INFERIORITY.
BESIDES, WE'RE THE ONES WHO SHOULD BE THANKING YOU. WE LUCKED OUT ON THIS DEAL.
YOU COLLECT CANCER SIMPLICIMUS VULGARIS?
SO YOU'RE A CONNOISSEUR OF THE LOCAL FAUNA! THE NAME'S DOMINIQUE LANDERNEAU, FILMMAKER. AND THIS IS RAYMOND PICHARD, MY CAMERAMAN.
YVES DUCROUET, SECRETARY-GENERAL OF GREENPEACE FRANCE.

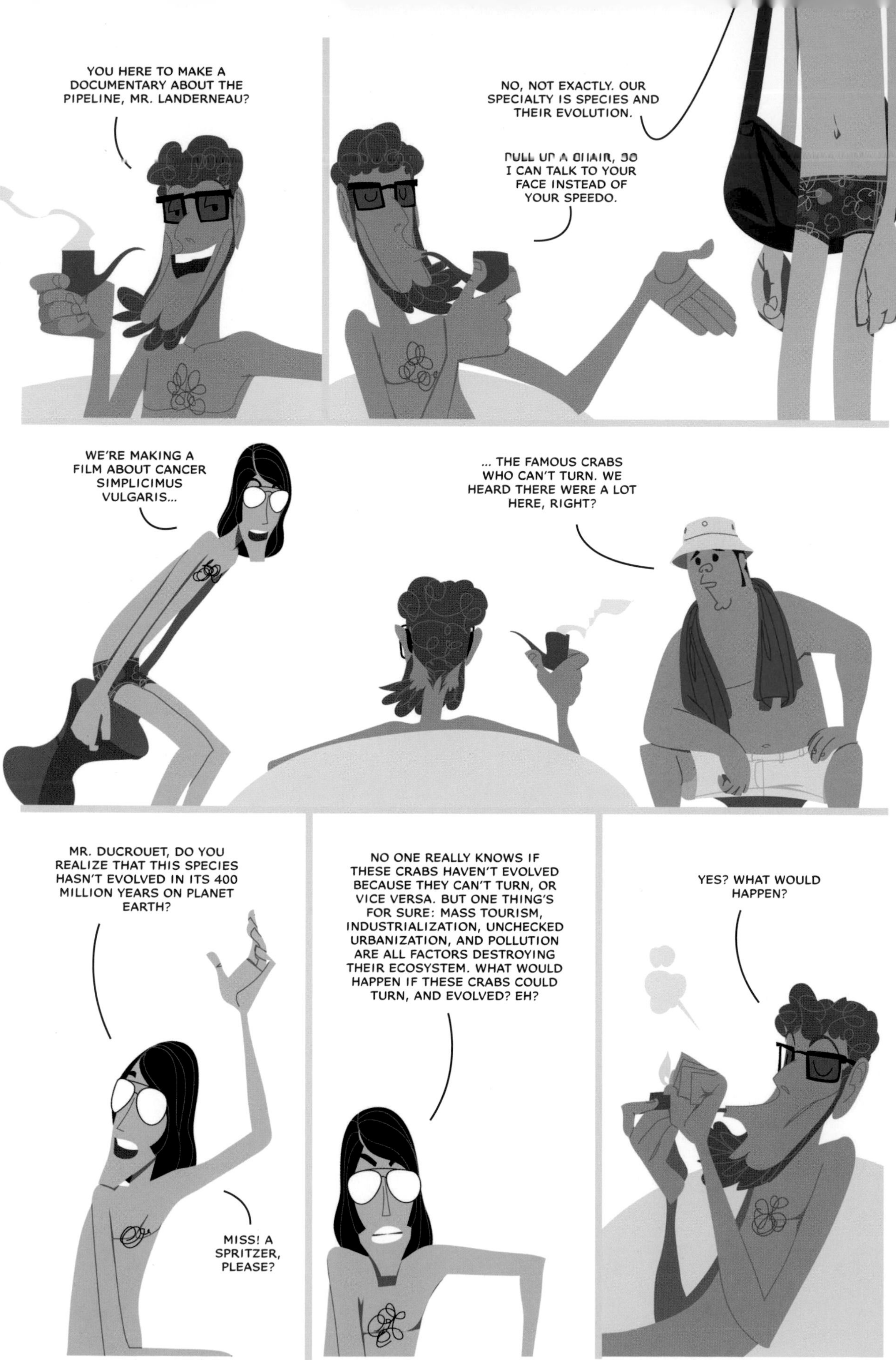
YOU HERE TO MAKE A DOCUMENTARY ABOUT THE PIPELINE, MR. LANDERNEAU?
NO, NOT EXACTLY. OUR SPECIALTY IS SPECIES AND THEIR EVOLUTION.
PULL UP A CHAIR, SO I CAN TALK TO YOUR FACE INSTEAD OF YOUR SPEEDO.
WE'RE MAKING A FILM ABOUT CANCER SIMPLICIMUS VULGARIS...
... THE FAMOUS CRABS WHO CAN'T TURN. WE HEARD THERE WERE A LOT HERE, RIGHT?
MR. DUCROUET, DO YOU REALIZE THAT THIS SPECIES HASN'T EVOLVED IN ITS 400 MILLION YEARS ON PLANET EARTH?
MISS! A SPRITZER, PLEASE?
NO ONE REALLY KNOWS IF THESE CRABS HAVEN'T EVOLVED BECAUSE THEY CAN'T TURN, OR VICE VERSA. BUT ONE THING'S FOR SURE: MASS TOURISM, INDUSTRIALIZATION, UNCHECKED URBANIZATION, AND POLLUTION ARE ALL FACTORS DESTROYING THEIR ECOSYSTEM. WHAT WOULD HAPPEN IF THESE CRABS COULD TURN, AND EVOLVED? EH?
YES? WHAT WOULD HAPPEN?

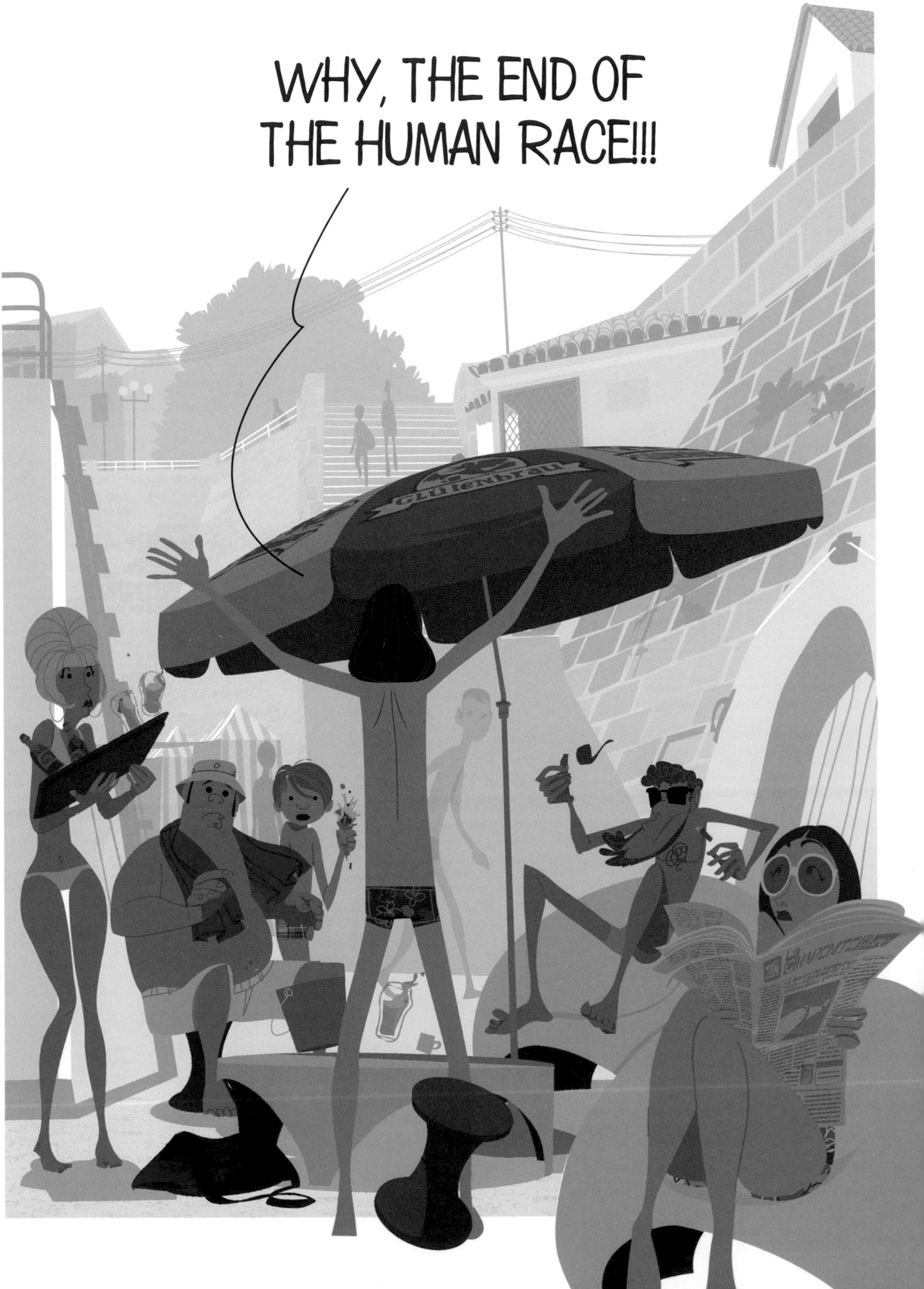
WHY, THE END OF THE HUMAN RACE!!!

SORRY—MY APOCALYPTIC SIDE.

PROFESSIONAL HAZARD.

IS SOMETHING BAD GOING TO HAPPEN?

UM... LET'S SAY THE CRABS MIGHT BECOME OUR NEW ENEMY.

LIKE JELLYFISH?

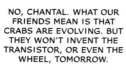

NO, CHANTAL. WHAT OUR FRIENDS MEAN IS THAT CRABS ARE EVOLVING. BUT THEY WON'T INVENT THE TRANSISTOR, OR EVEN THE WHEEL, TOMORROW.

IT'S A MUTANT SPECIES.

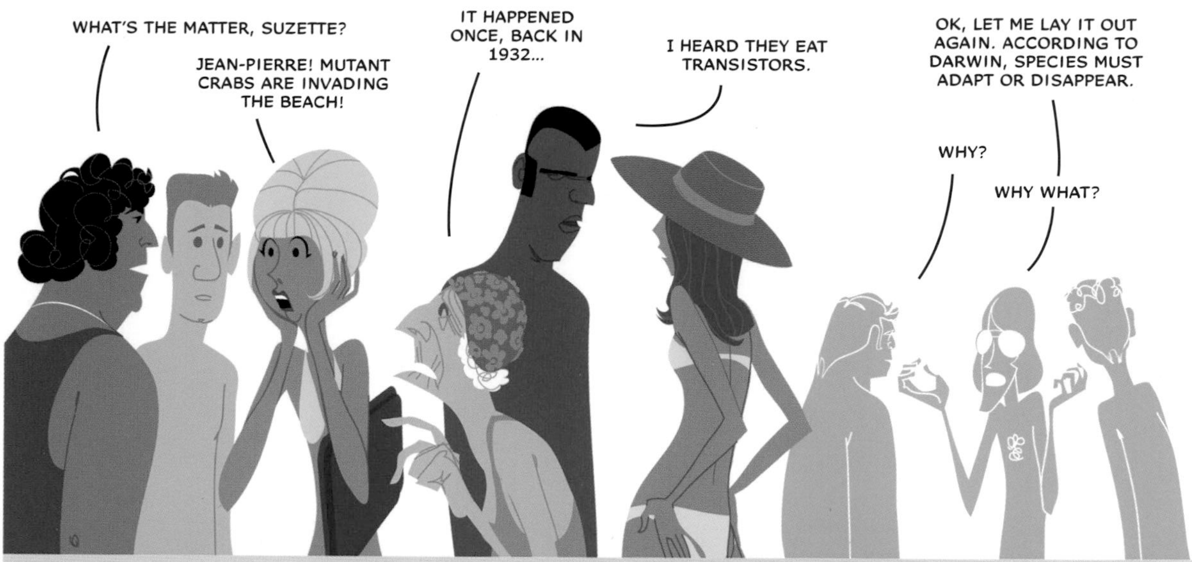
WHAT'S THE MATTER, SUZETTE?
JEAN-PIERRE! MUTANT CRABS ARE INVADING THE BEACH!
IT HAPPENED ONCE, BACK IN 1932...
I HEARD THEY EAT TRANSISTORS.
OK, LET ME LAY IT OUT AGAIN. ACCORDING TO DARWIN, SPECIES MUST ADAPT OR DISAPPEAR.
WHY?
WHY WHAT?

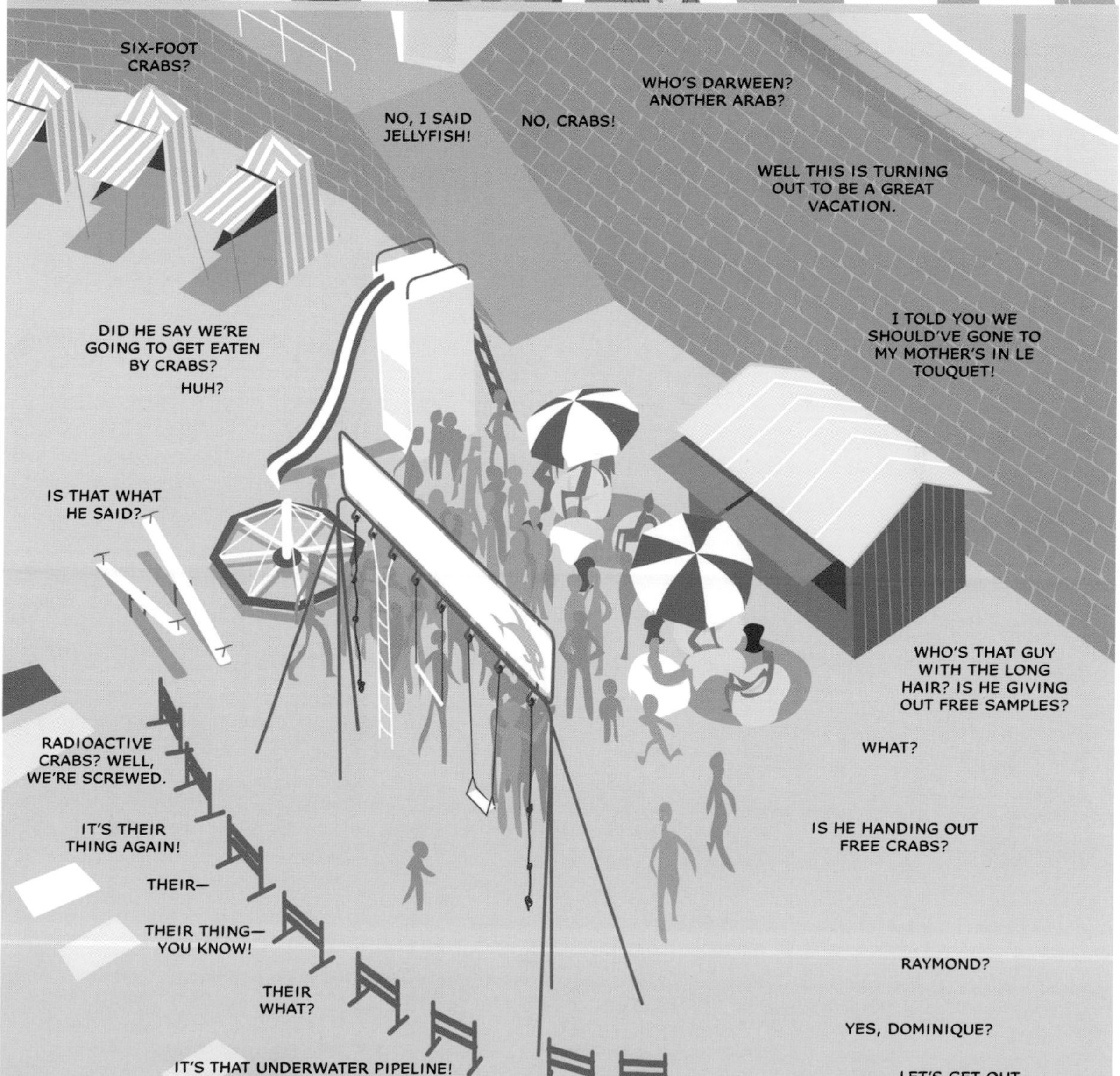
SIX-FOOT CRABS?
NO, I SAID JELLYFISH!
NO, CRABS!
WHO'S DARWEEN? ANOTHER ARAB?
WELL THIS IS TURNING OUT TO BE A GREAT VACATION.
DID HE SAY WE'RE GOING TO GET EATEN BY CRABS?
HUH?
I TOLD YOU WE SHOULD'VE GONE TO MY MOTHER'S IN LE TOUQUET!
IS THAT WHAT HE SAID?
WHO'S THAT GUY WITH THE LONG HAIR? IS HE GIVING OUT FREE SAMPLES?
WHAT?
RADIOACTIVE CRABS? WELL, WE'RE SCREWED.
IT'S THEIR THING AGAIN!
THEIR—
IS HE HANDING OUT FREE CRABS?
THEIR THING— YOU KNOW!
THEIR WHAT?
RAYMOND?
YES, DOMINIQUE?
IT'S THAT UNDERWATER PIPELINE! THEY'RE DOING EXPERIMENTS!
LET'S GET OUT OF HERE!

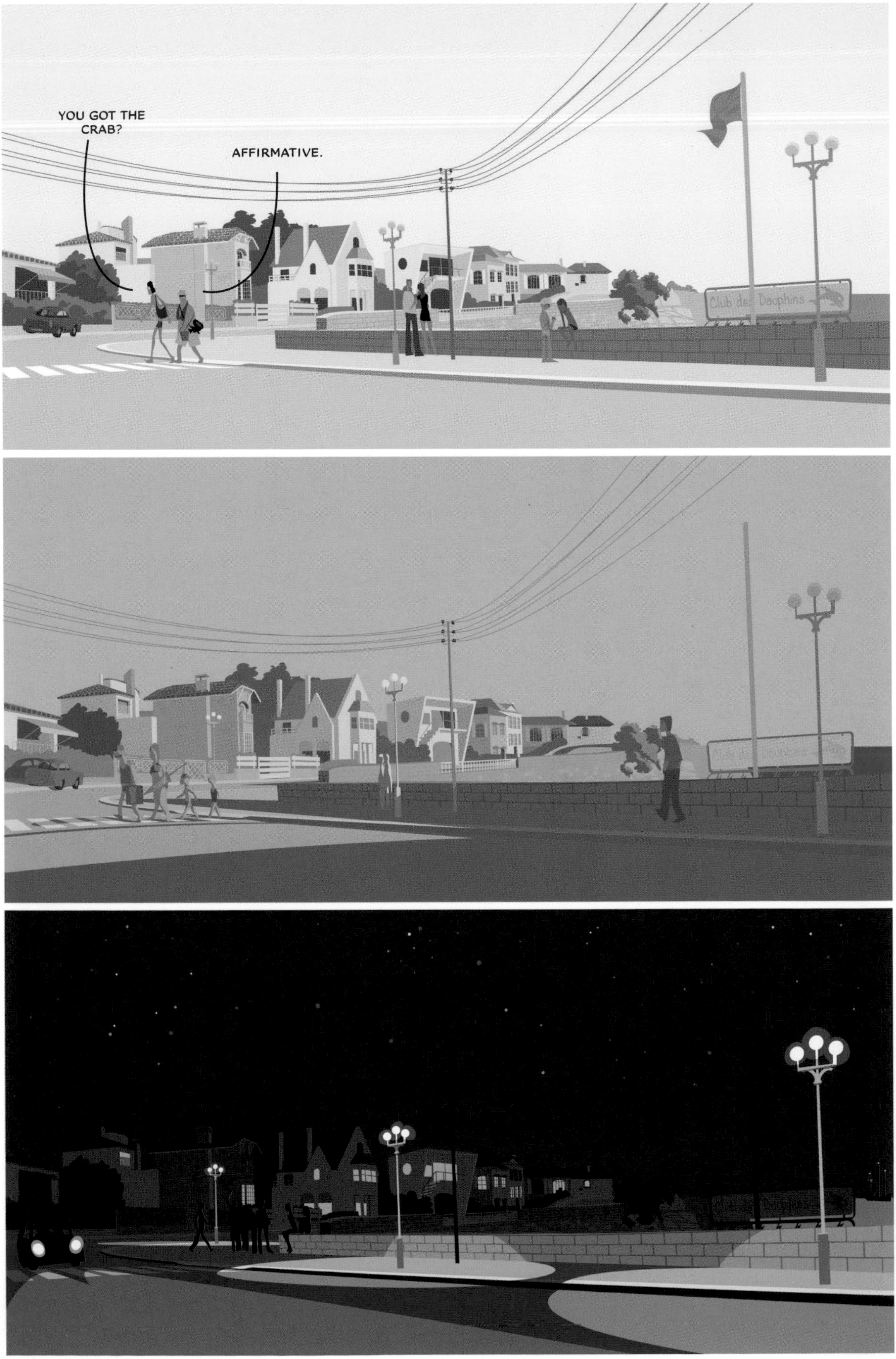
YOU GOT THE CRAB?
AFFIRMATIVE.
Club des Dauphins

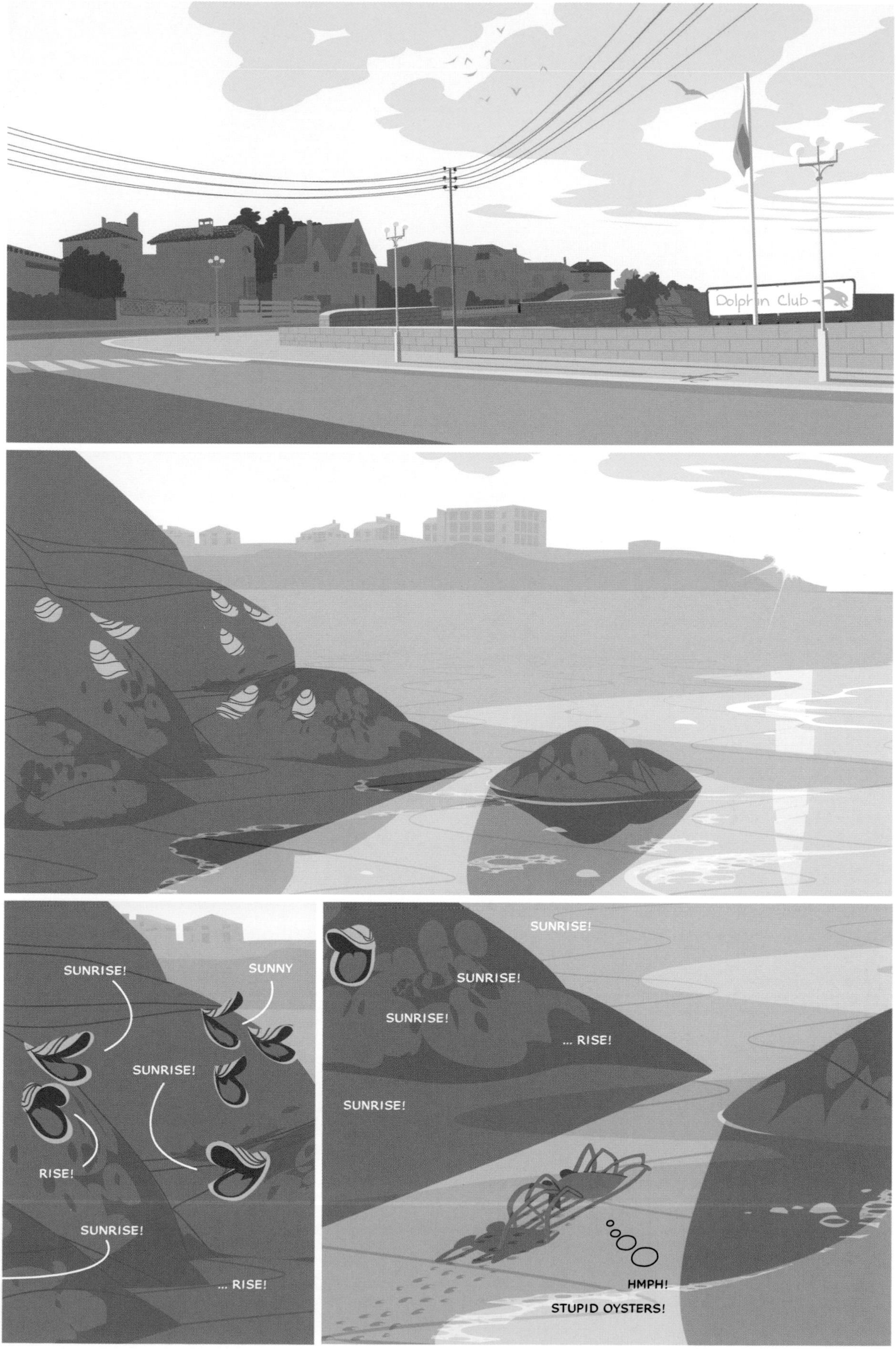
Dolphin Club
SUNRISE!
SUNNY
SUNRISE!
RISE!
SUNRISE!
... RISE!
SUNRISE!
SUNRISE!
SUNRISE!
... RISE!
SUNRISE!
HMPH!
STUPID OYSTERS!

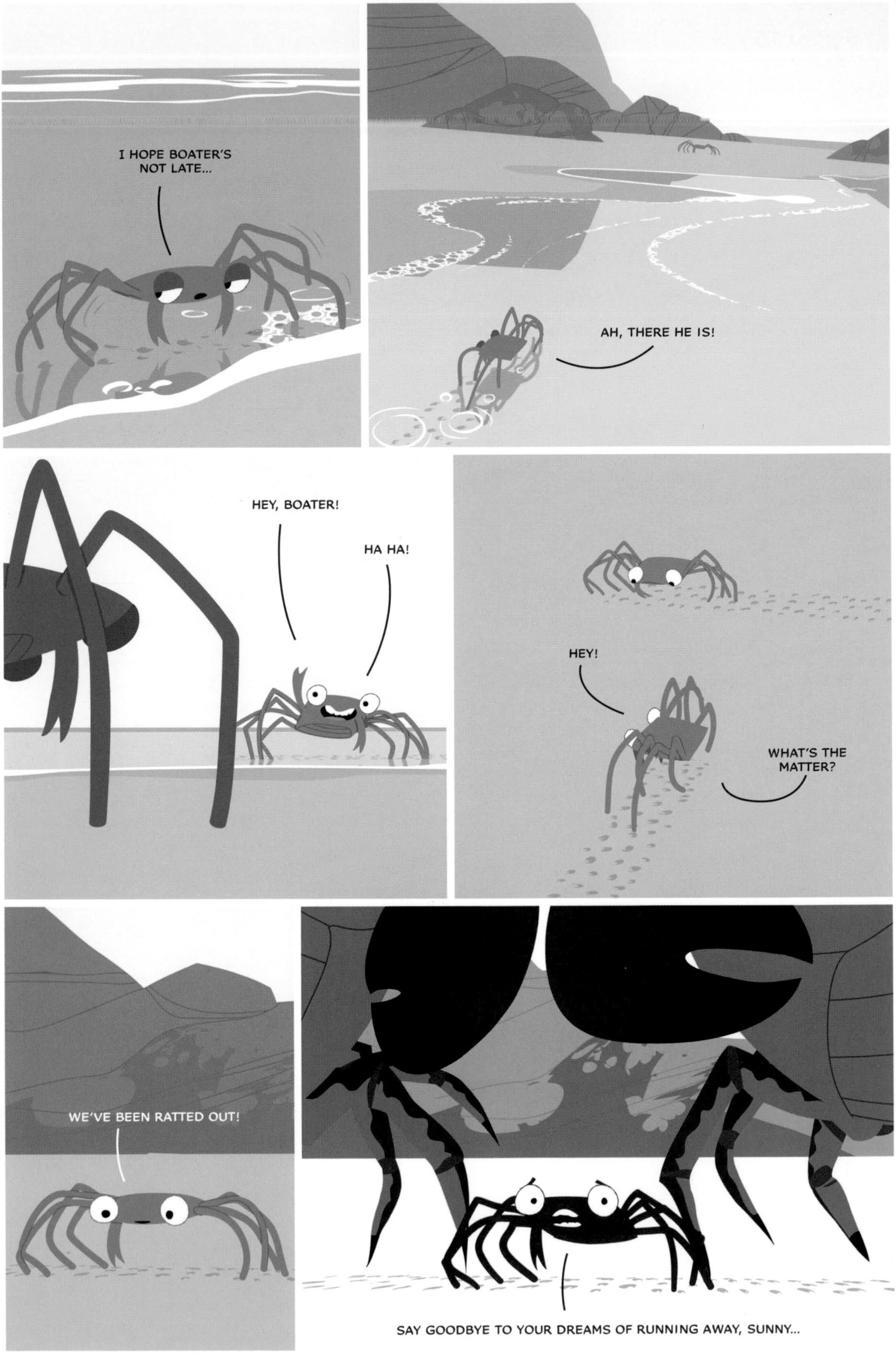
I HOPE BOATER'S NOT LATE...
AH, THERE HE IS!
HEY, BOATER!
HA HA!
HEY!
WHAT'S THE MATTER?
WE'VE BEEN RATTED OUT!
SAY GOODBYE TO YOUR DREAMS OF RUNNING AWAY, SUNNY...

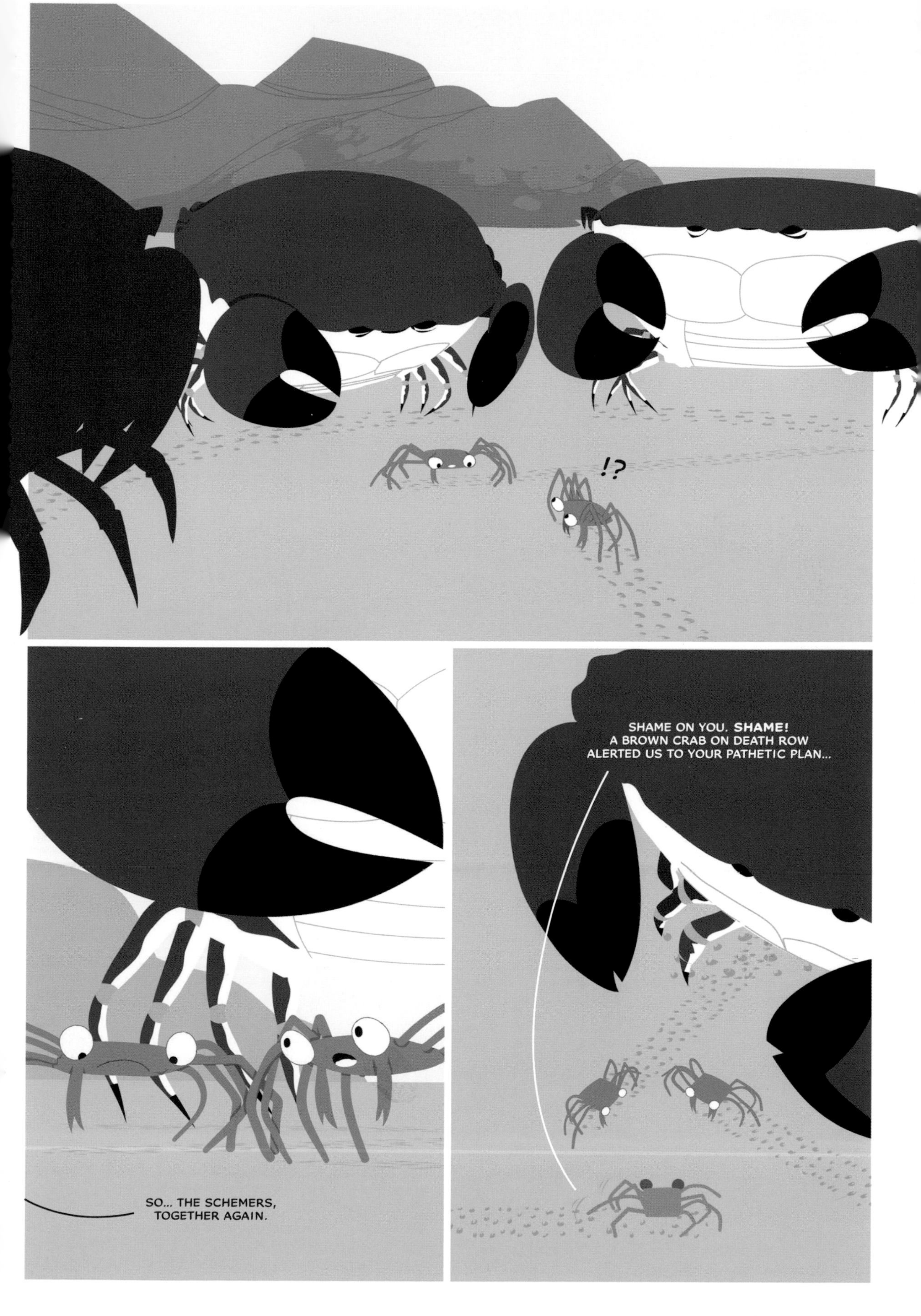
!?
SO... THE SCHEMERS, TOGETHER AGAIN.
SHAME ON YOU. SHAME! A BROWN CRAB ON DEATH ROW ALERTED US TO YOUR PATHETIC PLAN...

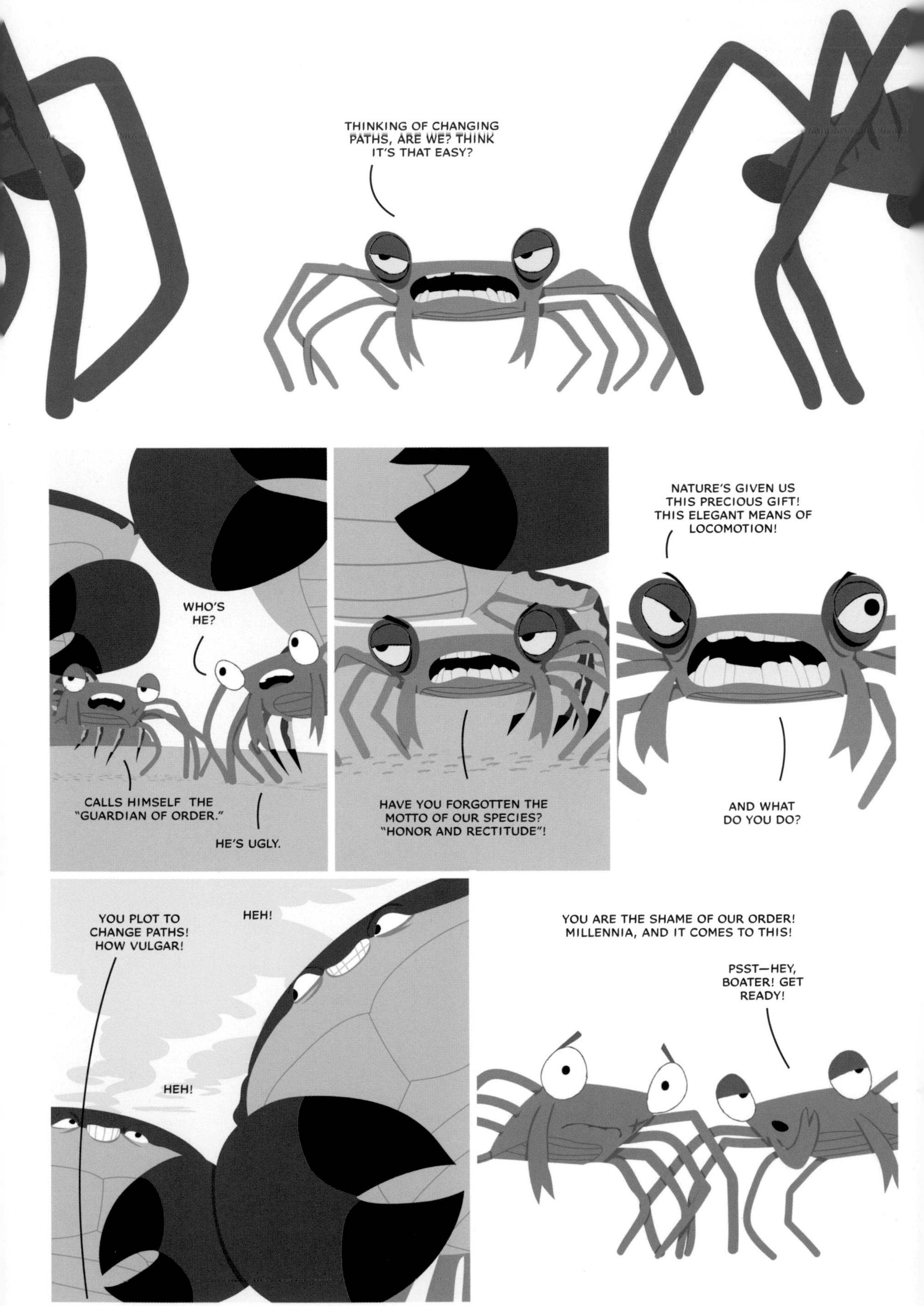
THINKING OF CHANGING PATHS, ARE WE? THINK IT'S THAT EASY?
WHO'S HE?
CALLS HIMSELF THE "GUARDIAN OF ORDER."
HE'S UGLY.
HAVE YOU FORGOTTEN THE MOTTO OF OUR SPECIES? "HONOR AND RECTITUDE"!
NATURE'S GIVEN US THIS PRECIOUS GIFT! THIS ELEGANT MEANS OF LOCOMOTION!
AND WHAT DO YOU DO?
YOU PLOT TO CHANGE PATHS! HOW VULGAR!
HEH!
HEH!
YOU ARE THE SHAME OF OUR ORDER! MILLENNIA, AND IT COMES TO THIS!
PSST—HEY, BOATER! GET READY!

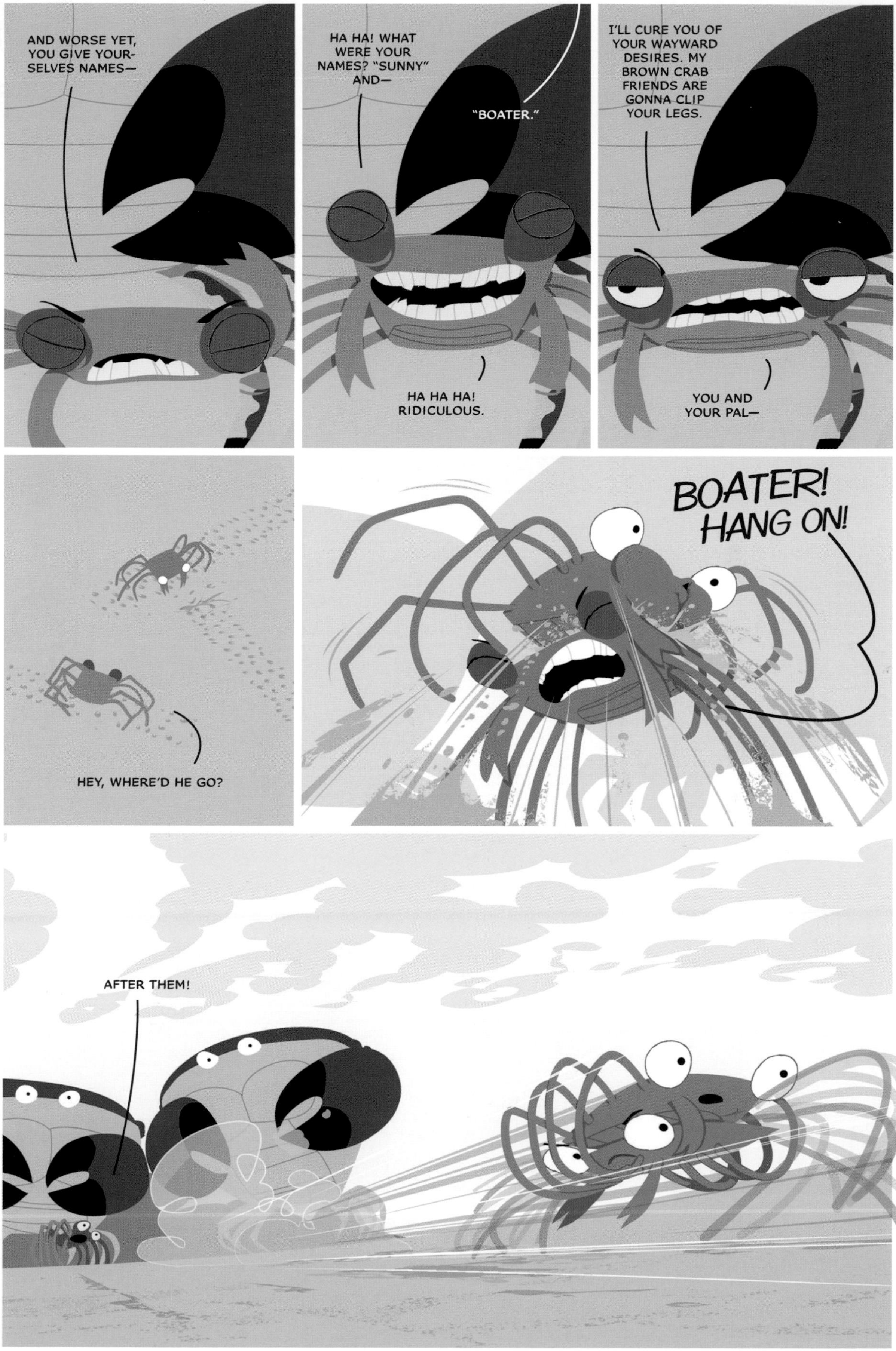
AND WORSE YET, YOU GIVE YOUR-SELVES NAMES—
HA HA! WHAT WERE YOUR NAMES? "SUNNY" AND—
"BOATER."
HA HA HA! RIDICULOUS.
I'LL CURE YOU OF YOUR WAYWARD DESIRES. MY BROWN CRAB FRIENDS ARE GONNA CLIP YOUR LEGS.
YOU AND YOUR PAL—
HEY, WHERE'D HE GO?
BOATER! HANG ON!
AFTER THEM!

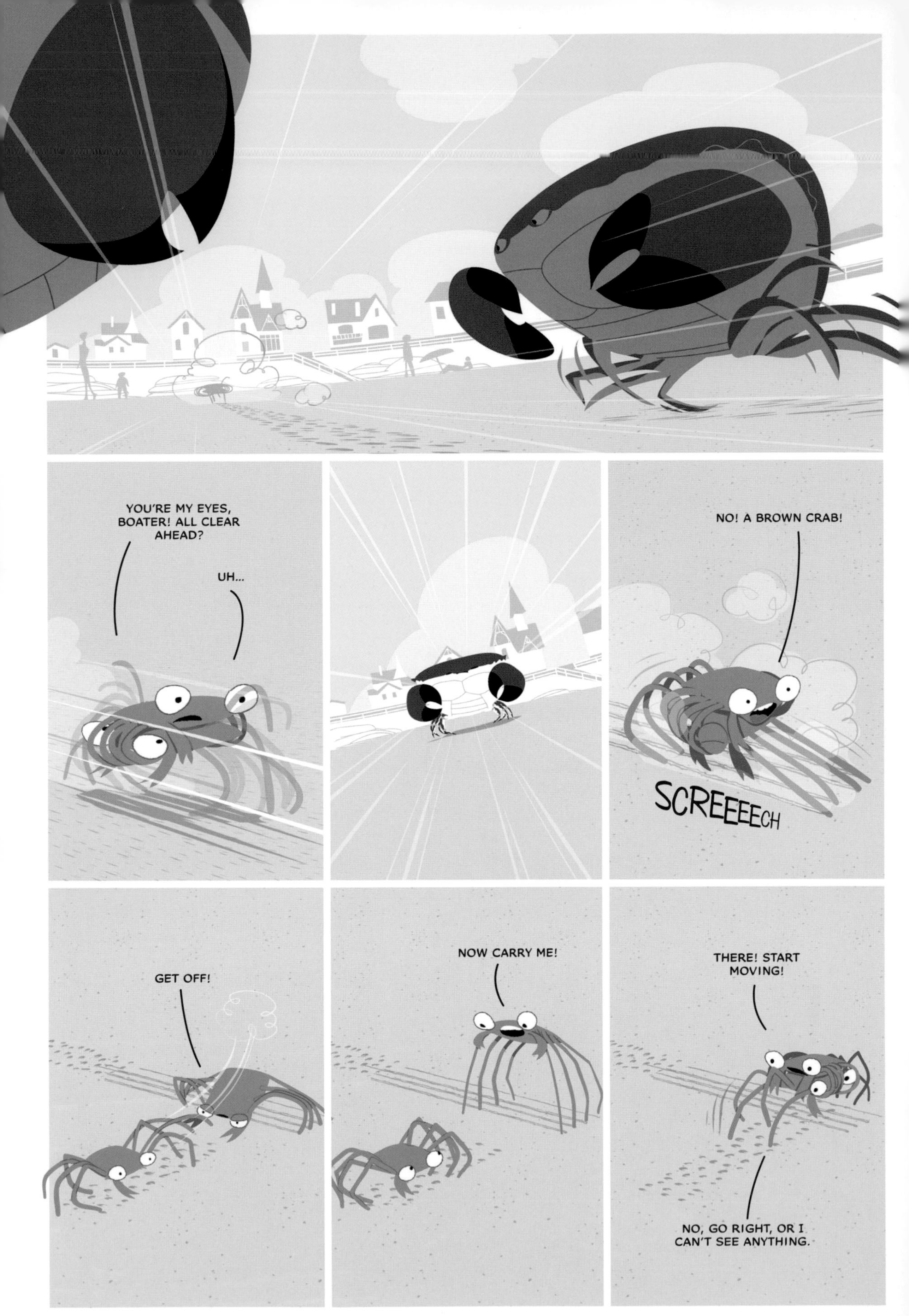

YOU'RE MY EYES, BOATER! ALL CLEAR AHEAD?
UH...
NO! A BROWN CRAB!
SCREEEEECH
GET OFF!
NOW CARRY ME!
THERE! START MOVING!
NO, GO RIGHT, OR I CAN'T SEE ANYTHING.

VROOOOM!
WHOA! YOU'RE FASTER THAN A SWORDFISH WITH A WHALER IN PURSUIT!
SO, UH—WHERE ARE WE GOING?
AWAY FROM THE BROWN CRABS.
RIGHT, SO—TOWARD THE HUMANS?
NOT SURE THIS IS THE BEST TRADE-OFF...

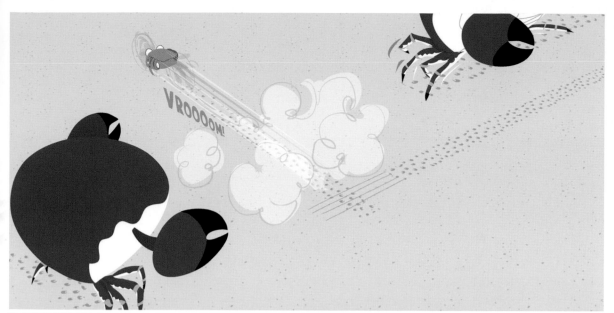

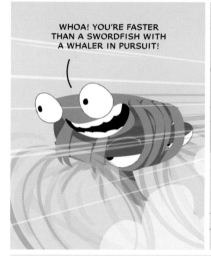

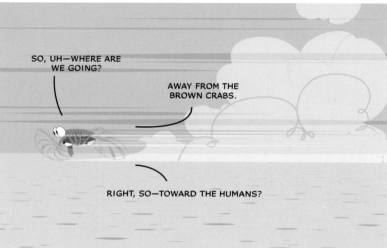

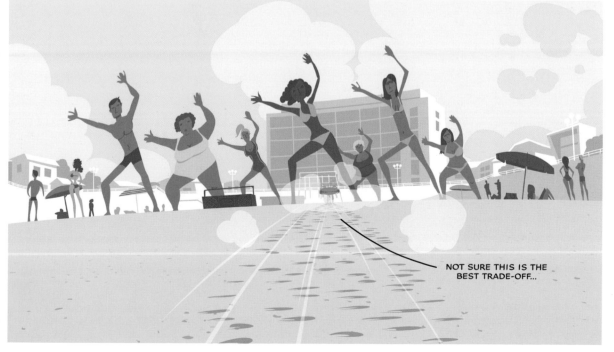

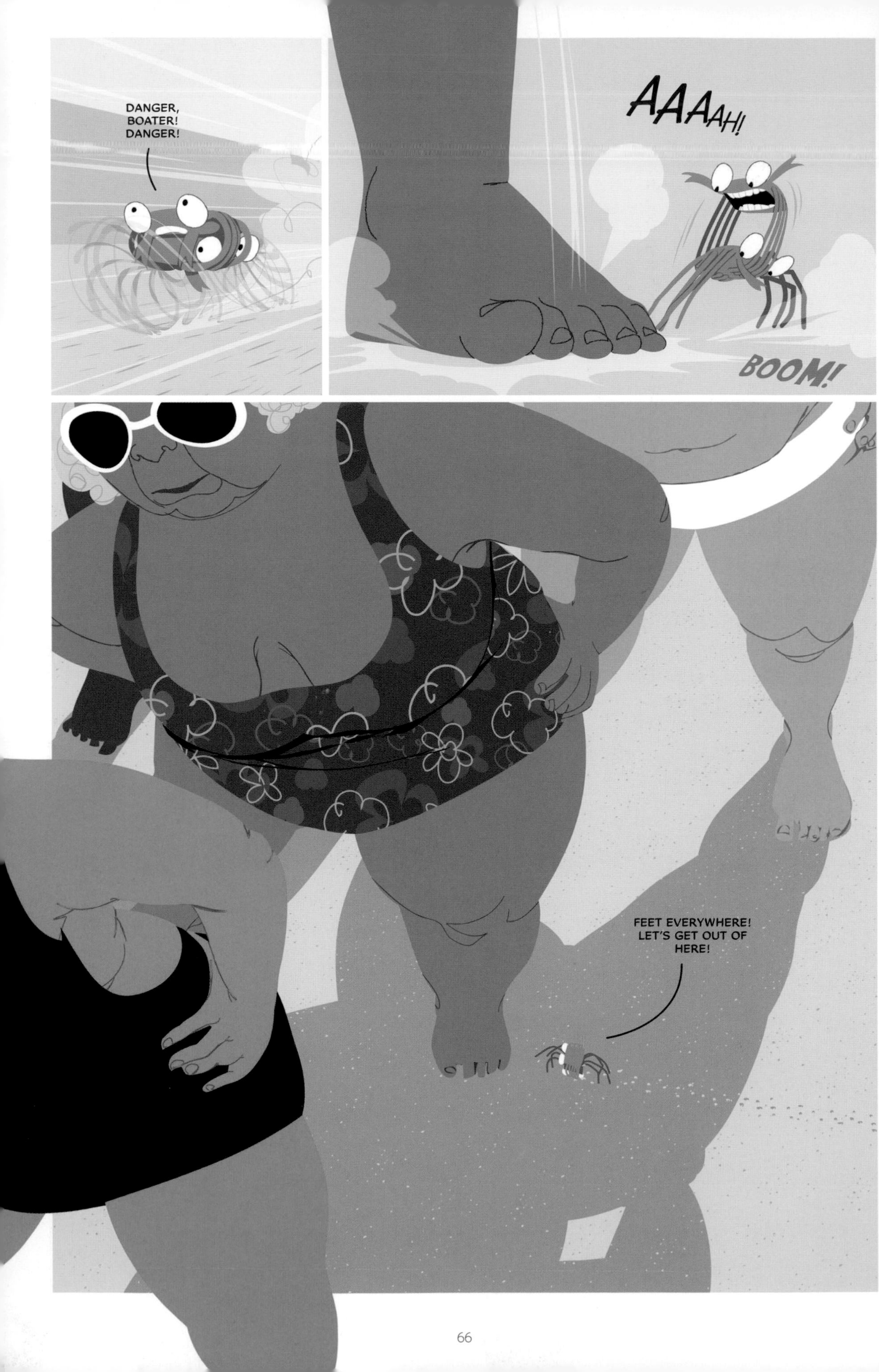
DANGER, BOATER! DANGER!
AAAAAH!
BOOM!
FEET EVERYWHERE! LET'S GET OUT OF HERE!

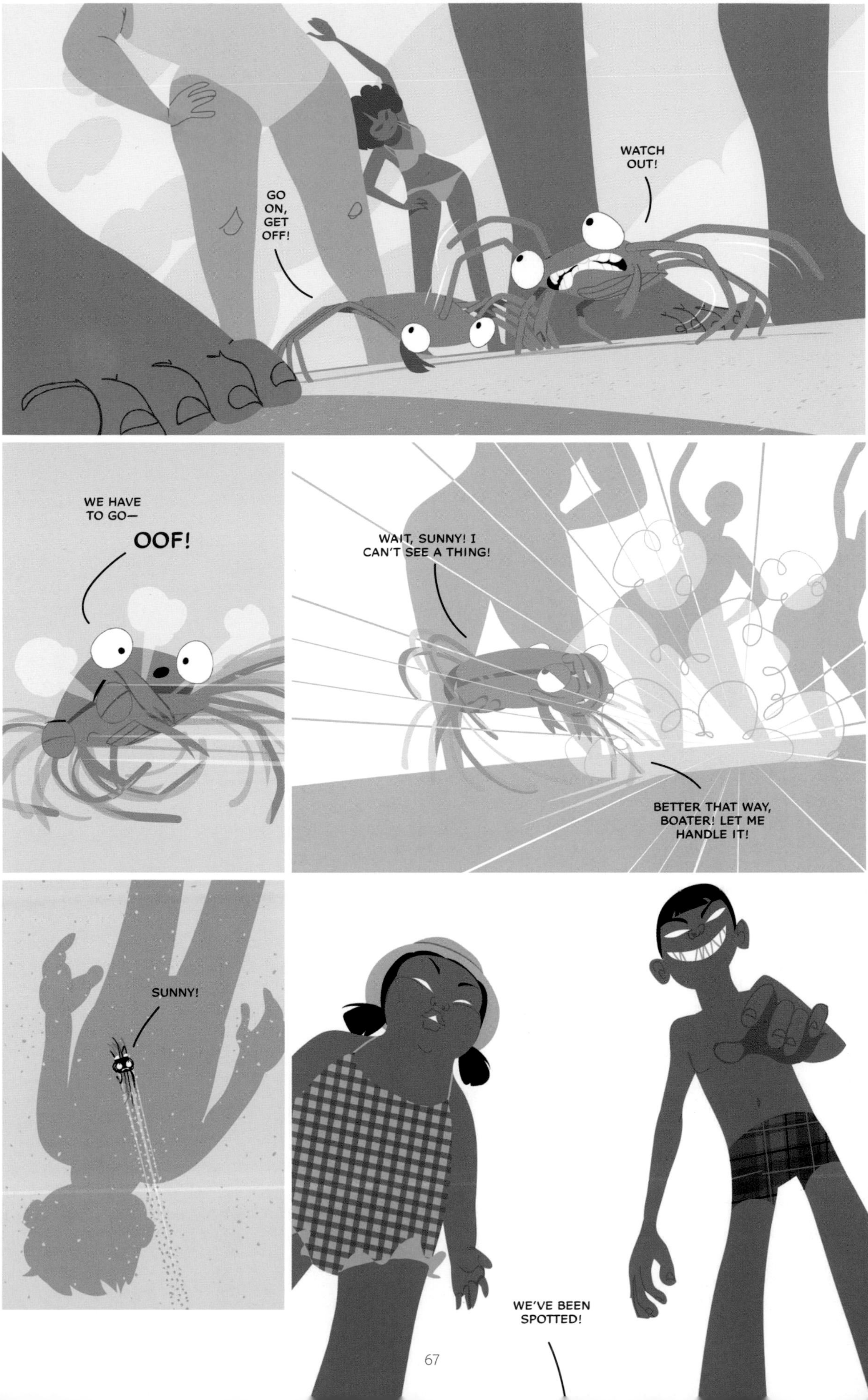
GO ON, GET OFF!
WATCH OUT!
WE HAVE TO GO—
OOF!
WAIT, SUNNY! I CAN'T SEE A THING!
BETTER THAT WAY, BOATER! LET ME HANDLE IT!
SUNNY!
WE'VE BEEN SPOTTED!

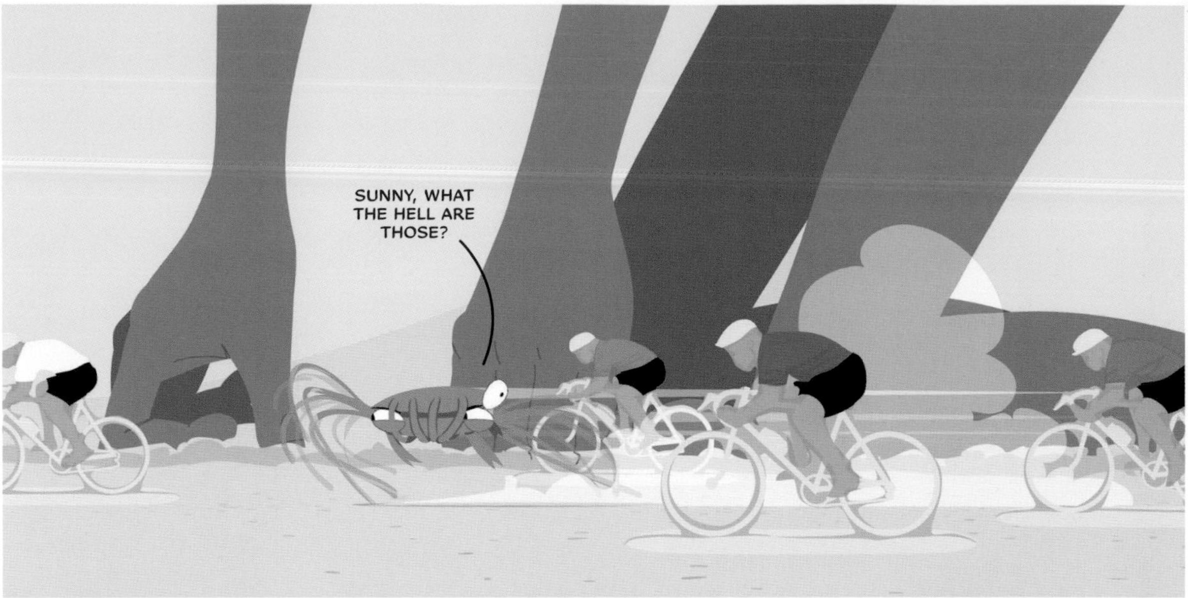
SUNNY, WHAT THE HELL ARE THOSE?

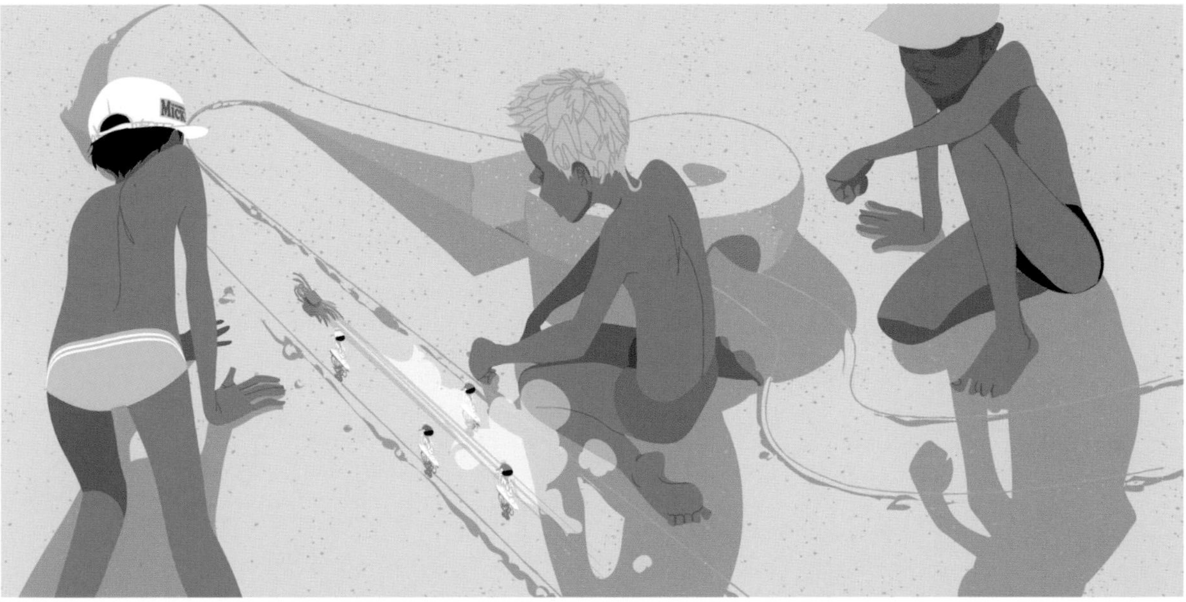

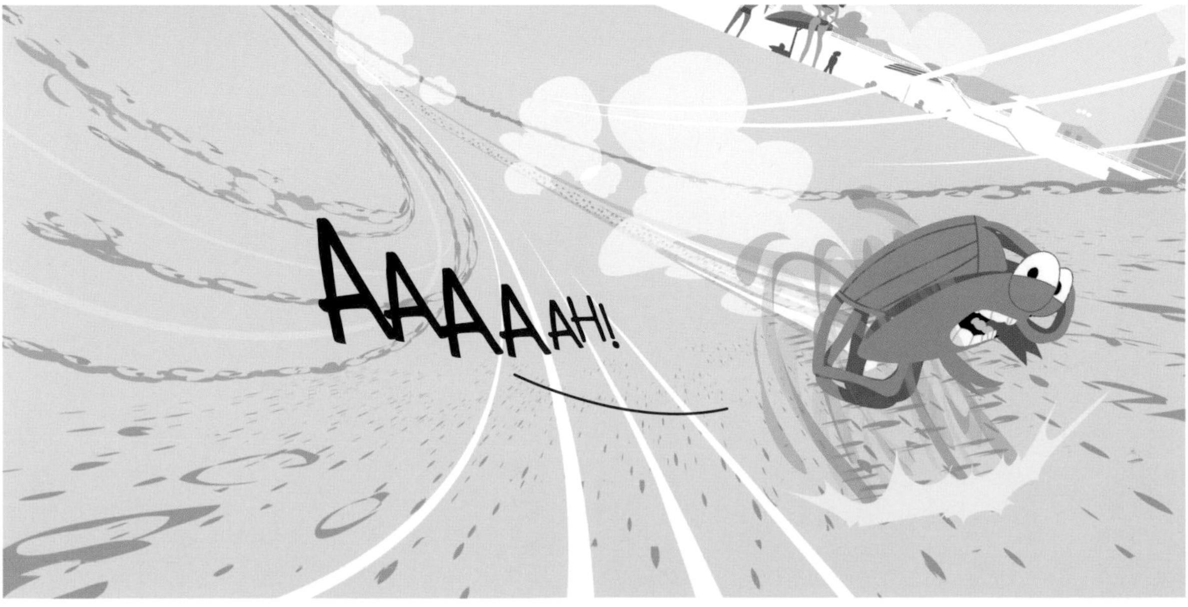
AAAAAAH!

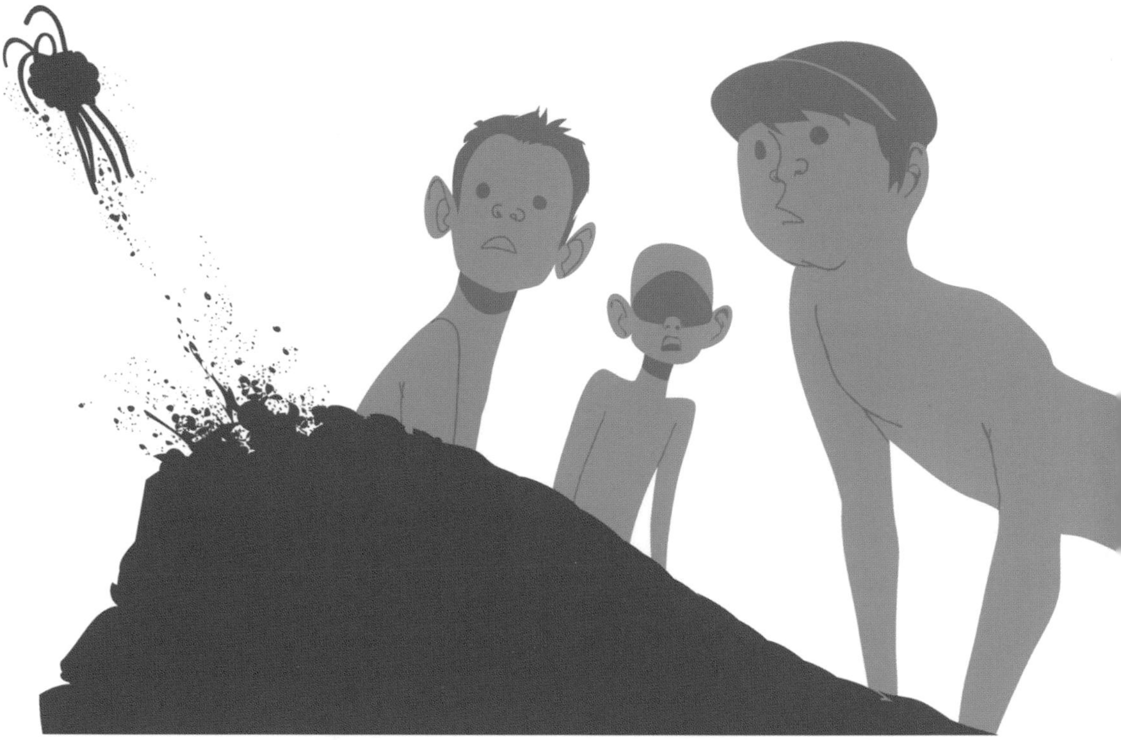

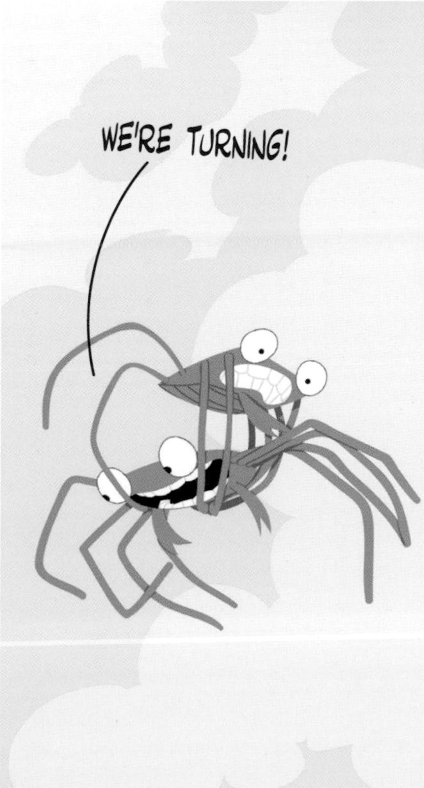
WE'RE TURNING!

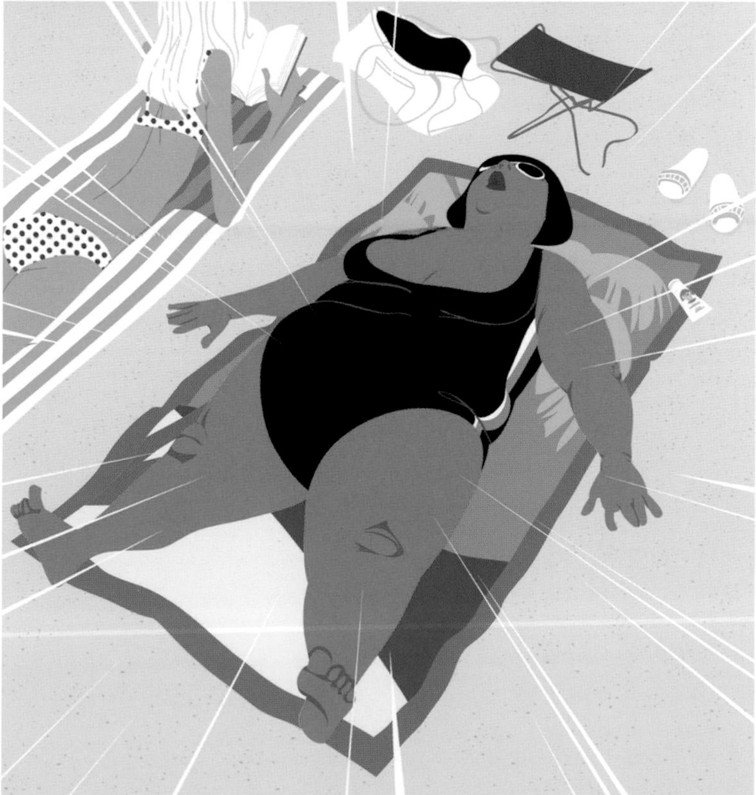

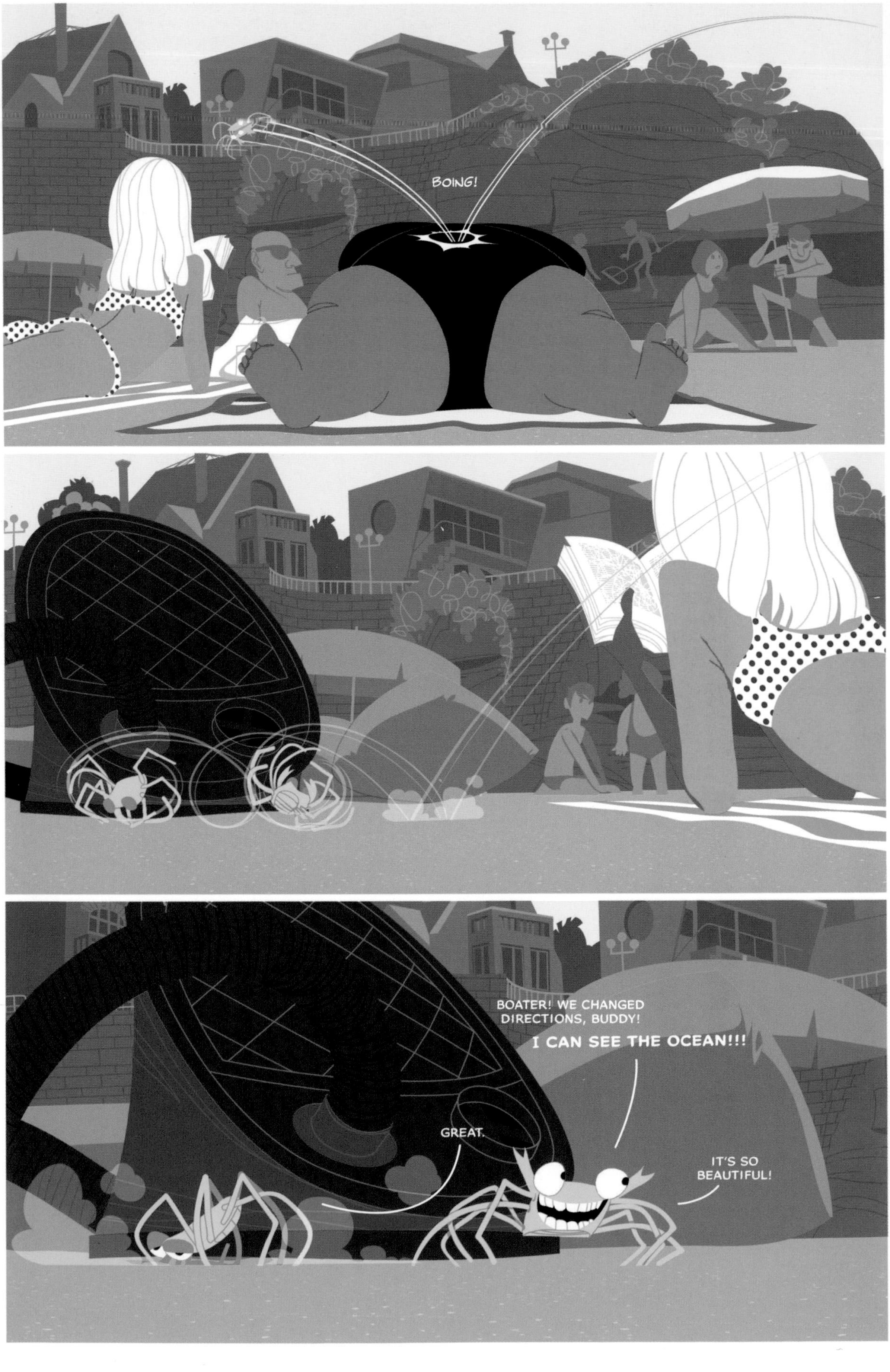
BOING!
BOATER! WE CHANGED DIRECTIONS, BUDDY!
I CAN SEE THE OCEAN!!!
GREAT.
IT'S SO BEAUTIFUL!

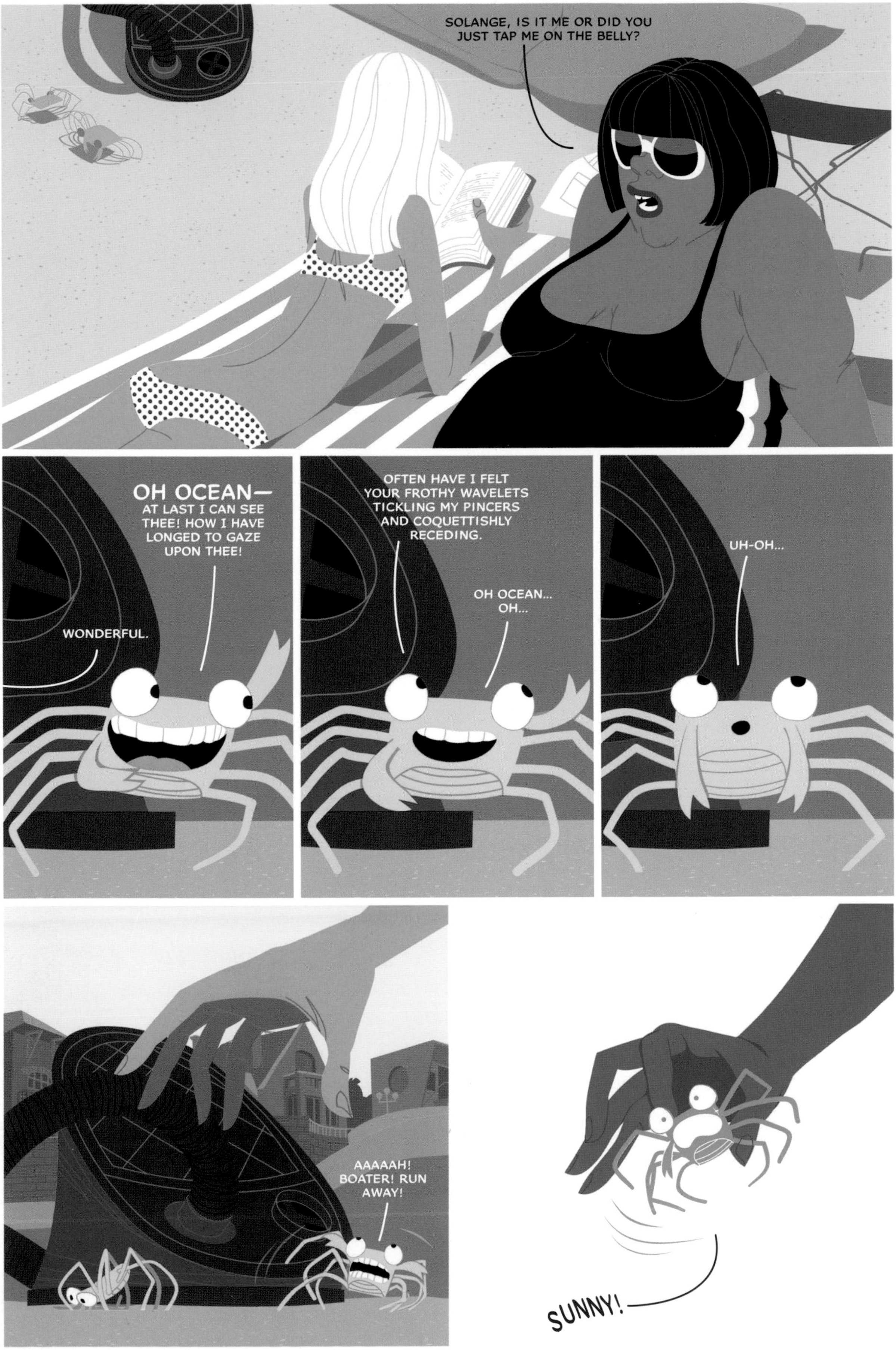
SOLANGE, IS IT ME OR DID YOU JUST TAP ME ON THE BELLY?
OH OCEAN— AT LAST I CAN SEE THEE! HOW I HAVE LONGED TO GAZE UPON THEE!
WONDERFUL.
OFTEN HAVE I FELT YOUR FROTHY WAVELETS TICKLING MY PINCERS AND COQUETTISHLY RECEDING.
OH OCEAN... OH...
UH-OH...
AAAAAH! BOATER! RUN AWAY!
SUNNY!

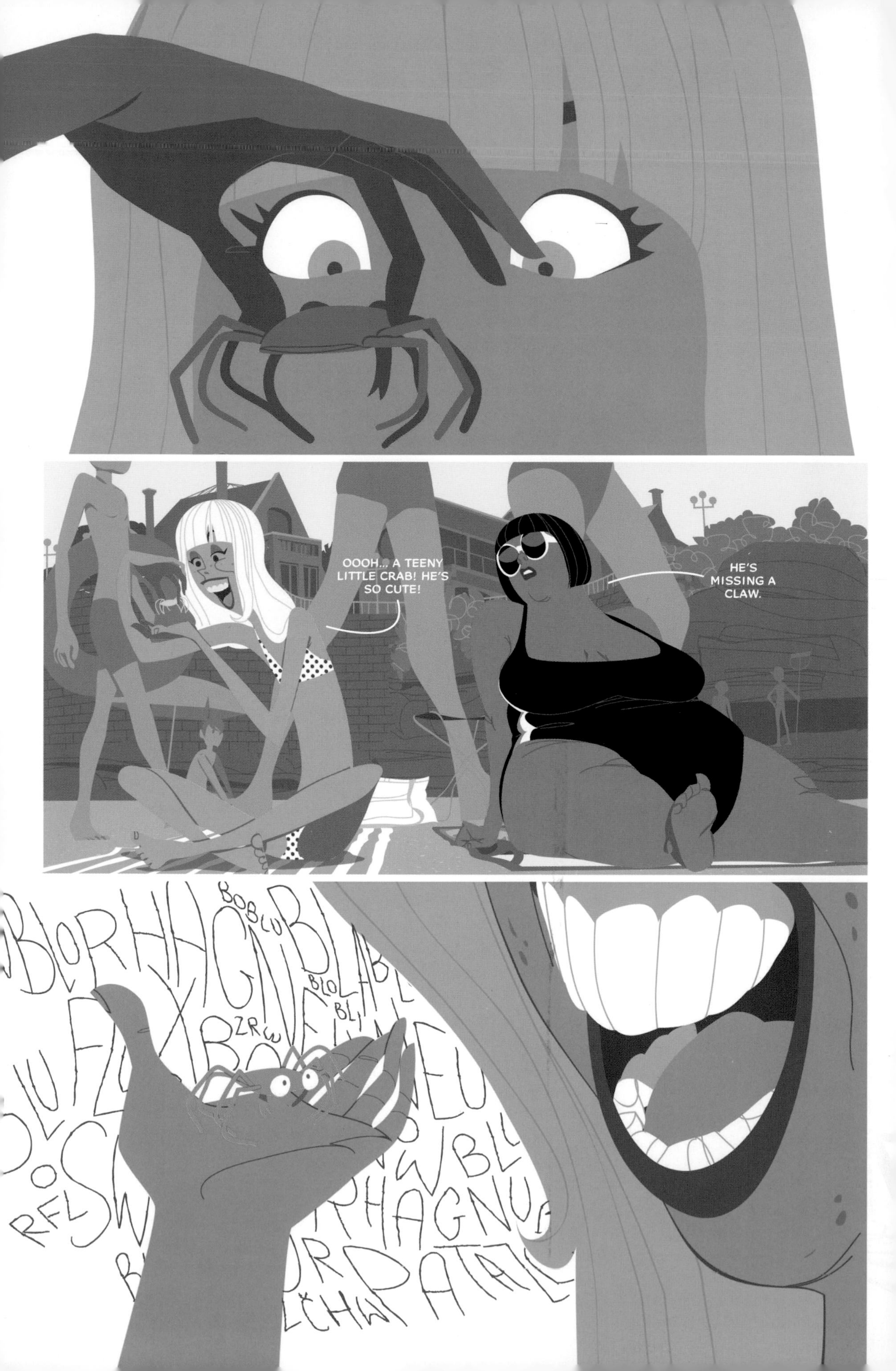
OOOH... A TEENY LITTLE CRAB! HE'S SO CUTE!
HE'S MISSING A CLAW.

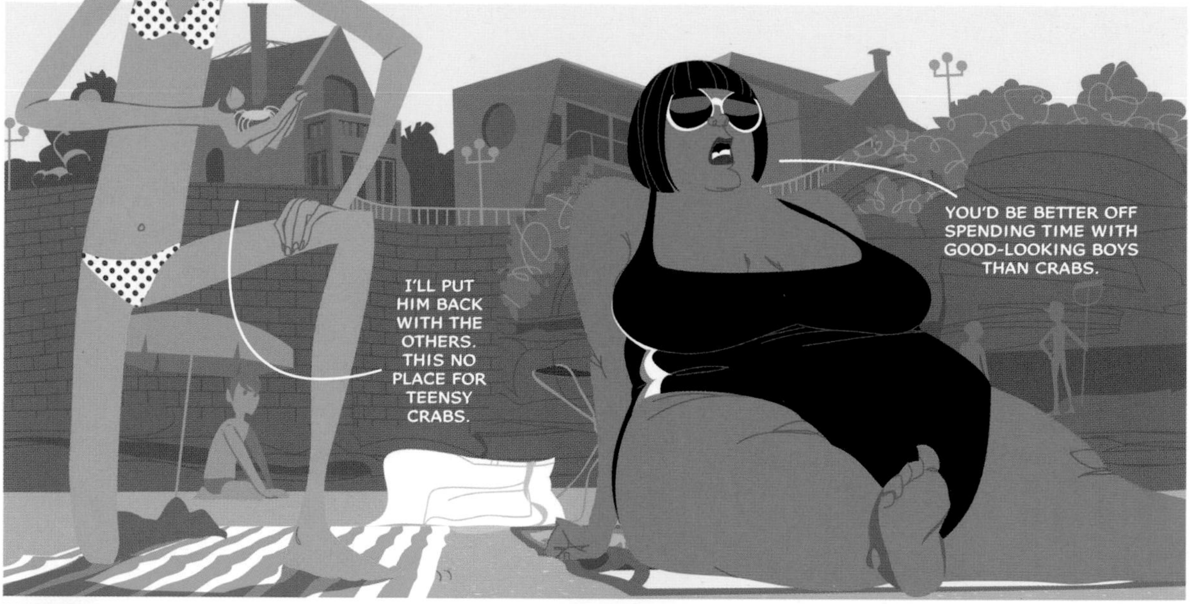
I'LL PUT HIM BACK WITH THE OTHERS. THIS NO PLACE FOR TEENSY CRABS.
YOU'D BE BETTER OFF SPENDING TIME WITH GOOD-LOOKING BOYS THAN CRABS.

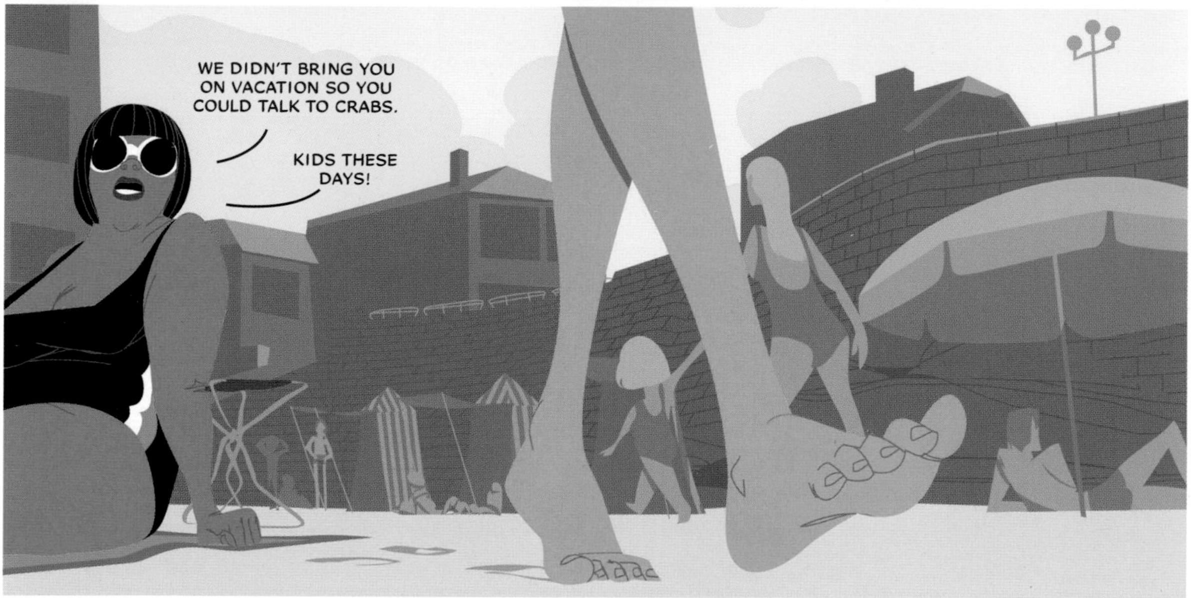
WE DIDN'T BRING YOU ON VACATION SO YOU COULD TALK TO CRABS.
KIDS THESE DAYS!

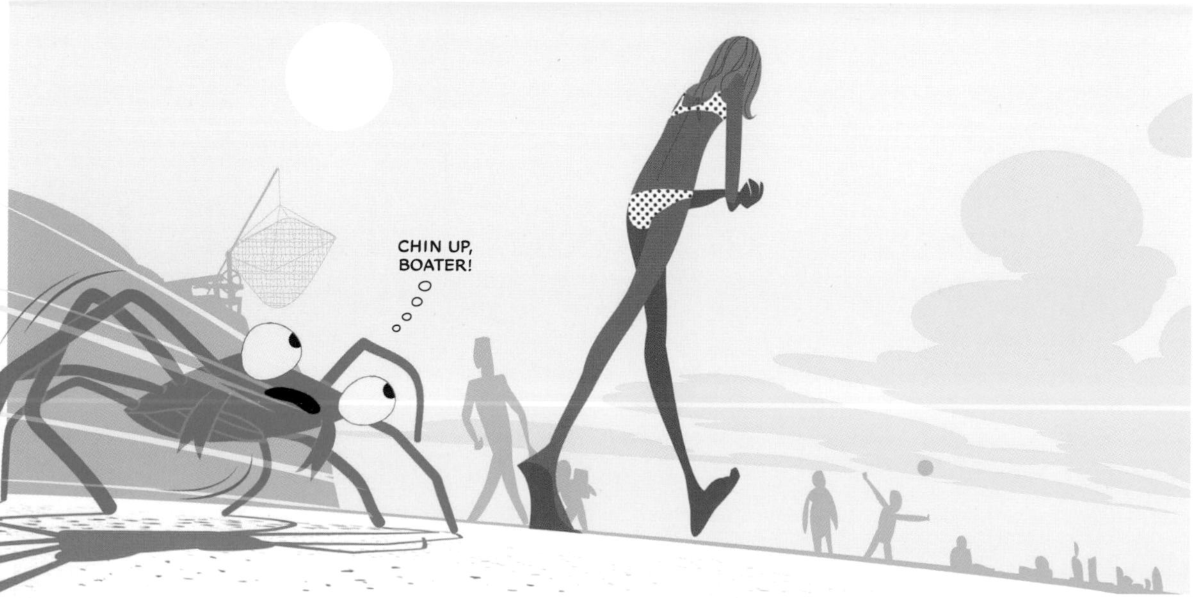
CHIN UP, BOATER!

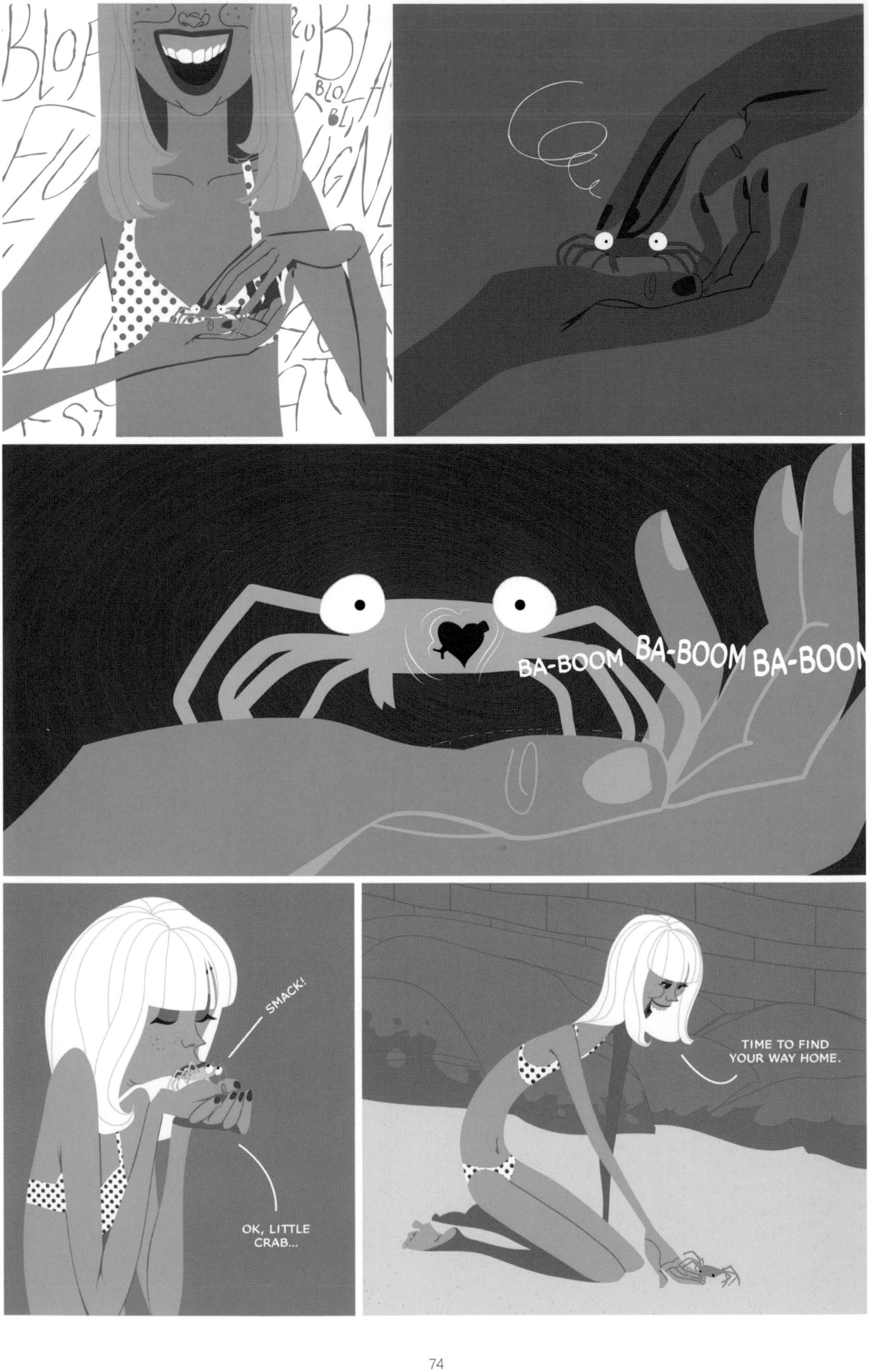
BA-BOOM
BA-BOOM
BA-BOO
SMACK!
OK, LITTLE CRAB...
TIME TO FIND YOUR WAY HOME.

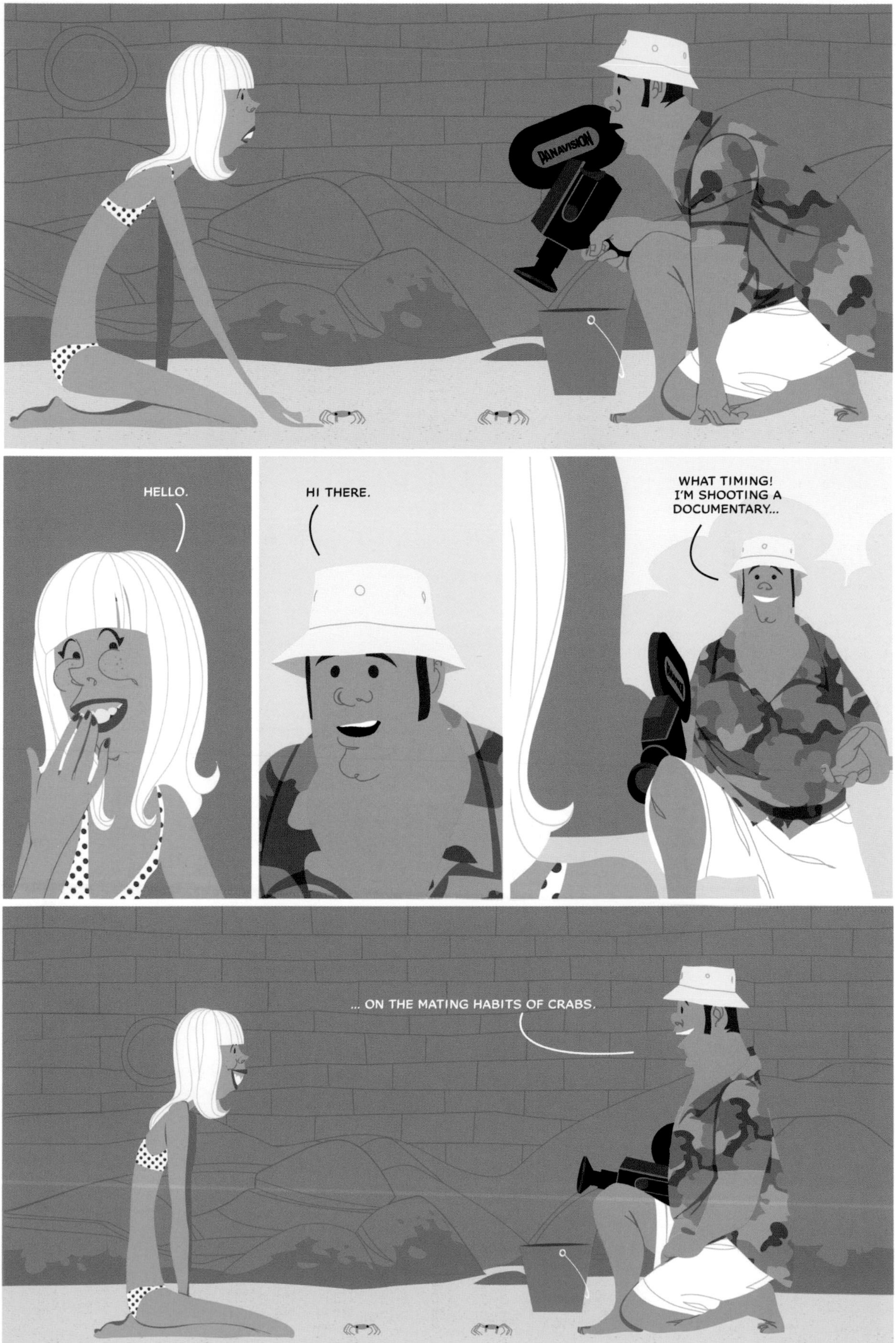
PANAVISION
HELLO.
HI THERE.
WHAT TIMING! I'M SHOOTING A DOCUMENTARY...
... ON THE MATING HABITS OF CRABS.

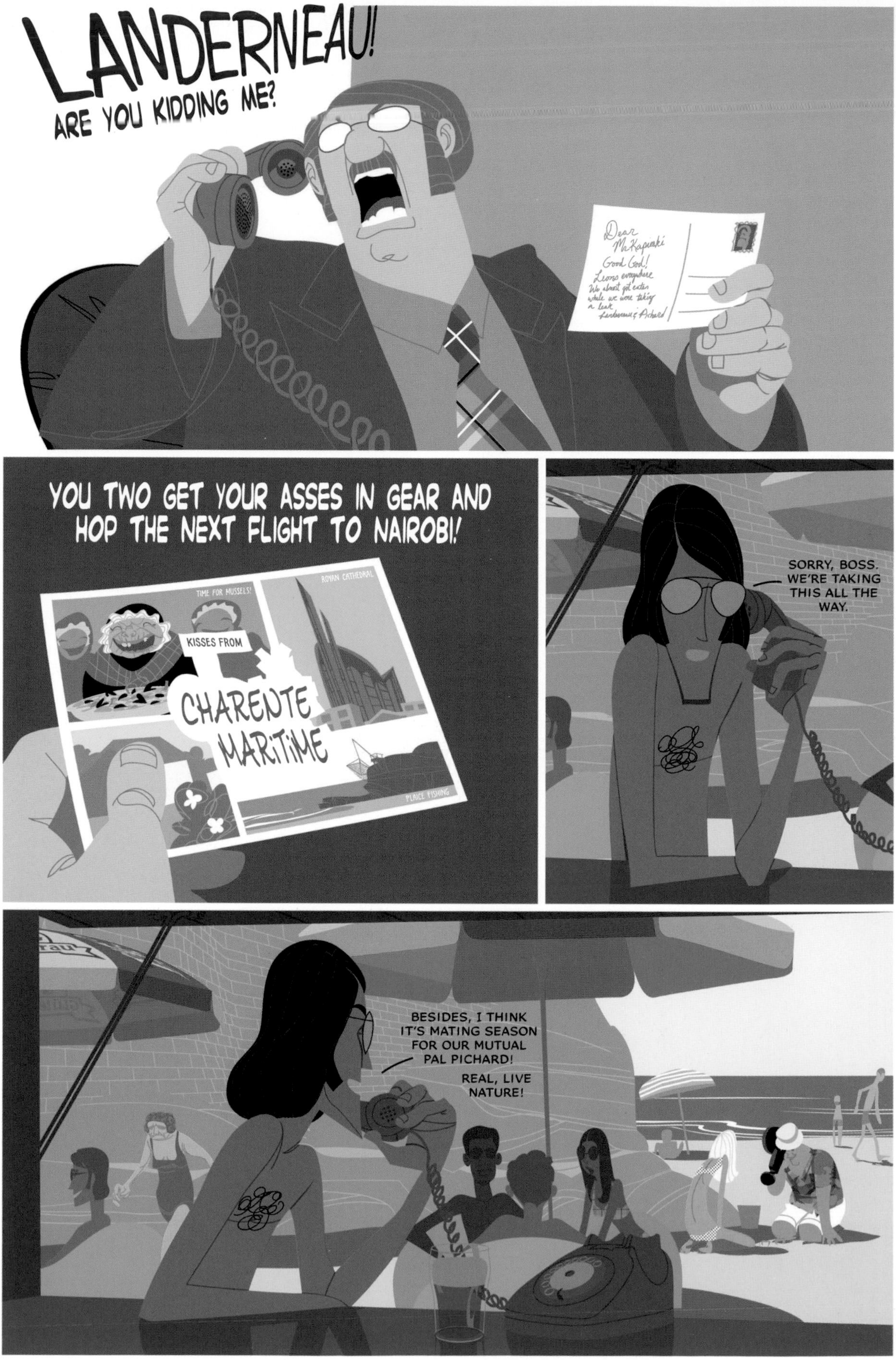
LANDERNEAU! ARE YOU KIDDING ME?
Dear
Good God!
We almost got eaten
while we were taking
a leak
YOU TWO GET YOUR ASSES IN GEAR AND HOP THE NEXT FLIGHT TO NAIROBI!
TIME FOR MUSSELS!
ROYAN CATHEDRAL
KISSES FROM
CHARENTE MARITIME
PLAICE FISHING
SORRY, BOSS. WE'RE TAKING THIS ALL THE WAY.
BESIDES, I THINK IT'S MATING SEASON FOR OUR MUTUAL PAL PICHARD!
REAL, LIVE NATURE!

YOU'RE NOT GETTING A CENT! GO STUFF YOURSELVES WITH CRABS! IT'LL ADD A CULINARY TOUCH TO YOUR STINKING...

BYE, BOSS!

CLICK

BEEP BEEP BEEP BEEP BEEP BEEP BEEP

GRUMBLE

KLANG!

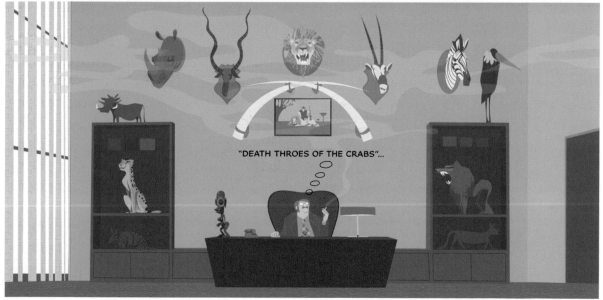

"DEATH THROES OF THE CRABS"...

NOT BAD AS TITLES GO...

"THE TRAGIC FATE OF A VANISHING SPECIES."

THROW IN CORRUPTION, GREENPEACE...

THIS CRAB STUFF COULD WORK! IT'S ACCESSIBLE, PEOPLE SEE CRABS EVERY DAY, IT SMACKS OF BEACH VACATIONS... BUT SOMETHING'S MISSING.

A HOT TOPIC.

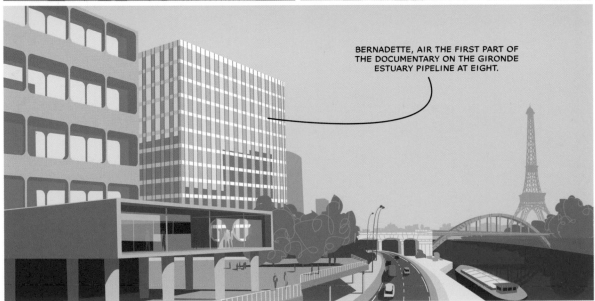

BERNADETTE, AIR THE FIRST PART OF THE DOCUMENTARY ON THE GIRONDE ESTUARY PIPELINE AT EIGHT.

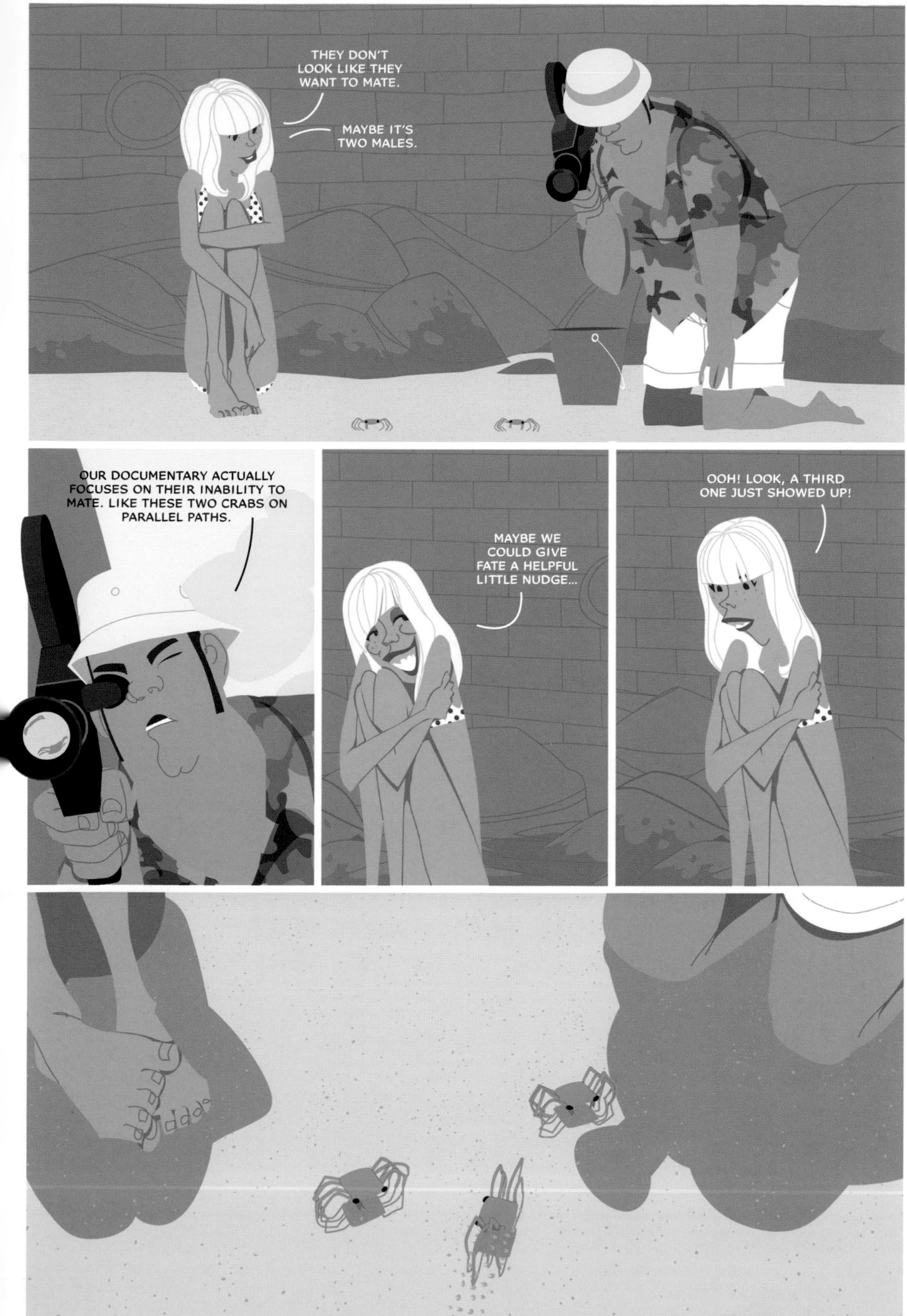
THEY DON'T LOOK LIKE THEY WANT TO MATE.
MAYBE IT'S TWO MALES.
OUR DOCUMENTARY ACTUALLY FOCUSES ON THEIR INABILITY TO MATE. LIKE THESE TWO CRABS ON PARALLEL PATHS.
MAYBE WE COULD GIVE FATE A HELPFUL LITTLE NUDGE...
OOH! LOOK, A THIRD ONE JUST SHOWED UP!

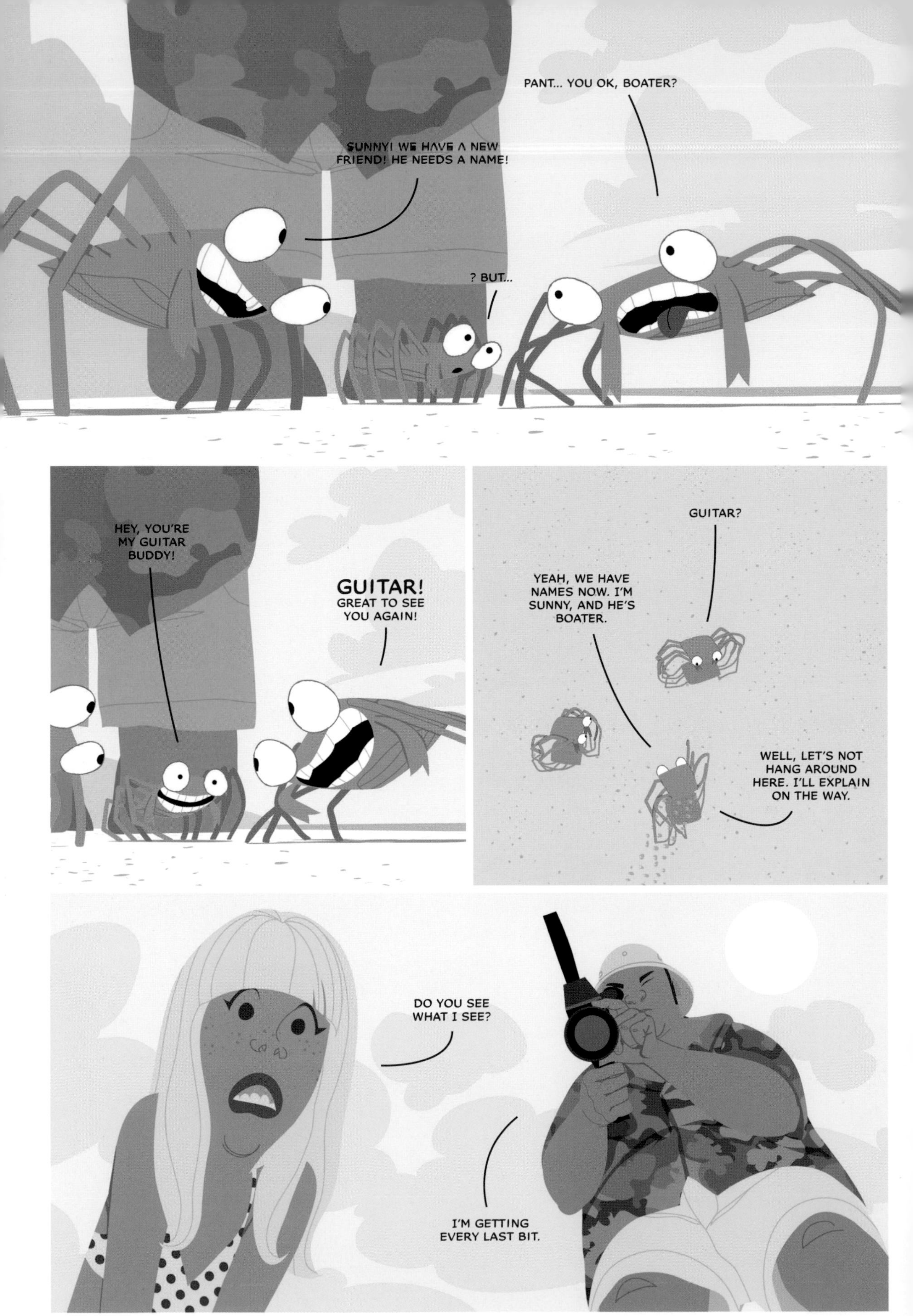
SUNNY! WE HAVE A NEW FRIEND! HE NEEDS A NAME!
PANT... YOU OK, BOATER?
? BUT...
HEY, YOU'RE MY GUITAR BUDDY!
GUITAR! GREAT TO SEE YOU AGAIN!
GUITAR?
YEAH, WE HAVE NAMES NOW. I'M SUNNY, AND HE'S BOATER.
WELL, LET'S NOT HANG AROUND HERE. I'LL EXPLAIN ON THE WAY.
DO YOU SEE WHAT I SEE?
I'M GETTING EVERY LAST BIT.

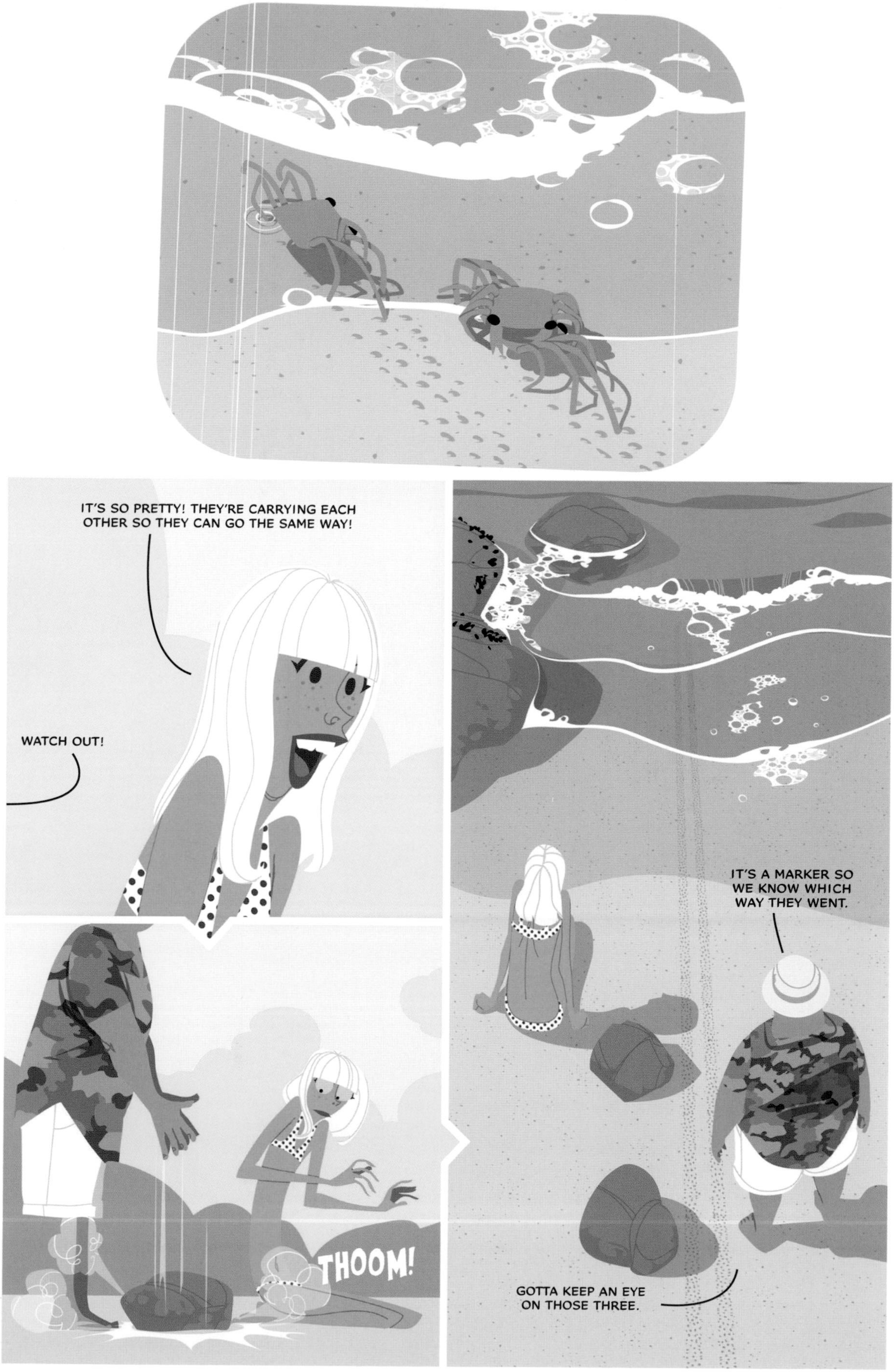
IT'S SO PRETTY! THEY'RE CARRYING EACH OTHER SO THEY CAN GO THE SAME WAY!
WATCH OUT!
THOOM!
IT'S A MARKER SO WE KNOW WHICH WAY THEY WENT.
GOTTA KEEP AN EYE ON THOSE THREE.

HONESTLY, GUYS...
THAT IS ONE CRAZY STORY!
SUNNY... IMAGINE IF YOU'D FIGURED THAT OUT BACK WHEN—
WOULDN'T HAVE WORKED, GUITAR. WE RAN PARALLEL.
SUNNY?
YES, BOATER?
I—
I'M POOPED. CAN I TAKE A BREAK?
SURE! SORRY. BUSY TALKING.
AHHH... NEVER BEEN HERE BEFORE. ROOMY, AIN'T IT?

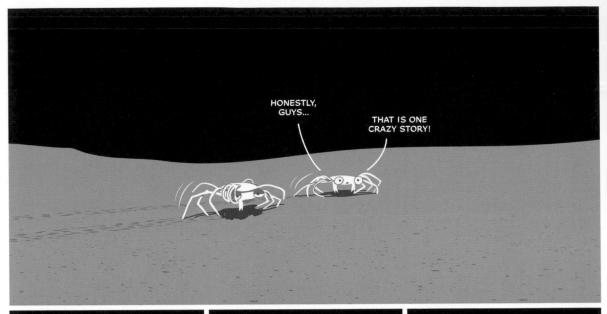

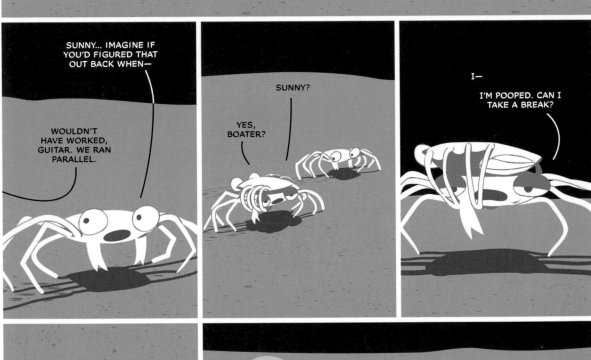

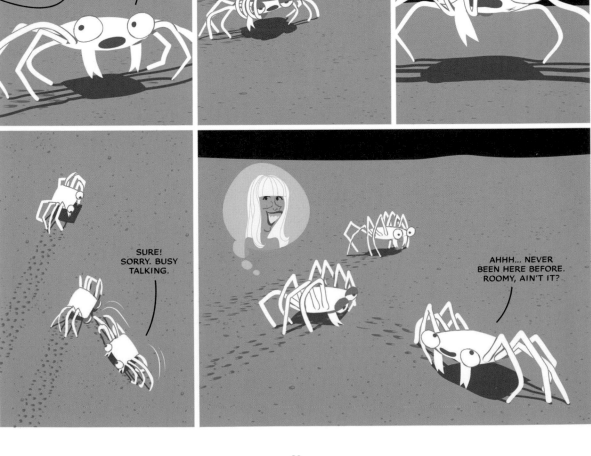

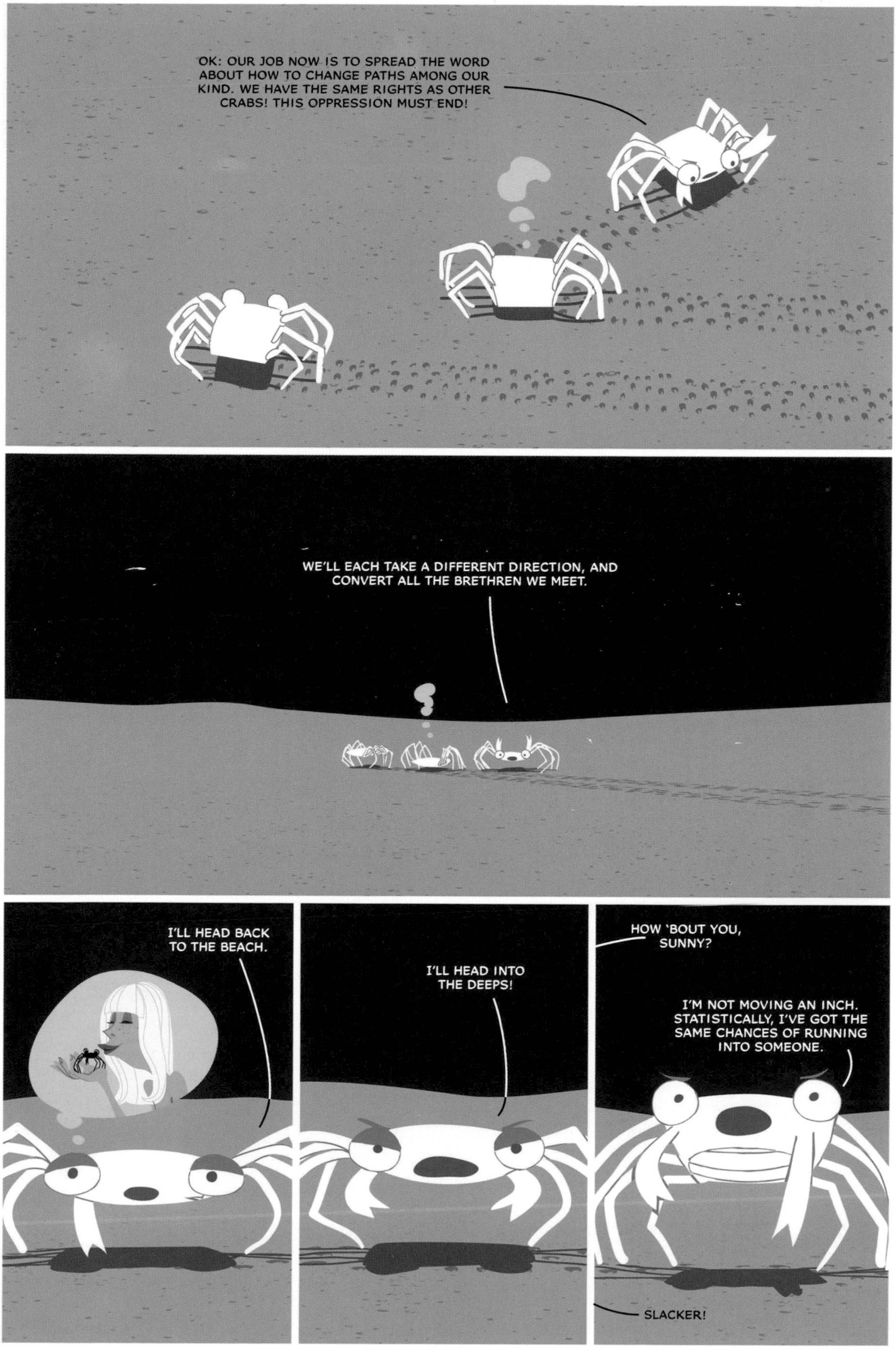
OK: OUR JOB NOW IS TO SPREAD THE WORD ABOUT HOW TO CHANGE PATHS AMONG OUR KIND. WE HAVE THE SAME RIGHTS AS OTHER CRABS! THIS OPPRESSION MUST END!
WE'LL EACH TAKE A DIFFERENT DIRECTION, AND CONVERT ALL THE BRETHREN WE MEET.
I'LL HEAD BACK TO THE BEACH.
I'LL HEAD INTO THE DEEPS!
HOW 'BOUT YOU, SUNNY?
I'M NOT MOVING AN INCH. STATISTICALLY, I'VE GOT THE SAME CHANCES OF RUNNING INTO SOMEONE.
SLACKER!

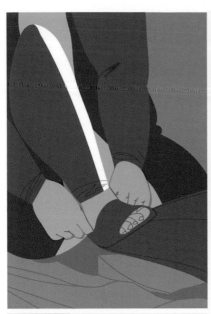

NOT GOING TO WATCH THE PORT GET BLOCKADED, MR. LANDERNEAU?

DON'T YOU FELLOWS HAVE TV IN YOUR HOTEL ROOM? LAST NIGHT AT 8, THERE WAS A SHOW ABOUT A PIPELINE BEING BUILT IN THE ESTUARY...

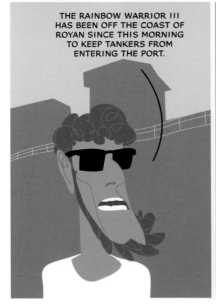

THE RAINBOW WARRIOR III HAS BEEN OFF THE COAST OF ROYAN SINCE THIS MORNING TO KEEP TANKERS FROM ENTERING THE PORT.

YOU'RE GOING TO MISS THE SCOOP OF THE SUMMER.

THANKS MR. DUCROUET, BUT WE'VE GOT THREE CRABS TO TRACK DOWN.

I KNOW IT'S DUMB, BUT...

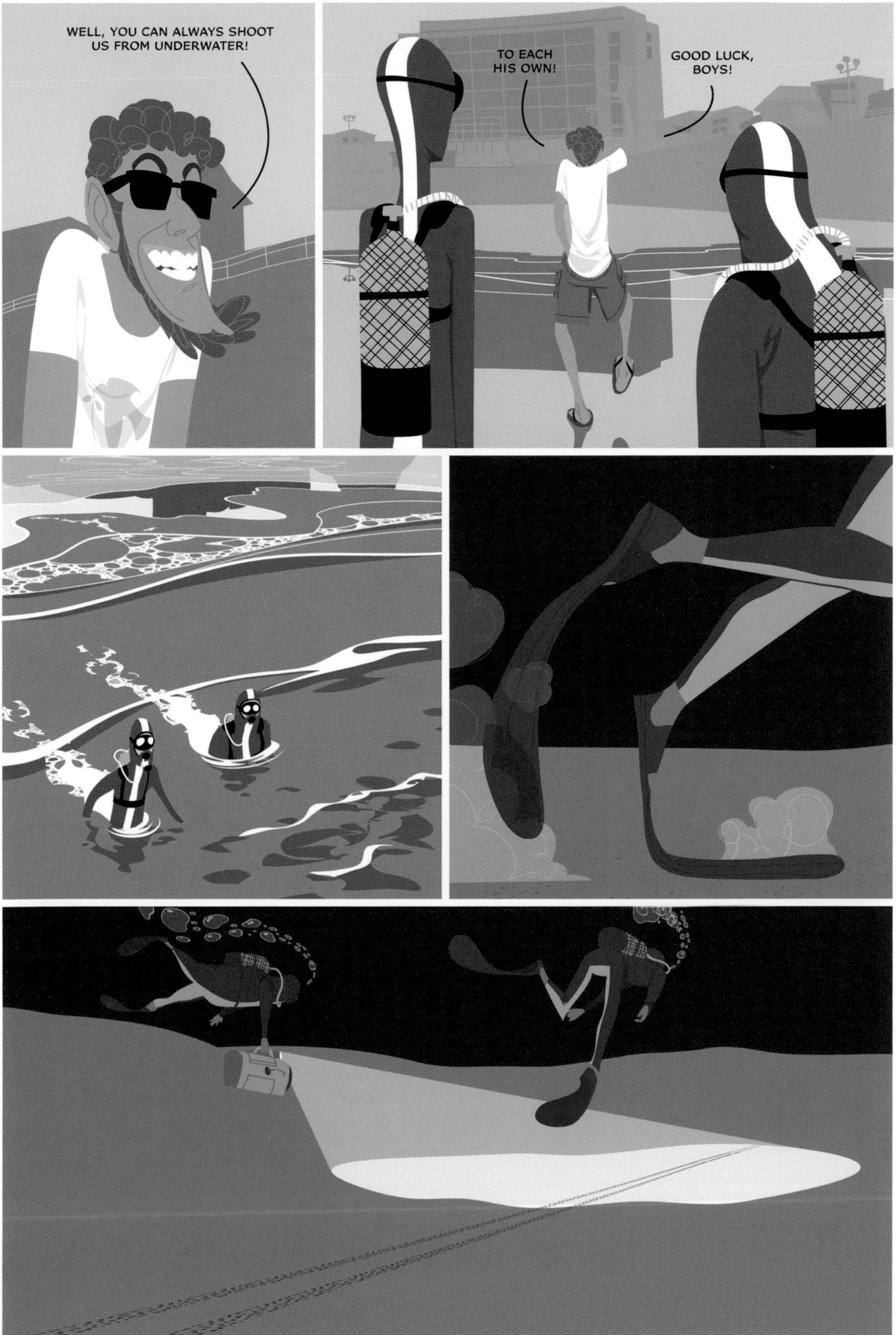
WELL, YOU CAN ALWAYS SHOOT US FROM UNDERWATER!
TO EACH HIS OWN!
GOOD LUCK, BOYS!

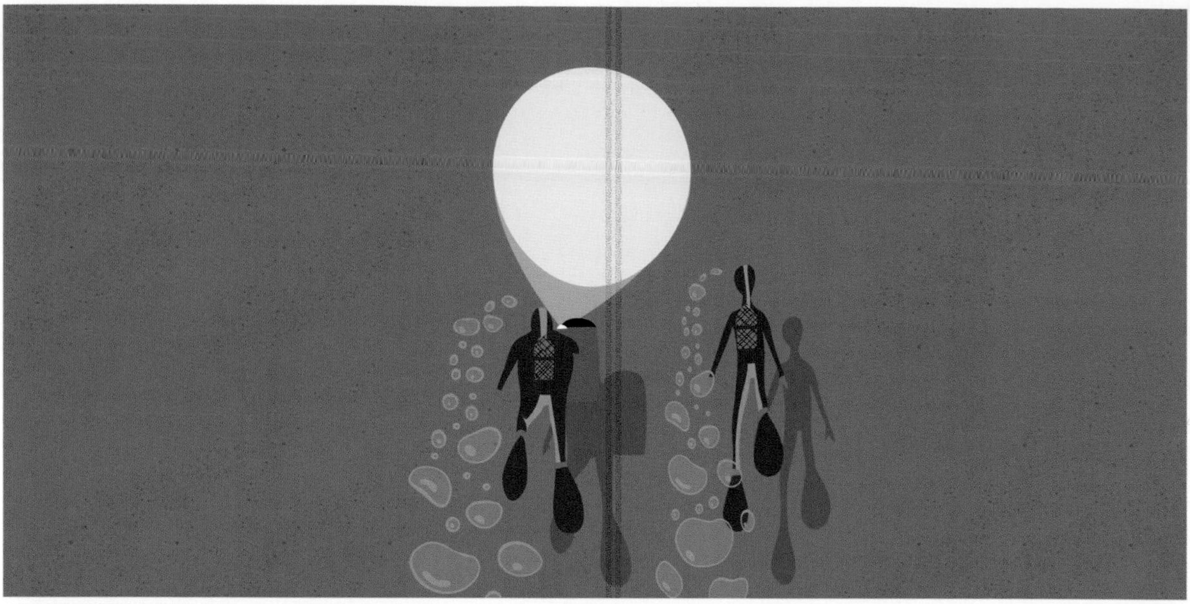

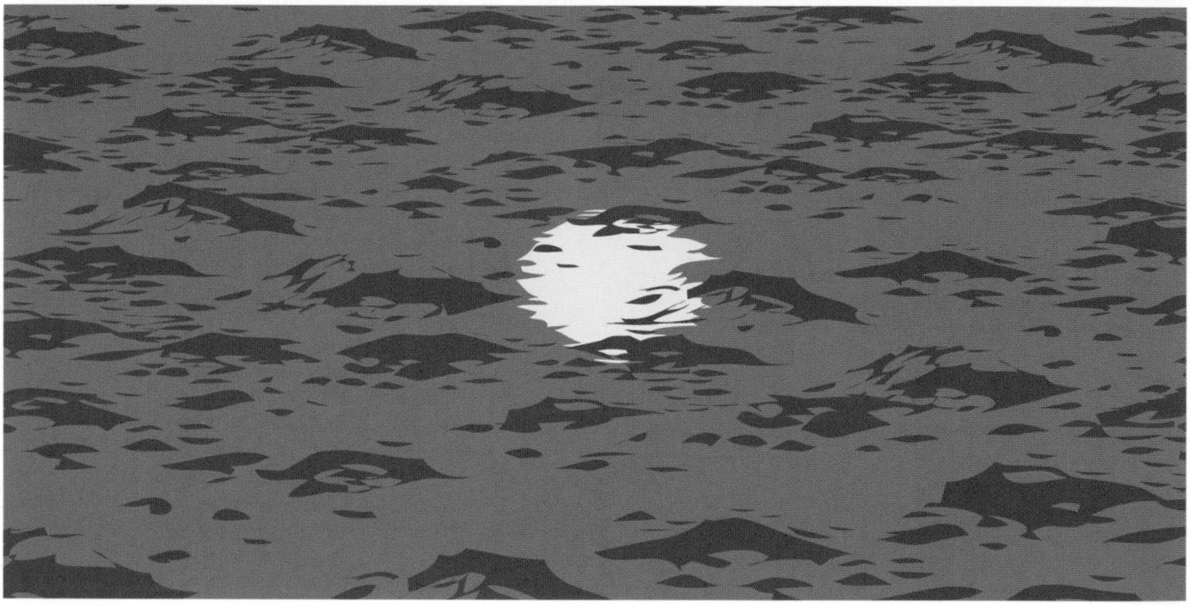

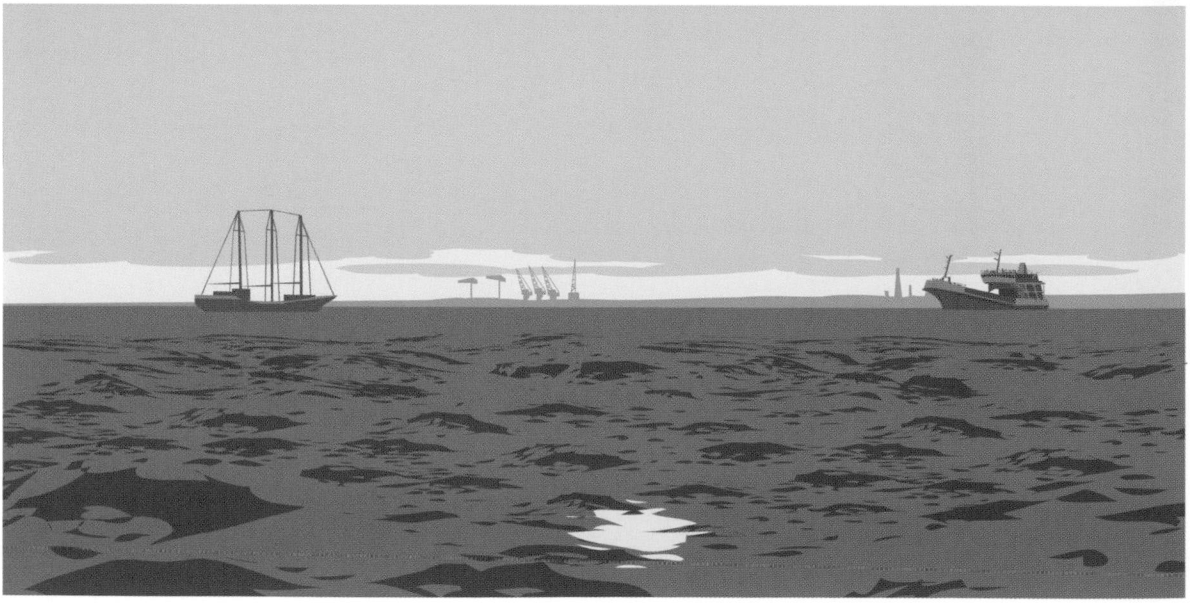

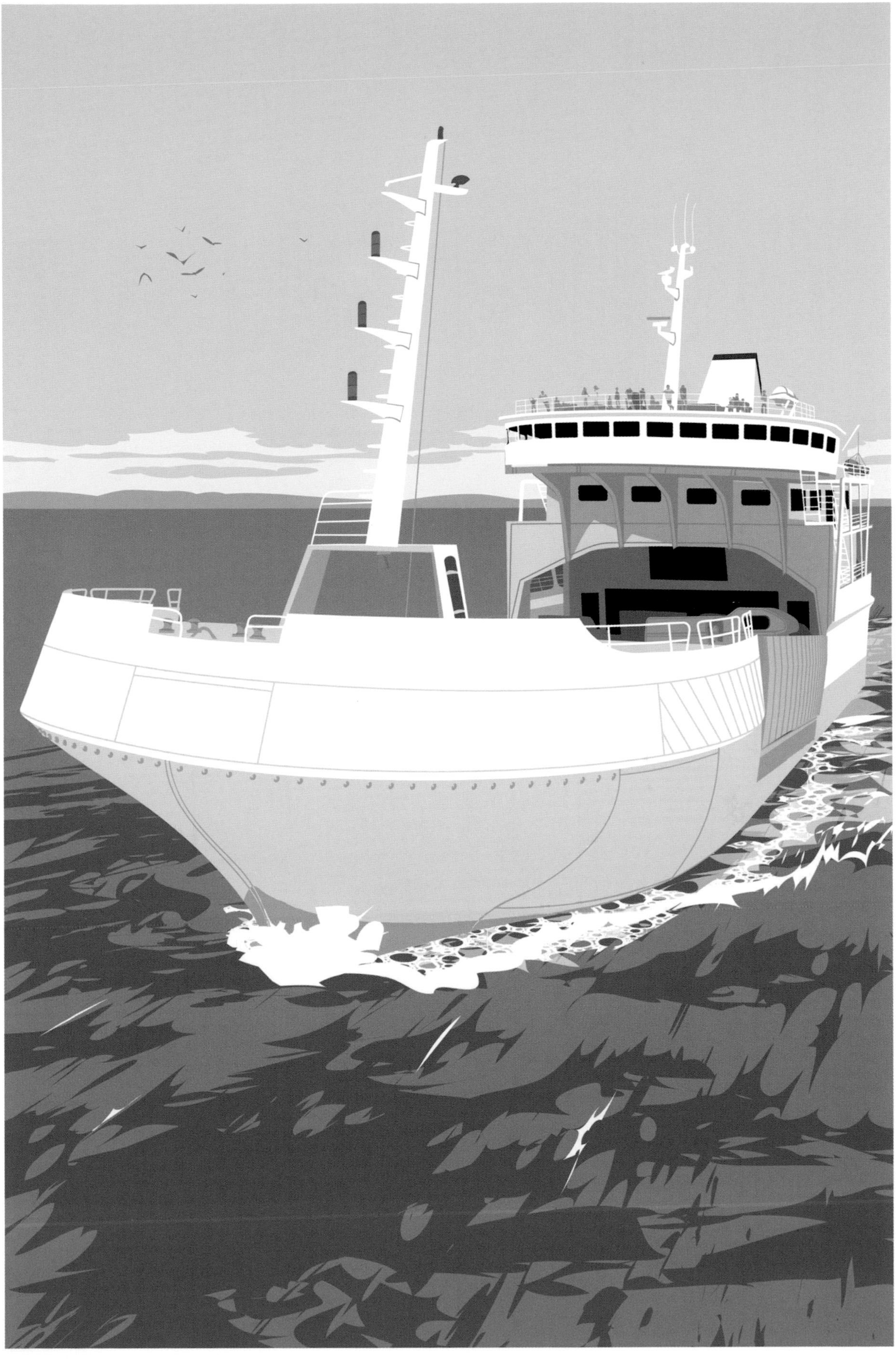

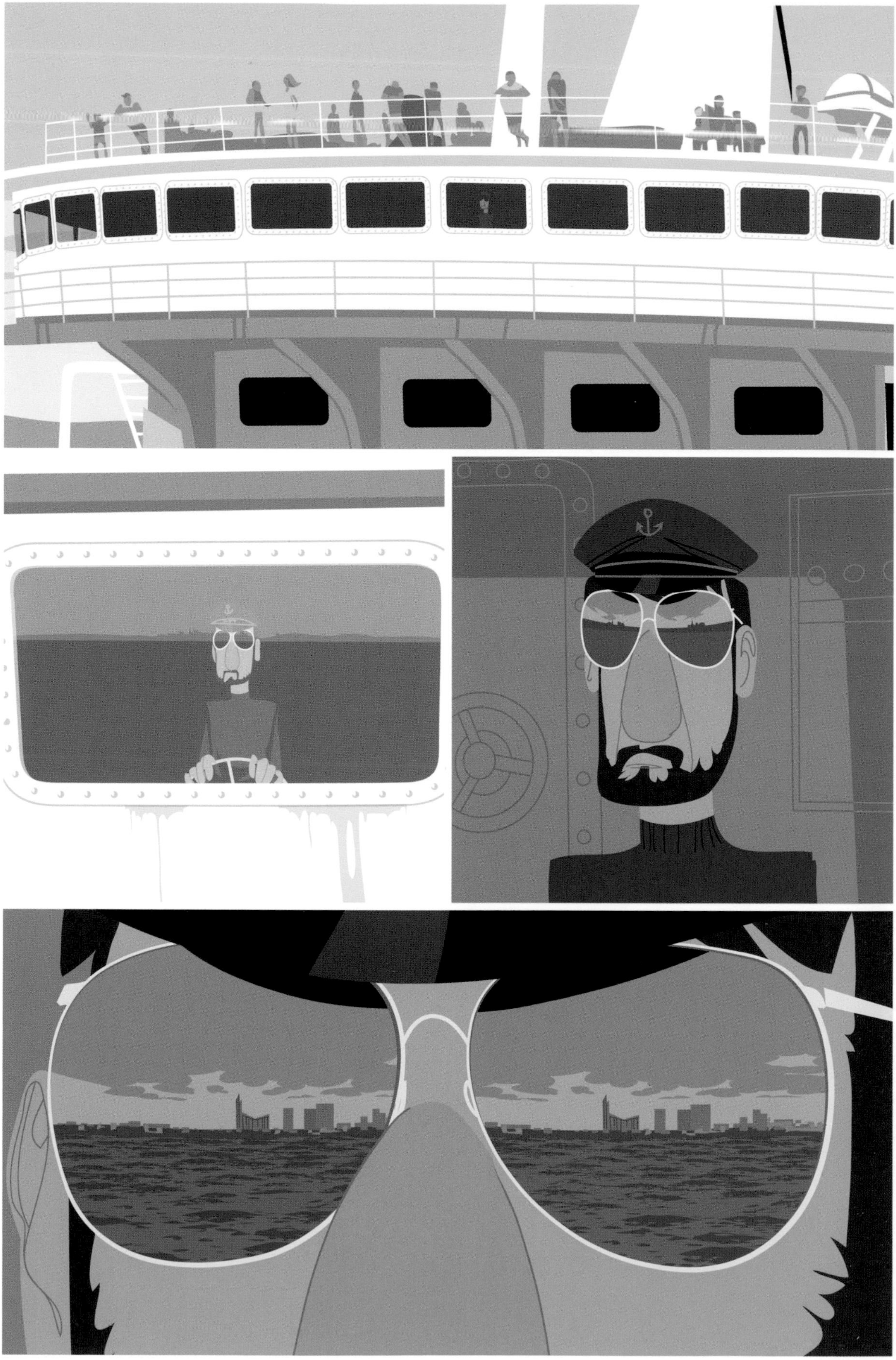

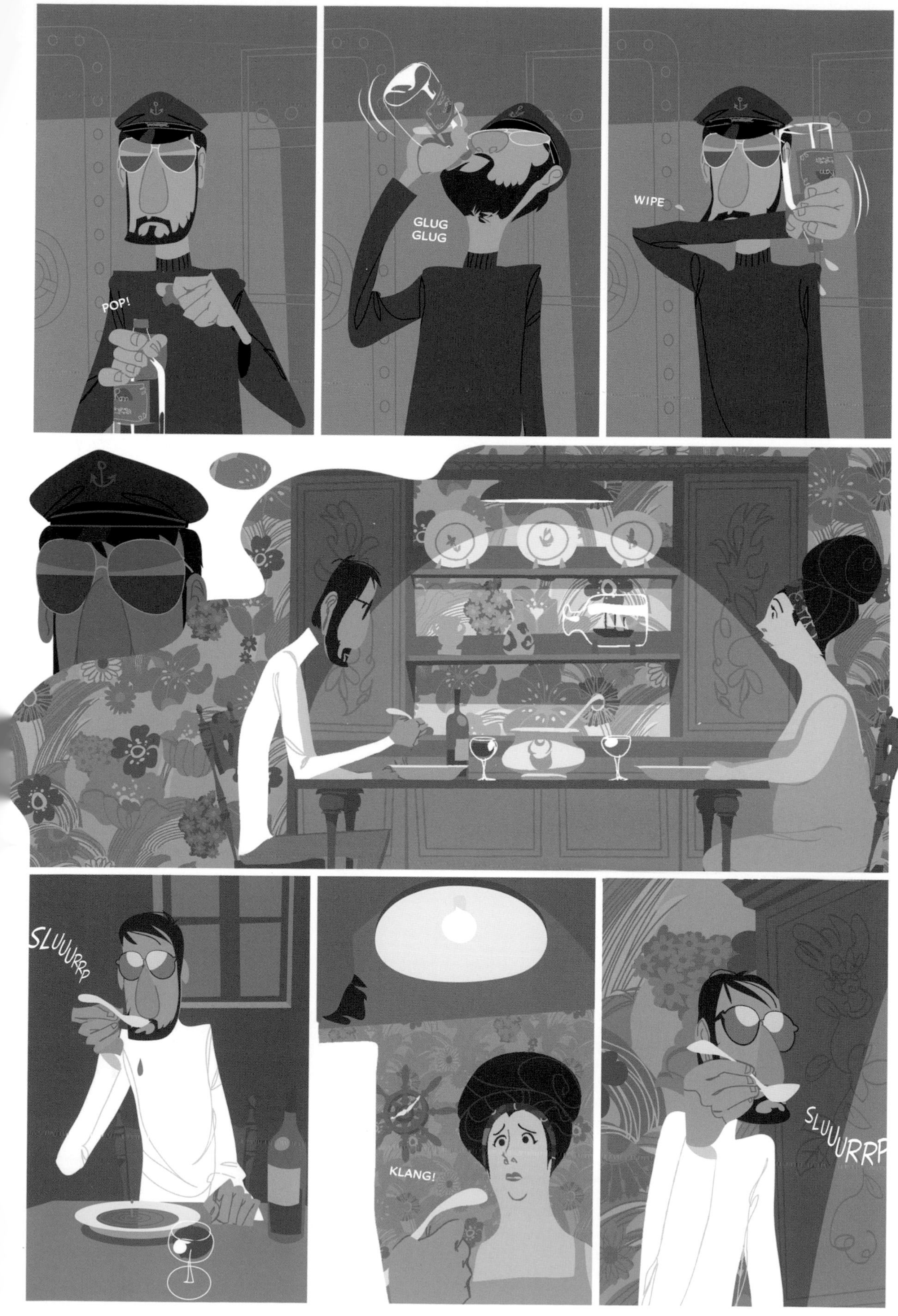
POP!
GLUG
GLUG
WIPE
SLUUURRP
KLANG!
SLUUURRP

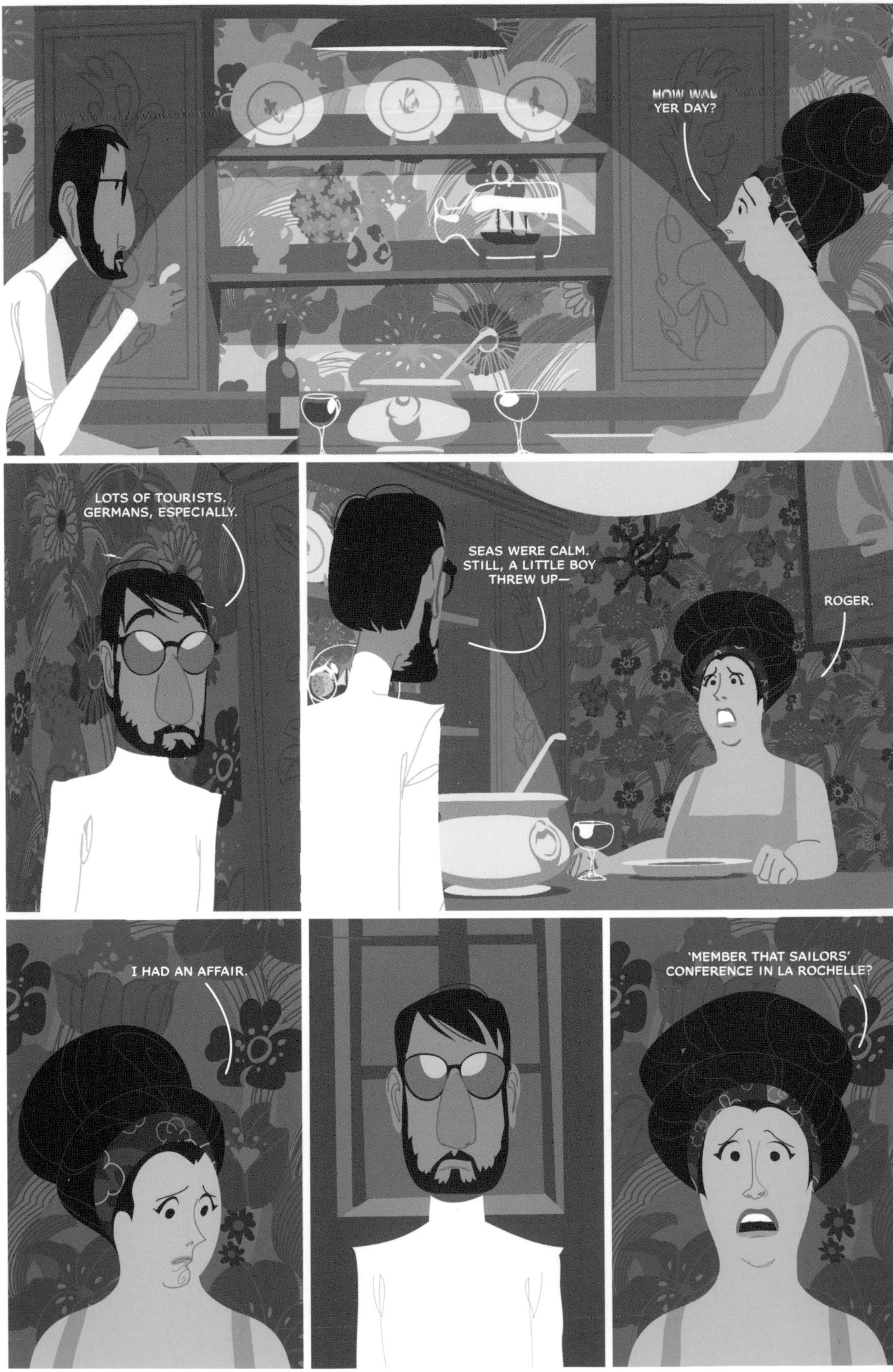
HOW WAS YER DAY?
LOTS OF TOURISTS. GERMANS, ESPECIALLY.
SEAS WERE CALM. STILL, A LITTLE BOY THREW UP—
ROGER.
I HAD AN AFFAIR.
'MEMBER THAT SAILORS' CONFERENCE IN LA ROCHELLE?

THERE WAS THIS BIG STRAPPIN' FELLOW THERE, GAETAN. HE WORKED FOR GREENPEACE. AFTER THE CONFERENCE, HE WROTE ME A LETTER FROM SINGAPORE. I WAS ALL MIXED-UP. NOBODY HAD EVER WRITTEN ME FROM SO FAR AWAY BEFORE. WE MET UP A FEW TIMES IN LA ROCHELLE. I TOLD YOU I WAS GOIN' TO SEE MY MAMA, BUT THAT WAS A LIE.

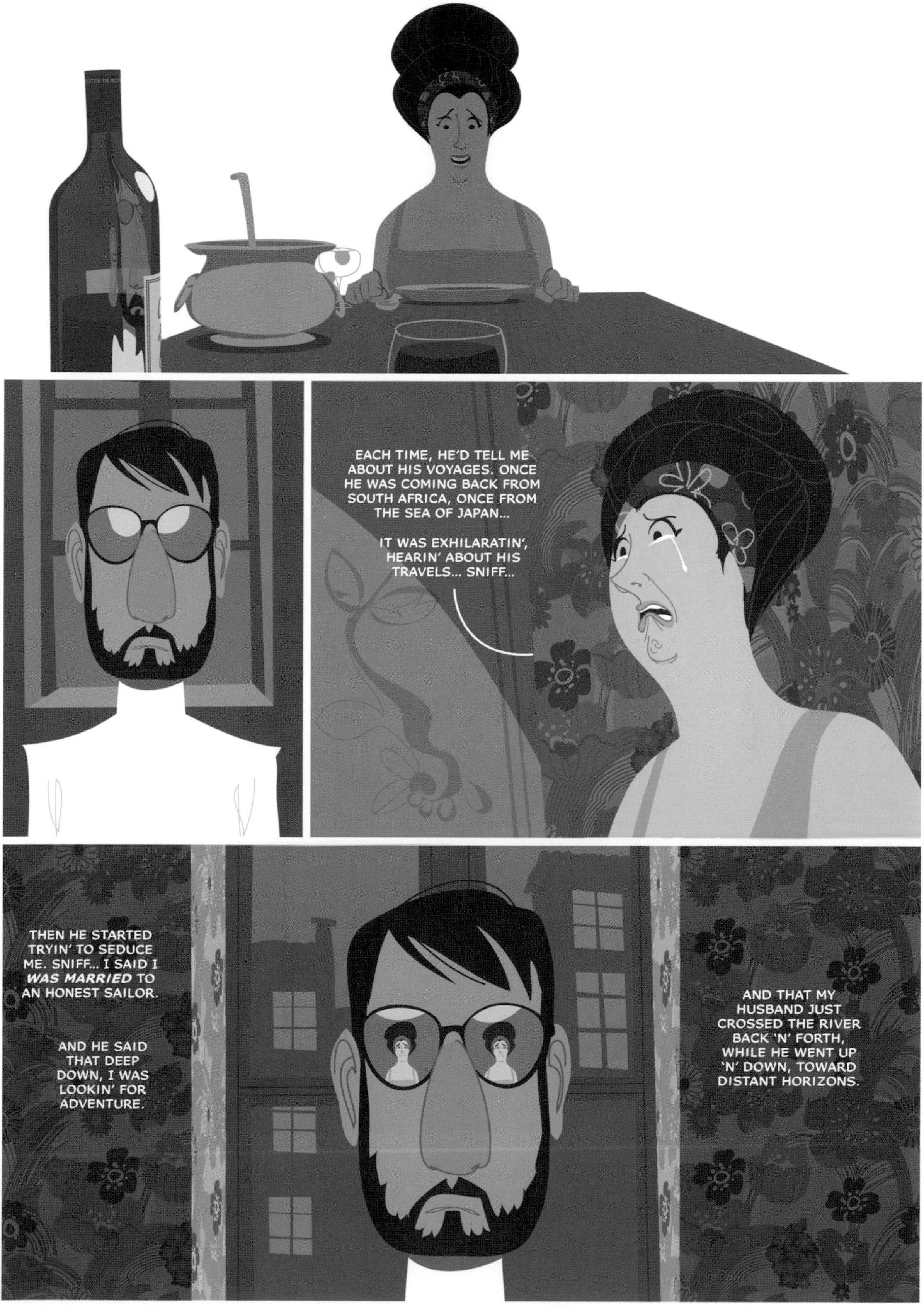
EACH TIME, HE'D TELL ME ABOUT HIS VOYAGES. ONCE HE WAS COMING BACK FROM SOUTH AFRICA, ONCE FROM THE SEA OF JAPAN...
IT WAS EXHILARATIN', HEARIN' ABOUT HIS TRAVELS... SNIFF...
THEN HE STARTED TRYIN' TO SEDUCE ME. SNIFF... I SAID I ***WAS MARRIED*** TO AN HONEST SAILOR.
AND HE SAID THAT DEEP DOWN, I WAS LOOKIN' FOR ADVENTURE.
AND THAT MY HUSBAND JUST CROSSED THE RIVER BACK 'N' FORTH, WHILE HE WENT UP 'N' DOWN, TOWARD DISTANT HORIZONS.

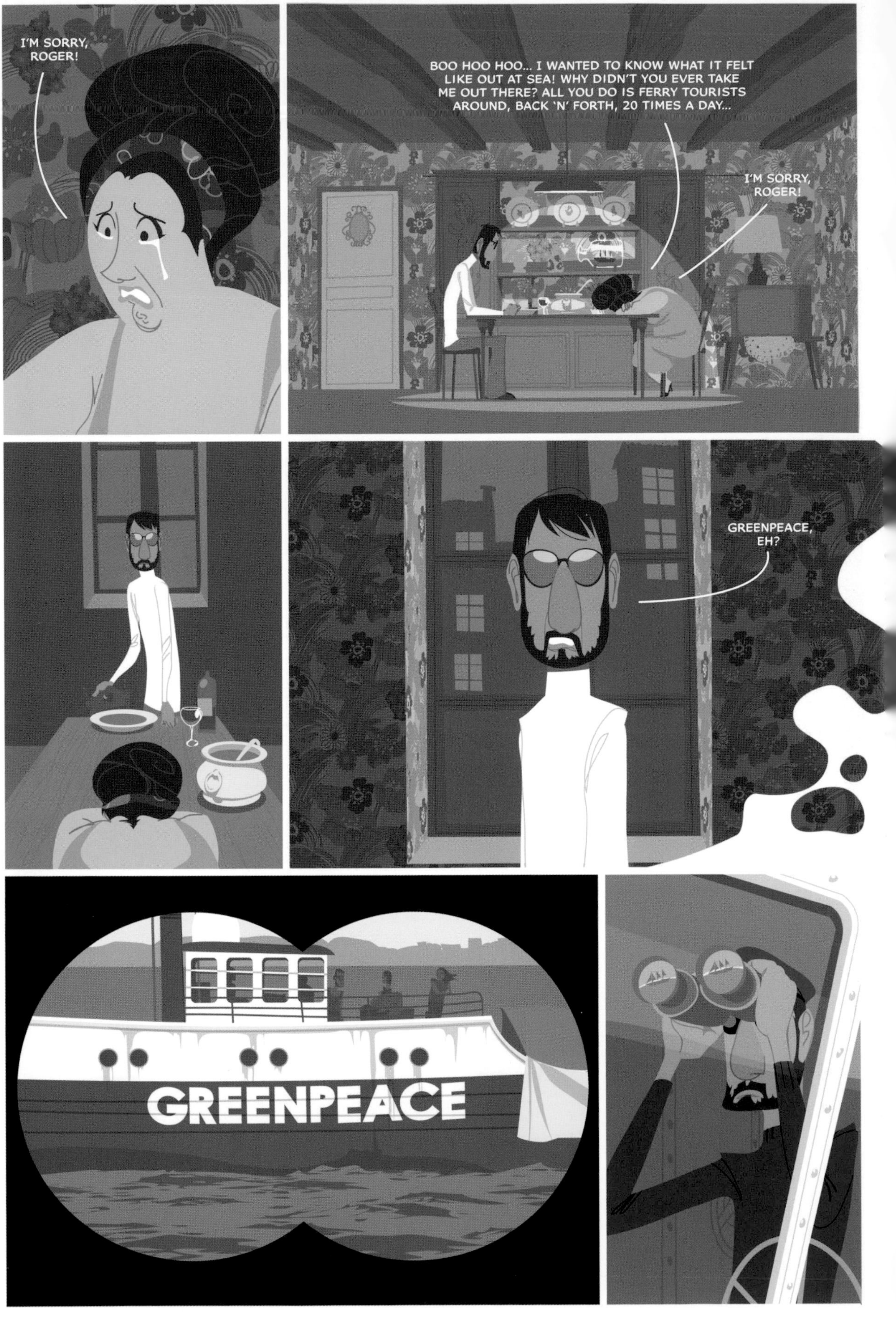
I'M SORRY, ROGER!
BOO HOO HOO... I WANTED TO KNOW WHAT IT FELT LIKE OUT AT SEA! WHY DIDN'T YOU EVER TAKE ME OUT THERE? ALL YOU DO IS FERRY TOURISTS AROUND, BACK 'N' FORTH, 20 TIMES A DAY...
I'M SORRY, ROGER!
GREENPEACE, EH?
GREENPEACE

THOSE HIPPIES ARE KEEPING US FROM THE TANKERS.
CRIPES. BETTER STEP ASIDE AND LET US HONEST GUYS DO OUR JOB.
OR I'LL UP AND RAM YOUR BOAT.
GREENPEACE
NO PIPELINE
CALM WATERS...
WAVE HELLO TO THE TOURISTS ON THE BOAT!
?
UH, ROGER... WHEN I SAID I'D RAM THEM...

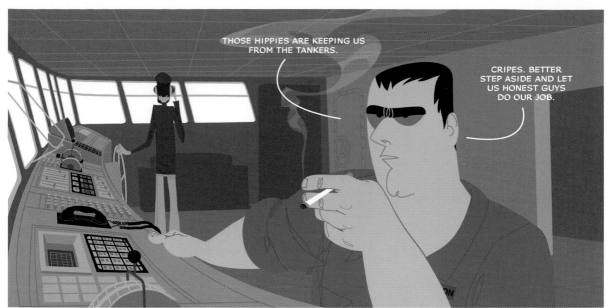

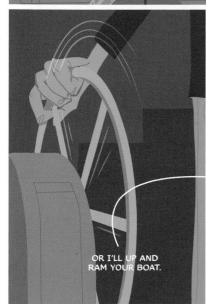

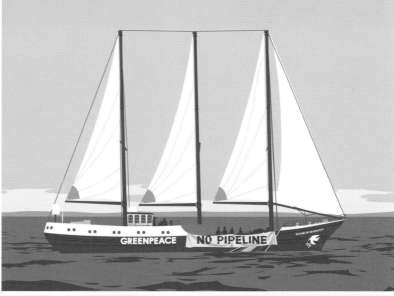

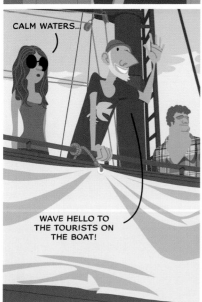

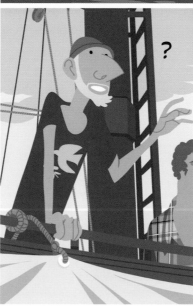

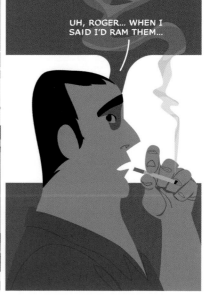

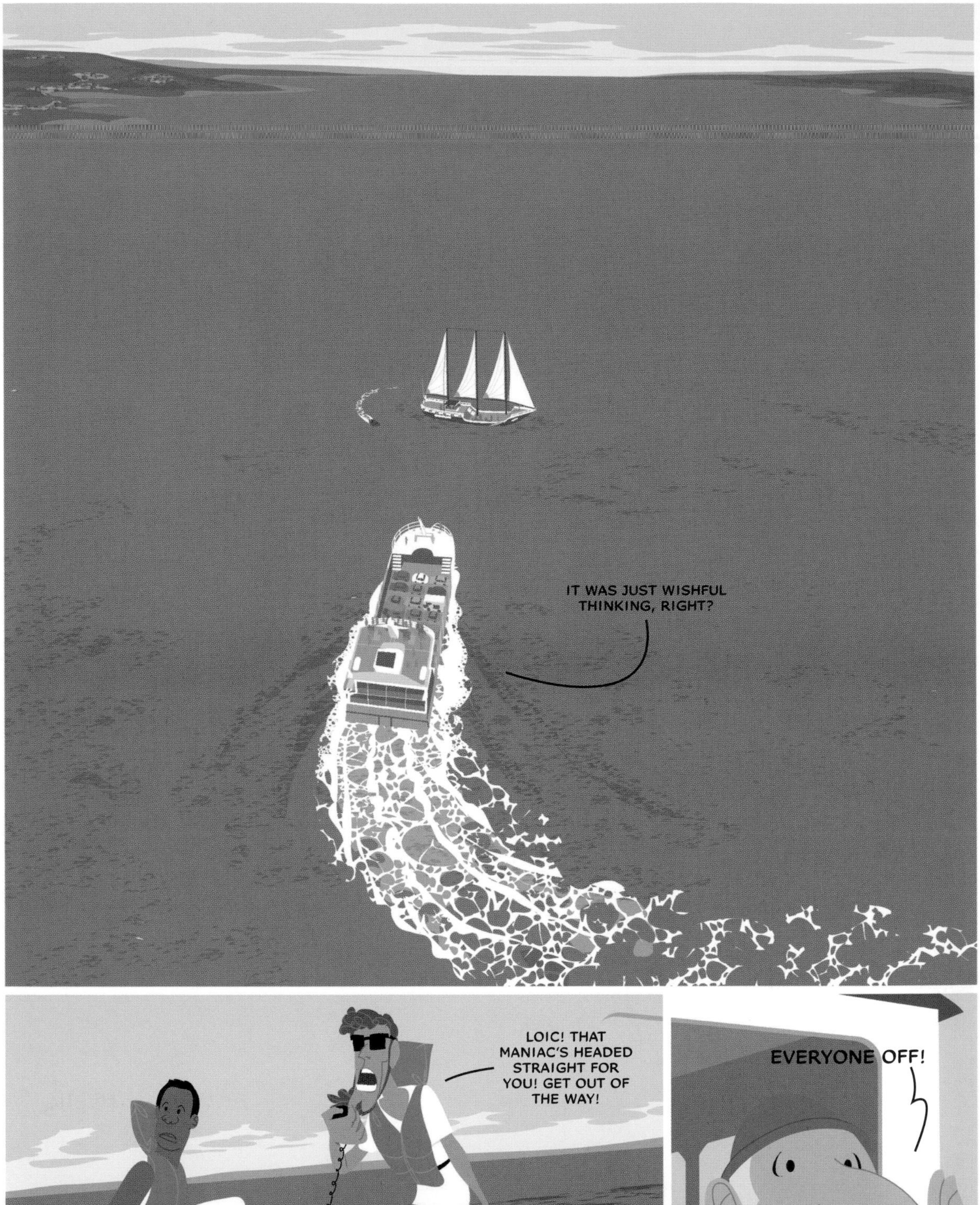
IT WAS JUST WISHFUL THINKING, RIGHT?

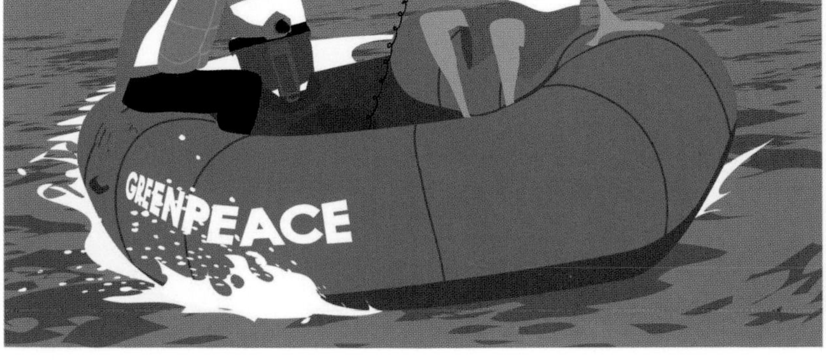
LOIC! THAT MANIAC'S HEADED STRAIGHT FOR YOU! GET OUT OF THE WAY!
GREENPEACE

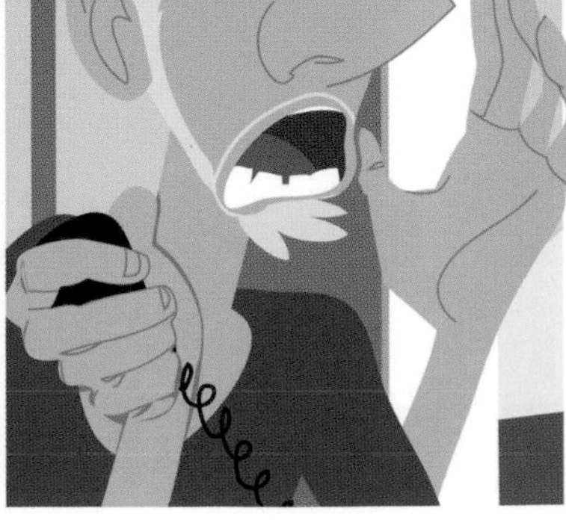
EVERYONE OFF!

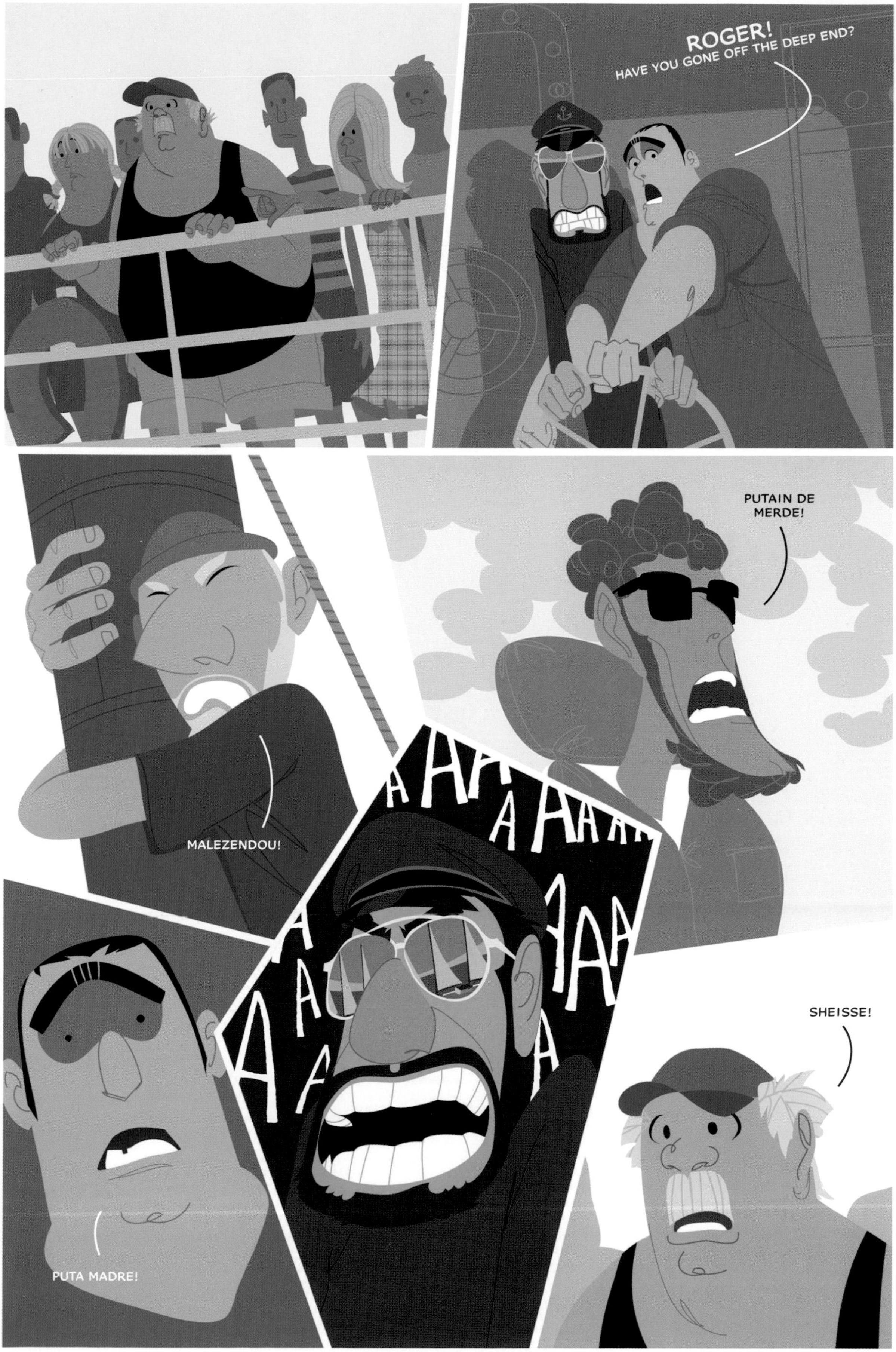
ROGER!
HAVE YOU GONE OFF THE DEEP END?
PUTAIN DE MERDE!
MALEZENDOU!
AAAAAAAAAAAAAAAAA
SHEISSE!
PUTA MADRE!

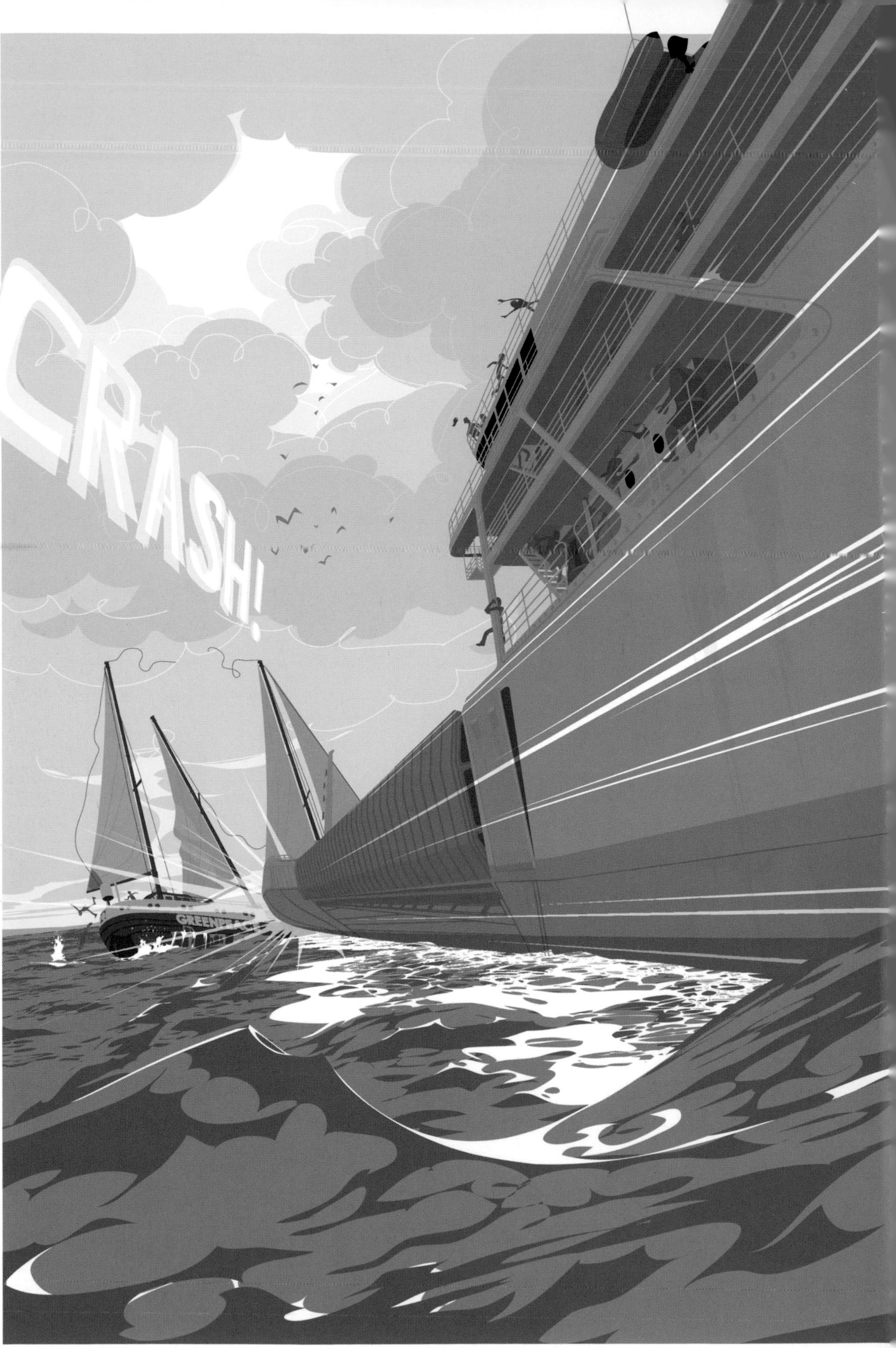
CRASH!
GREENPEACE

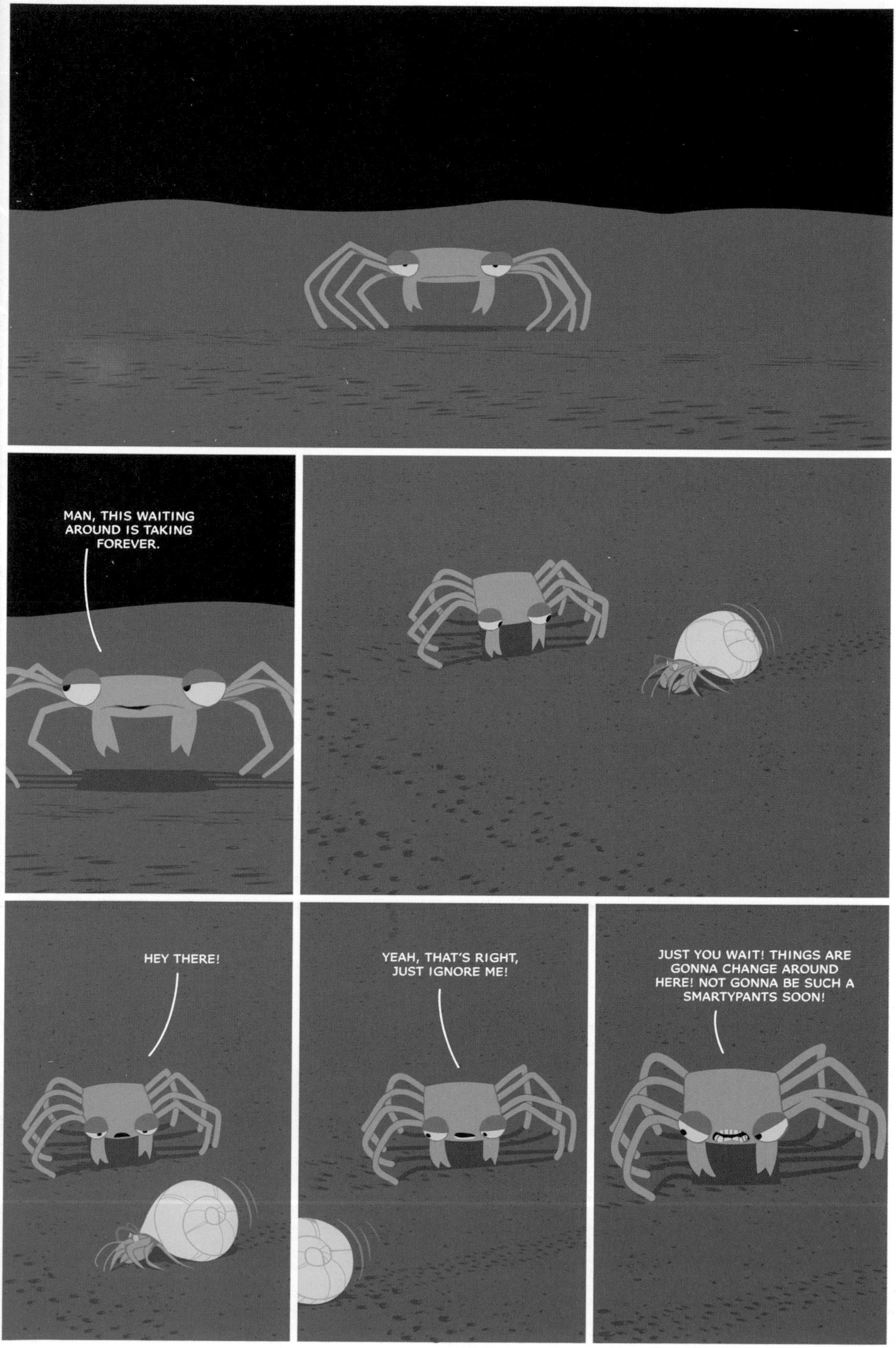
MAN, THIS WAITING AROUND IS TAKING FOREVER.
HEY THERE!
YEAH, THAT'S RIGHT, JUST IGNORE ME!
JUST YOU WAIT! THINGS ARE GONNA CHANGE AROUND HERE! NOT GONNA BE SUCH A SMARTYPANTS SOON!

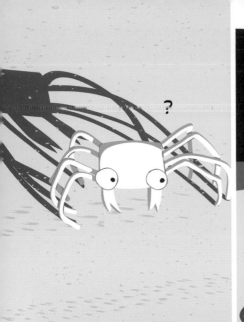

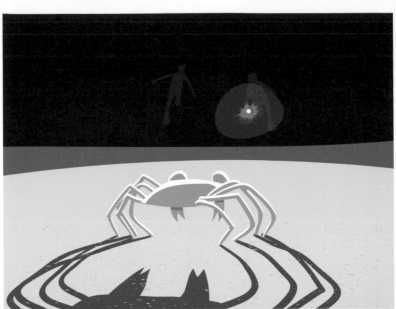

HEY! WHAT THE—?!

TRY AND SCARE ME ALL YOU WANT! I AIN'T MOVING!
AW, C'MON!

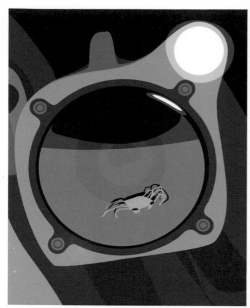

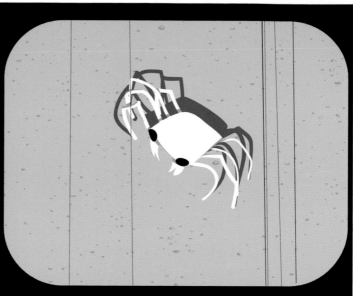

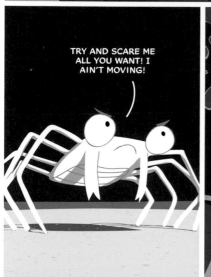

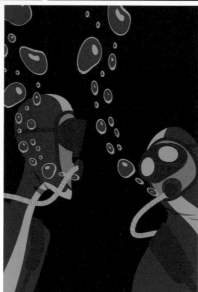

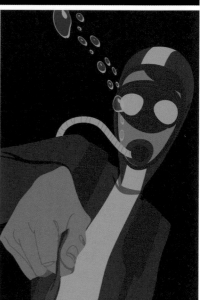

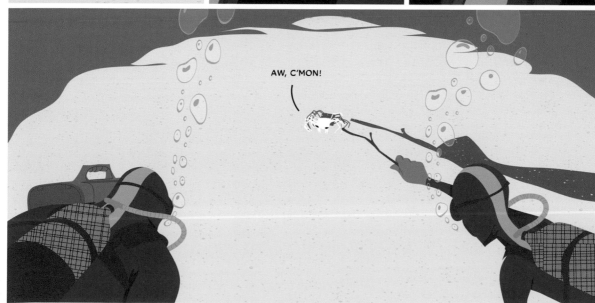

THESE HUMANS HAVE GOTTA BE IN LEAGUE WITH THE BROWN CRABS.
HA HA! THE ENEMY RETREATS!
BLUNK

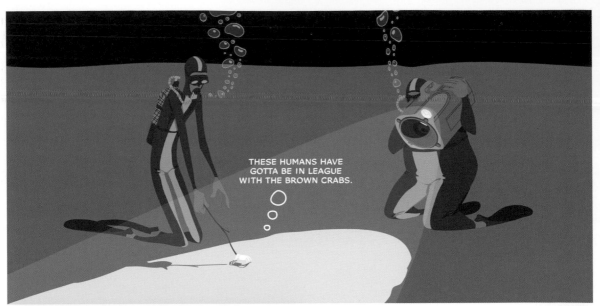

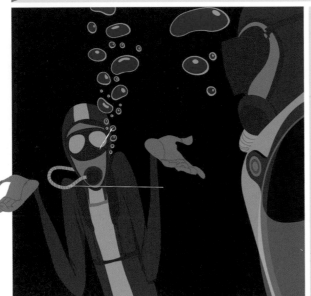

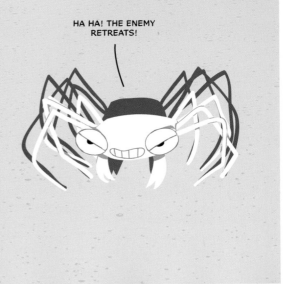

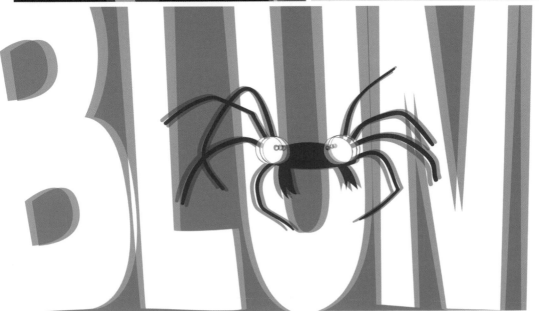

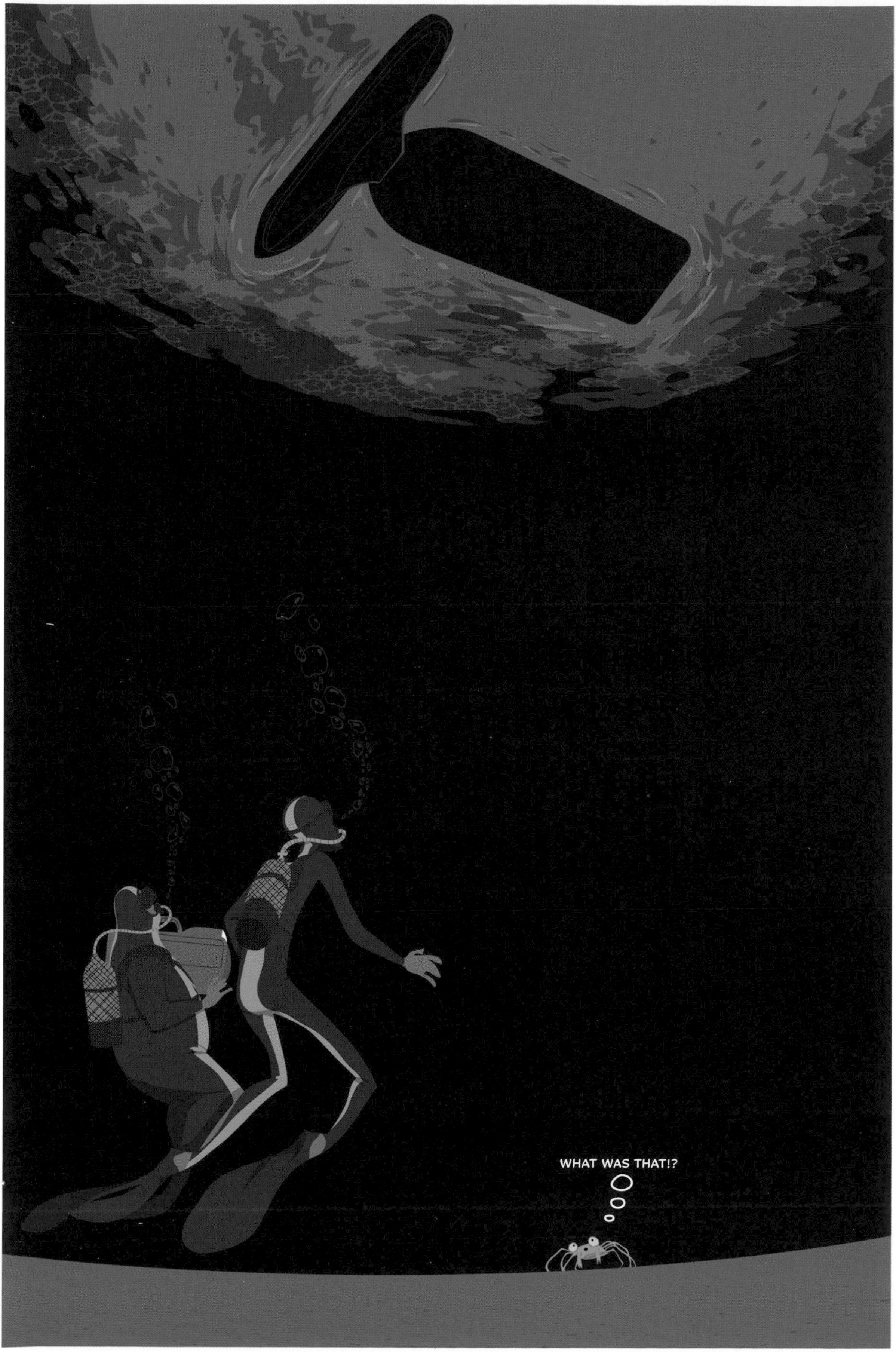
WHAT WAS THAT!?

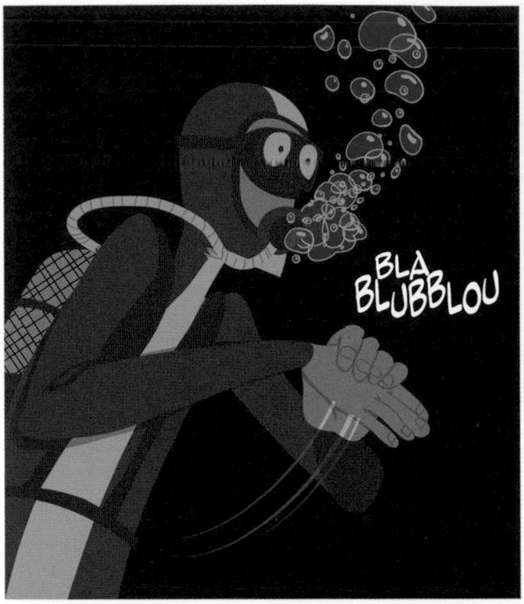
BLA BLUBBLOU
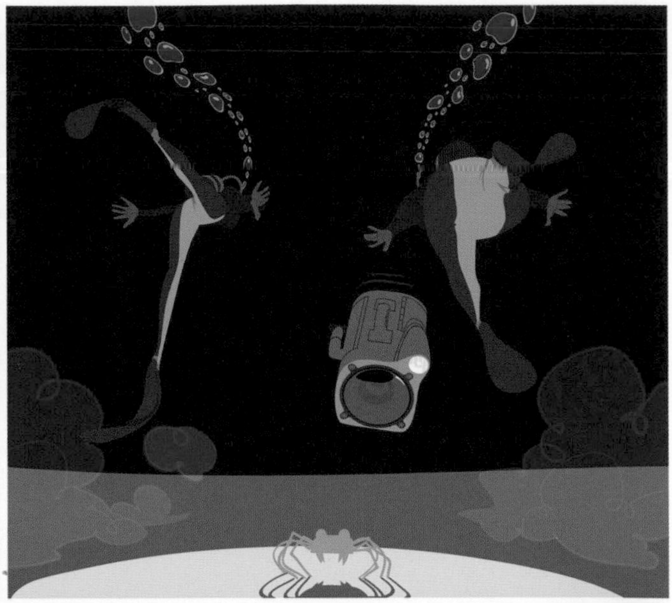
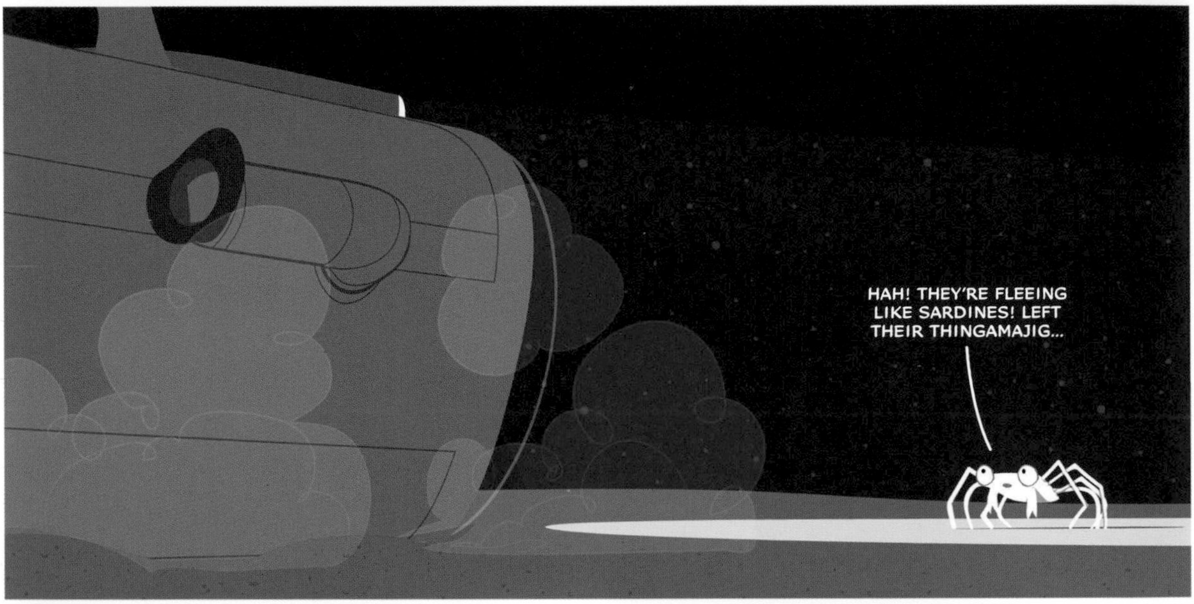
HAH! THEY'RE FLEEING LIKE SARDINES! LEFT THEIR THINGAMAJIG...
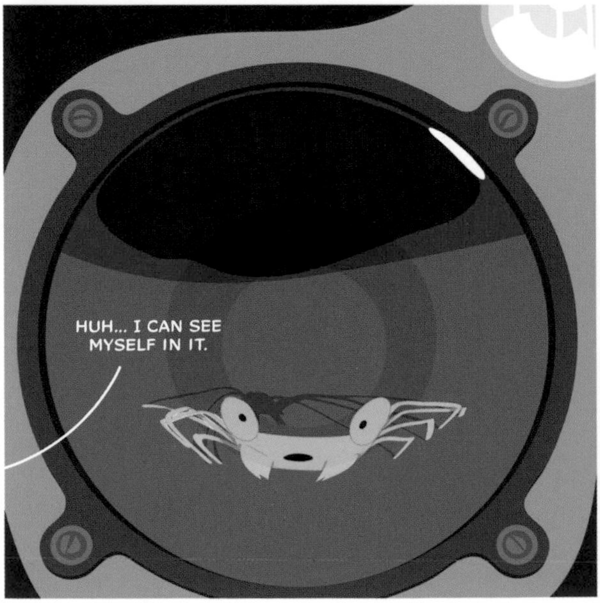
HUH... I CAN SEE MYSELF IN IT.
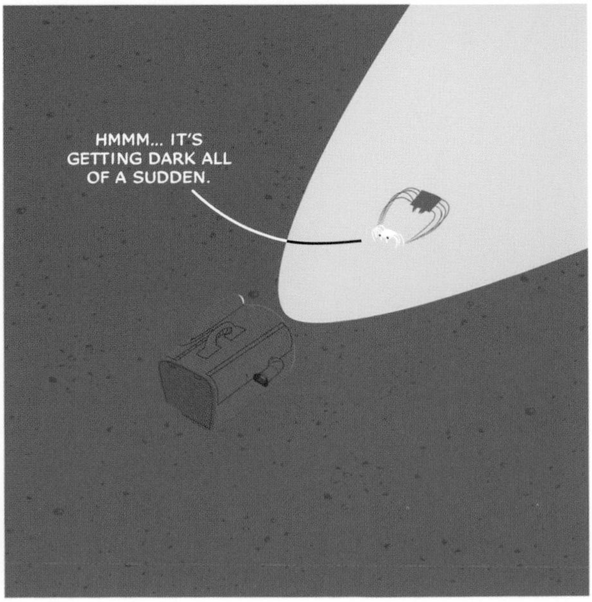
HMMM... IT'S GETTING DARK ALL OF A SUDDEN.

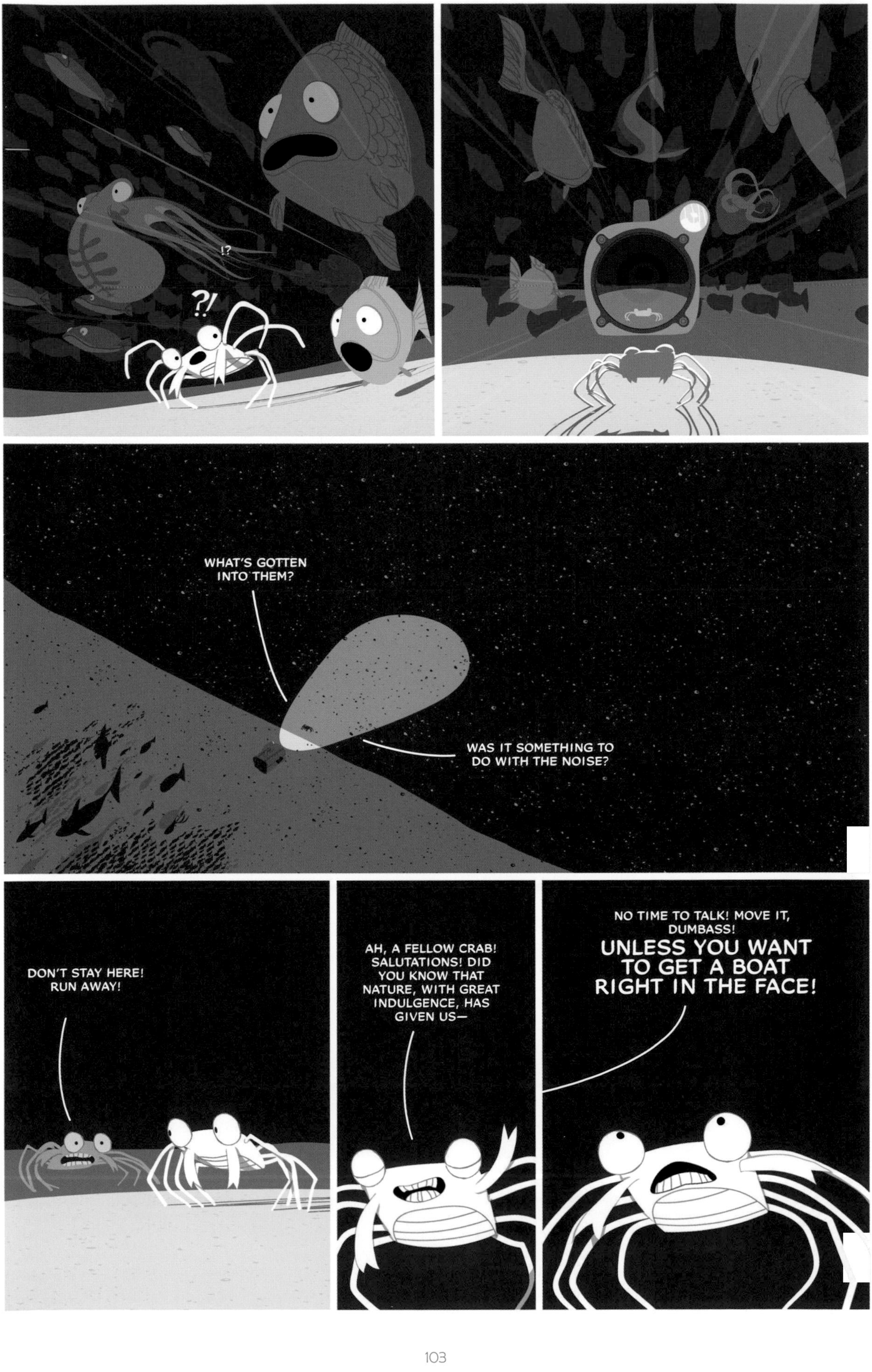
!?
?!
WHAT'S GOTTEN INTO THEM?
WAS IT SOMETHING TO DO WITH THE NOISE?
DON'T STAY HERE! RUN AWAY!
AH, A FELLOW CRAB! SALUTATIONS! DID YOU KNOW THAT NATURE, WITH GREAT INDULGENCE, HAS GIVEN US—
NO TIME TO TALK! MOVE IT, DUMBASS!
UNLESS YOU WANT TO GET A BOAT RIGHT IN THE FACE!

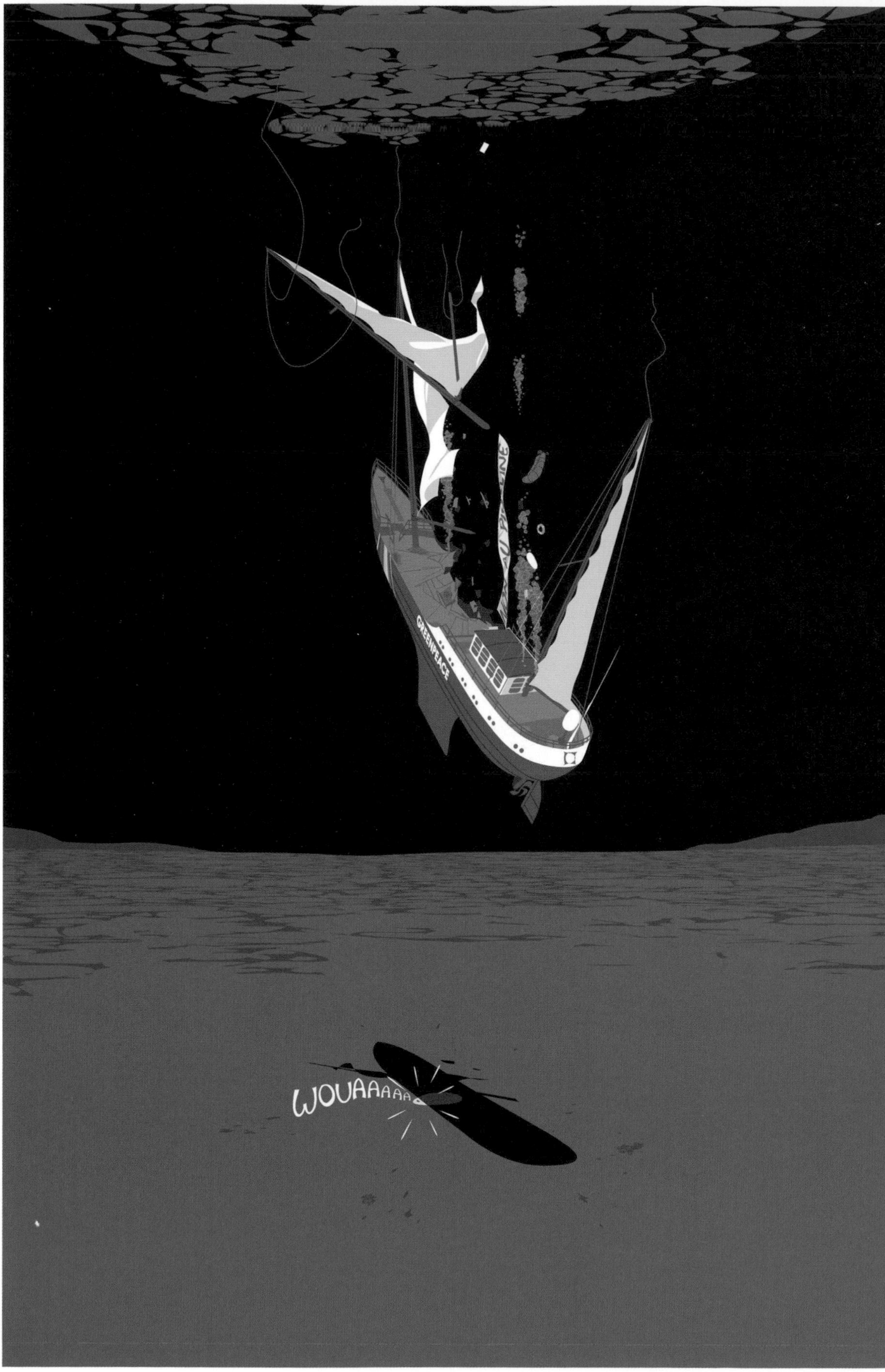
GREENPEACE
WOUAAAAAAA

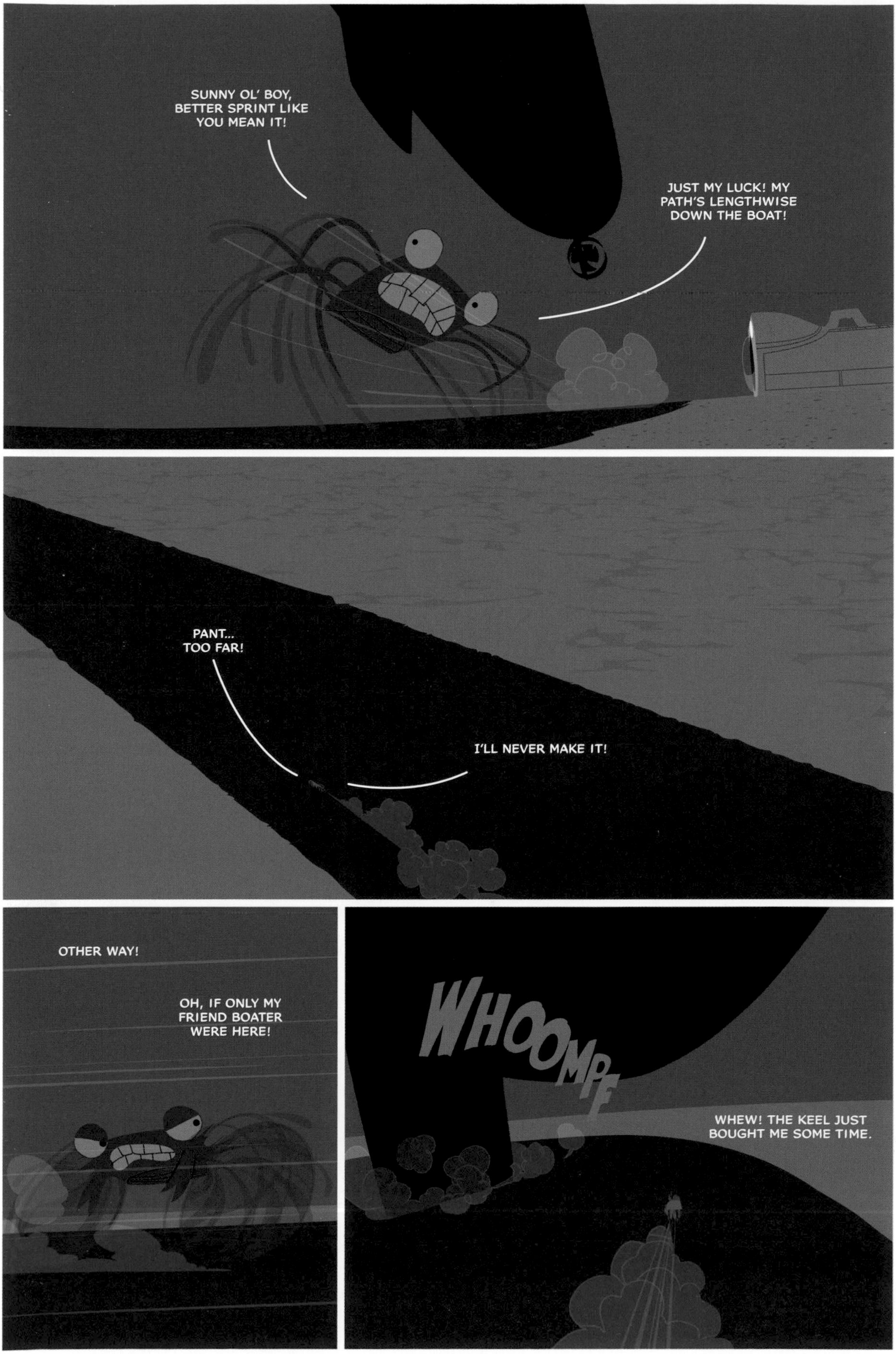
SUNNY OL' BOY, BETTER SPRINT LIKE YOU MEAN IT!
JUST MY LUCK! MY PATH'S LENGTHWISE DOWN THE BOAT!
PANT... TOO FAR!
I'LL NEVER MAKE IT!
OTHER WAY!
OH, IF ONLY MY FRIEND BOATER WERE HERE!
WHOOMPF
WHEW! THE KEEL JUST BOUGHT ME SOME TIME.

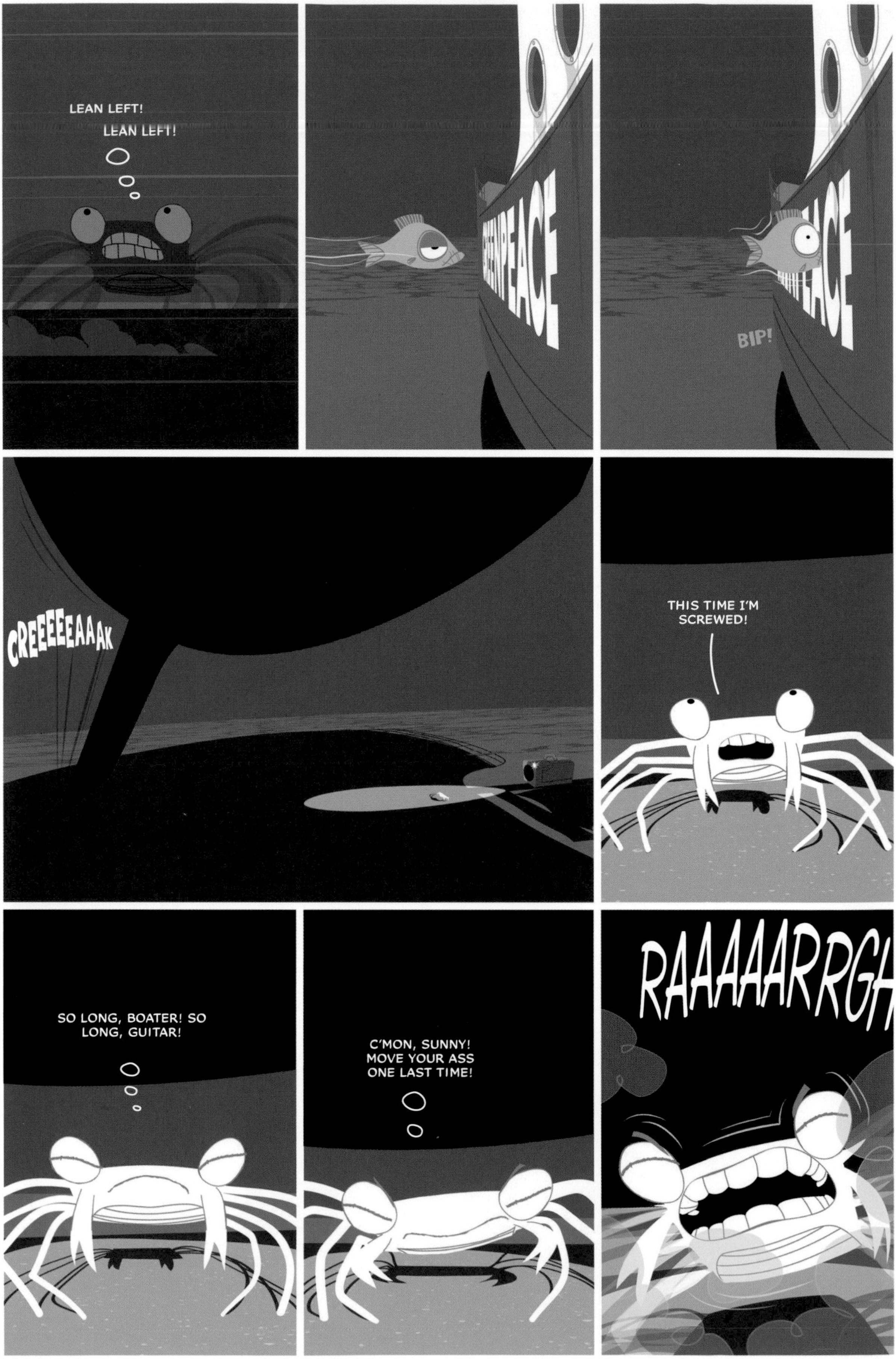

LEAN LEFT!
LEAN LEFT!
BIP!
CREEEEEAAAK
THIS TIME I'M SCREWED!
SO LONG, BOATER! SO LONG, GUITAR!
C'MON, SUNNY! MOVE YOUR ASS ONE LAST TIME!
RAAAAARRGH

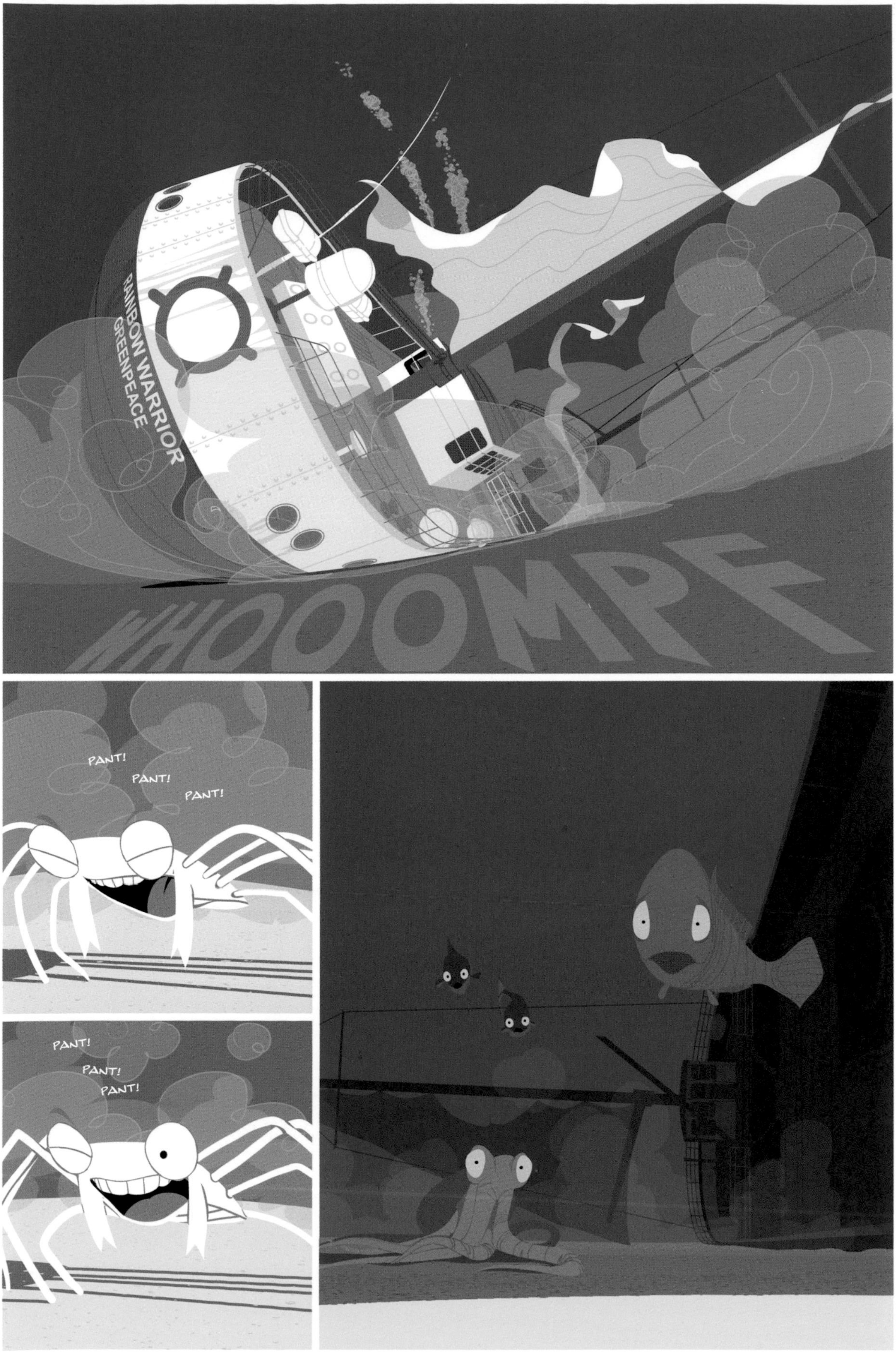
RAINBOW WARRIOR
GREENPEACE
WHOOOMPF
PANT!
PANT!
PANT!
PANT!
PANT!
PANT!

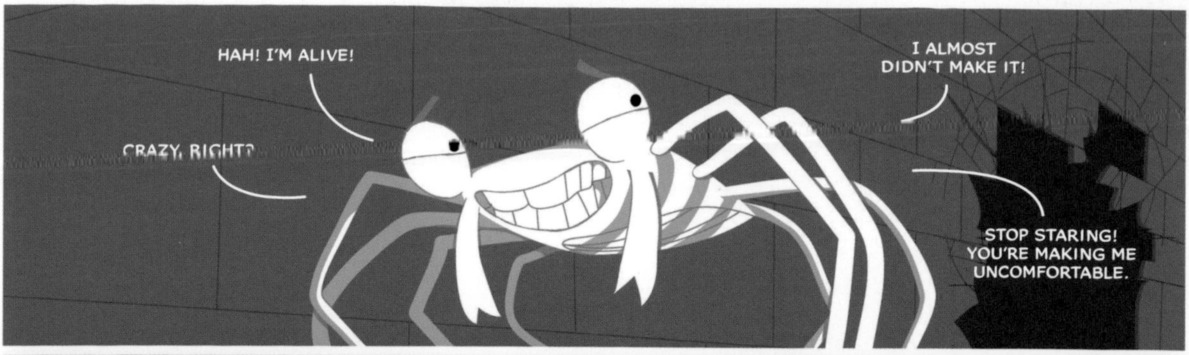
HAH! I'M ALIVE!
CRAZY, RIGHT?
I ALMOST DIDN'T MAKE IT!
STOP STARING! YOU'RE MAKING ME UNCOMFORTABLE.

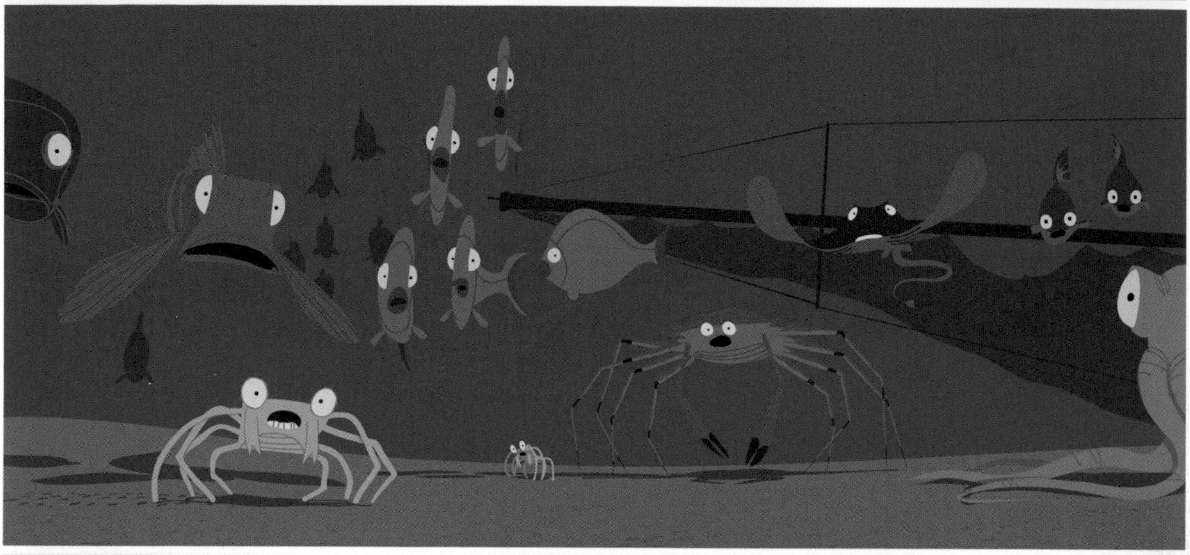

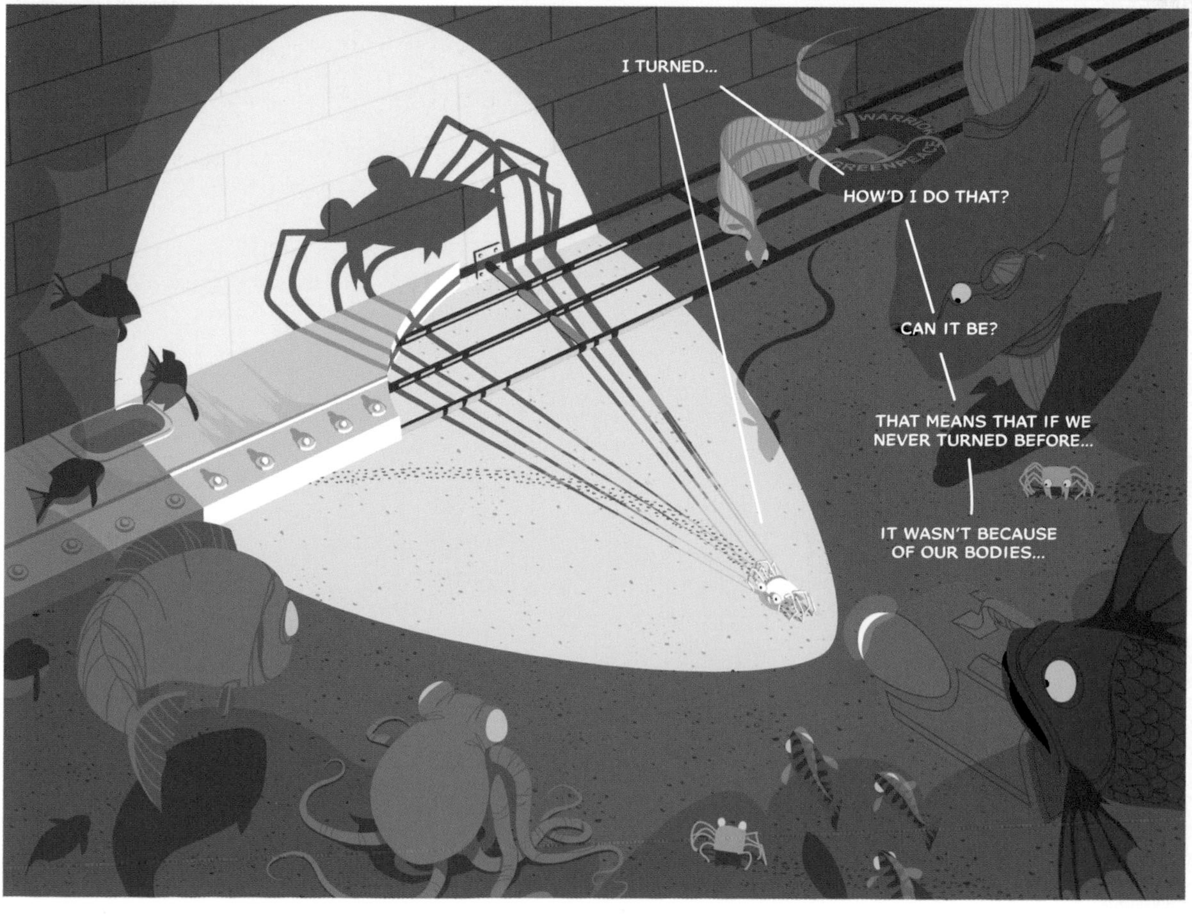
I TURNED...
HOW'D I DO THAT?
CAN IT BE?
THAT MEANS THAT IF WE NEVER TURNED BEFORE...
IT WASN'T BECAUSE OF OUR BODIES...

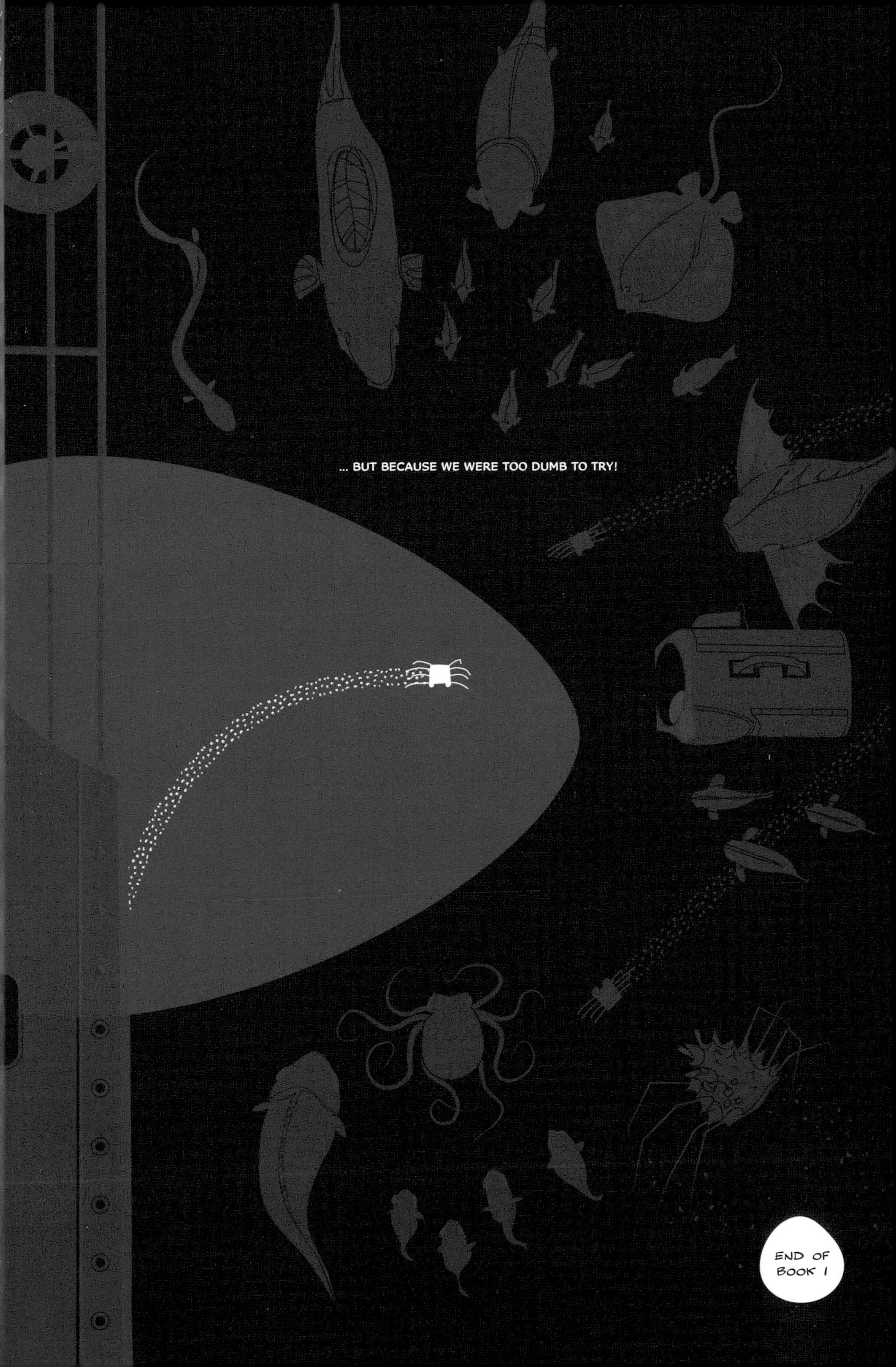
... BUT BECAUSE WE WERE TOO DUMB TO TRY!
END OF BOOK 1

ABOUT THE AUTHOR

Brittany, 1977: Arthur De Pins is born.

Years go by... here he is, studying Decorative Arts, designing flyers and doing sketches at events. Party promoters Wombat talent-spot him, opening many doors: magazines like **Max** and **Technikart**, not to mention the Lezilus Agency.

After a brief foray into video games, Arthur's career takes off, thanks to momentum from his first short film, **Géraldine**. His third, **Revolution of the Crabs (La Révolution des Crabes)**, is crowned with success: more than fifty prizes, including the Audience Favorite at the 2004 Annecy Festival.

At the same time, the ninth art entices him: **Guilty Pleasures (Pêchés mignons)** flirts with taboos and dodges hang-ups with humor and skill, tackling sexuality from a female perspective.

Two more series followed: **March of the Crabs (La marche du Crabe)** inspired by the short film, and **Zombillenium**, a macabre satire of the corporate world, currently being adapted into a feature-length animated film.

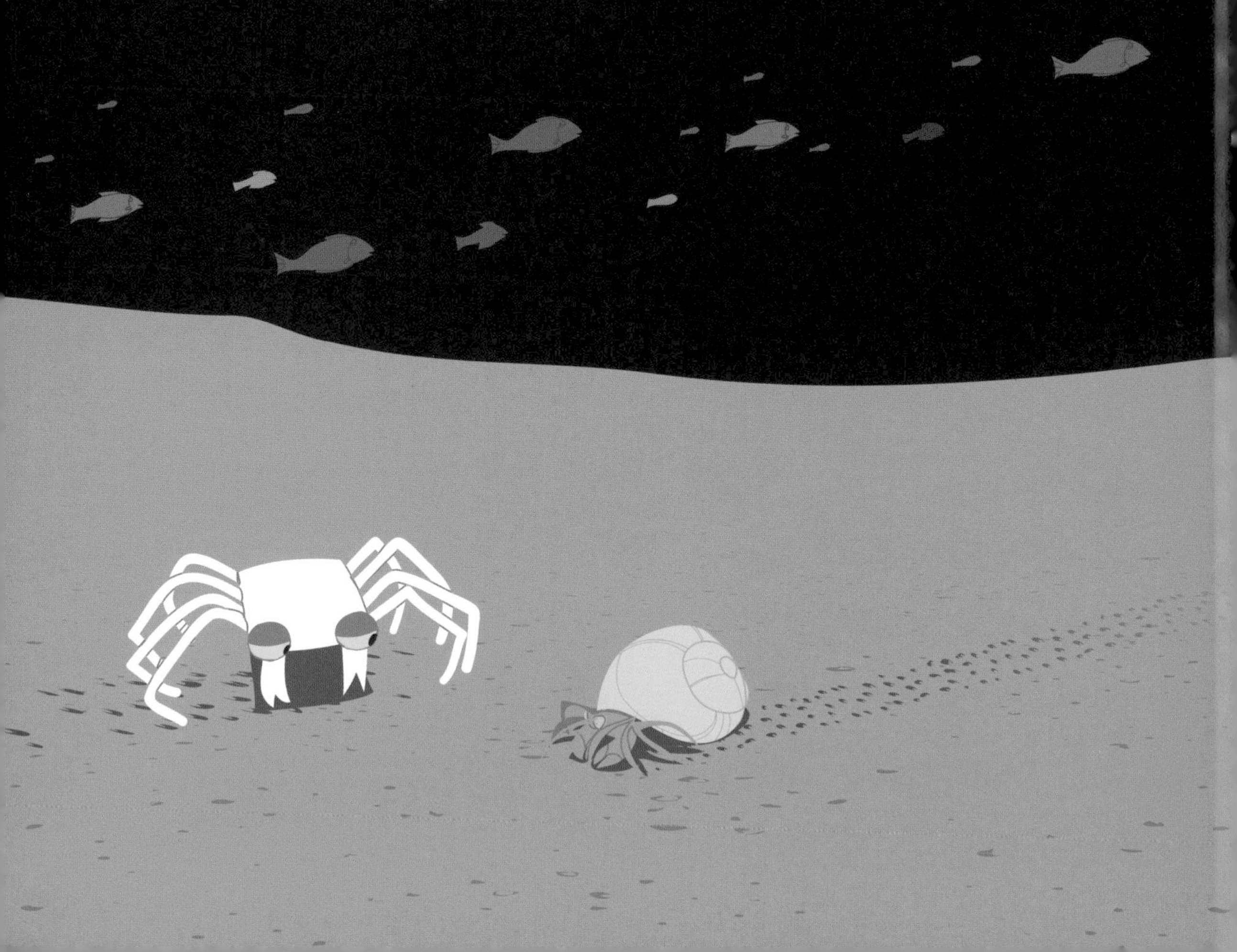